POLICY ENTREPRENEURSHIP IN EDUCATION

Policy Entrepreneurship in Education aims to build the confidence and skills of education academics in securing higher impact for their work. It offers guidance and identifies methods of capturing and measuring impact, as well as practical advice in helping academics engage policy makers and influence society with their research.

Written specifically for the field of education, the book utilises domestic and international examples to illustrate those policy entrepreneurship activities which advance impact and appeal to international audiences, who are increasingly concerned with how higher education studies in education can make a difference on the ground.

Combining theory and practice, the book employs a practical approach to doing policy entrepreneurship. It is a unique offering that will appeal to all who have an academic or practical interest in policy change and how to affect this.

James Arthur is Director of the Jubilee Centre for Character and Virtues and Deputy Pro Vice Chancellor (Staffing) at the University of Birmingham, UK.

POLICY ENTREPRENEURSHIP IN EDUCATION

Engagement, Influence and Impact

James Arthur

Routledge
Taylor & Francis Group

LONDON AND NEW YORK

First published 2018
by Routledge
2 Park Square, Milton Park, Abingdon, Oxon OX14 4RN

and by Routledge
711 Third Avenue, New York, NY 10017

Routledge is an imprint of the Taylor & Francis Group, an informa business

© 2018 James Arthur

British Library Cataloguing in Publication Data
A catalogue record for this book is available from the British Library

Library of Congress Cataloging-in-Publication Data
A catalog record for this book has been requested

ISBN: 978-1-138-21459-0 (hbk)
ISBN: 978-1-138-21460-6 (pbk)
ISBN: 978-1-315-44564-9 (ebk)

Typeset in Bembo
by Saxon Graphics Ltd, Derby

Dedication
To Jack and Pina Templeton

CONTENTS

ACKNOWLEDGEMENTS

During the writing of this book I have been fortunate in my surroundings: I thank my colleagues in the Jubilee Centre for Character and Virtues and those associated with us, including Kristján Kristjánsson, Aidan Thompson, Tom Harrison and David Lorimer for many helpful comments on the later drafts of this book. I owe a debt of gratitude to Lord O'Shaughnessy for his continued wise and critical counsel and for writing the generous Foreword. I am particularly indebted to Joseph Ward, an associate research fellow in the Centre, who helped me carry out the early background research for this project and provided essential administrative and intellectual support along the way. His careful eye and sensitive ear proved crucial time and again. However, the book's deficiencies are entirely my own.

FOREWORD

There was a time when academics thought great thoughts in their university departments, but the purchase of those ideas on the outside world was limited. Those days are – happily – gone. Whether it is due to the changing nature of higher education, the priority placed in the Research Excellence Framework on creating impact, or on the greater desire of governments to have an evidence-based approach, the time of the academic policy entrepreneur is here.

It is harder to think of someone who, in recent years, has fulfilled this role more fully than Professor James Arthur. The Jubilee Centre for Character and Virtues, the research institute he created, has arguably created more direct policy change in the UK and elsewhere than any other. Where six years ago the debate about the purpose of education was focused solely on academic achievements, thanks to the Jubilee Centre's pioneering work it is now accepted at all levels, from Ministers and officials through to teachers and parents, that the development of a broad set of virtues like kindness, service, curiosity and resilience should be at the centre of a good education.

Like all overnight successes, the foundations of the Jubilee Centre's impact were laid over many years and they provide the case study of policy entrepreneurship. It starts with a clear desire to work in the public realm and a belief that the academy should be in the business of informing and enlightening government. Some would dispute this normative assumption, but as someone who struggled for years to encourage academics to be engaged in public policy, I can say that it is one that most policy makers truly welcome.

Layered on to obligation to engage are three further critical elements. First, the ability to 'trial run' some of the ideas. Professor Arthur's early work in citizenship was important in its own right, but it also provided the opportunity to hone policy proposals over time and to see how politicians and officials react to them. Citizenship was a forerunner to values-led education, which led to character education and then discussions of virtue. Each one of these steps would have been impossible without its predecessor.

The second important factor is the independence that derives from having an autonomous base away from government. Many of the people and organisations who want to change policy are often after something that will benefit them, what we would call lobbying. Despite its reputation this is a perfectly respectable business so long as it is done transparently and according to norms of good behaviour, as set out in the Nolan Principles. The Jubilee Centre is in an altogether different position. It doesn't need anything from the government, and it gains no particular benefit from the policies it seeks to promote. It can, in negotiating parlance, walk away from the deal if it doesn't like the terms. This provides it with exceptional moral authority in the marketplace for ideas.

Finally, no policy entrepreneur can be successful without building strong relationships with those in positions of authority. All successful enterprises need a great product, but they also need a great sales team. Policy makers can sometimes be capricious and, as the book states, policy making can be a rough and ready business. This conforms to what Professor Arthur calls a humanist model of society, one in which Ministers are grappling with hundreds of problems at the same time, with often poor information and limited capacity. Any successful policy entrepreneur, therefore, needs to be able to put themselves in the shoes of the policy makers they seek to work with, see things from their point of view, and be prepared to offer solutions – however imperfect – rather than simply more problems. Do this and you won't just get one meeting with the Minister or senior official, but a long and productive relationship.

I thoroughly recommend this excellent book, which not only clarifies the nature of policy entrepreneurship but offers practical lessons to others who would seek to emulate the impact created by Professor Arthur and the Jubilee Centre. At a time when divisions are being exposed within nations around the world, there is a greater need than ever for our finest minds to be engaged in the process of better policy making.

Lord James O'Shaughnessy
Former Director of Policy
10 Downing Street

INTRODUCTION

[T]here is a dispute among those who agree that the most choiceworthy life is that accompanied by virtue as to whether the political and active way of life is choiceworthy, or rather that which is divorced from all external things – that involving some sort of study, for example – which some assert is the only philosophic way of life. For it is evident that these two ways of life are the ones intentionally chosen by those human beings who are most ambitious with a view to virtue, both in former times and at present; the two I mean are the political and the philosophic.

Aristotle, Politics, *Book 7, Ch. 2*

The human race will have no respite from evils until those who are really philosophers acquire political power or until, through some divine dispensation, those who rule and have political authority in the cities become real philosophers.

Plato, The Republic *(326a–326b)*

Outline of the book

The main aim of this book is to propose a conceptual framework to describe and explain the influence of policy entrepreneurs on the formulation and design of public policy. In this context, the book defines the *policy entrepreneur*, identifies the main characteristics of their entrepreneurial activities, describes strategies which the policy entrepreneur may employ, and characterises a model of successful and effective policy entrepreneurship. The book emphasises the importance of policy entrepreneurs in the public policy arena, and conveys insights into the conditions for their activity, their motivations and principal strategies. The theoretical framework and corresponding insights concerning the processes of institutional change in public policy are presented in relation to the design of the current English character education policy, which is presented as a case study. The book considers how education policy is made and the factors that lie behind the formation of this particular education policy. The case study of the origins of the Jubilee Centre for Character and Virtues illustrates how academics can change and influence policy.

Preliminary considerations

Mary Ann Glendon (2011: IX) opens *The Forum and the Tower* with Aristotle's words above from his *Politics*. Aristotle states that both the intellectual and the politician are two vocations that pursue virtue and are worthy choices in life. Glendon's book is concerned with bridging the distance between 'the forum' (where political decisions are made) and 'the tower' (where academics, intellectuals, scholars and researchers devote themselves to the disinterested quest for knowledge). Glendon (2011: *ibid.*) considers 'the difficult skills required, the temperament suited for one or the other way of life, and the relationship of the study of politics to its practice' between researchers and policy makers. She considers the gap between these two worlds and observes that this distance between academics and policy makers is not new, but rather is as old as academe itself. Academics have always talked to other academics, and policy makers have always talked to other policy makers, but they have, more often than not, pulled in different directions. Many academics do not try to reach beyond the ivory tower, content with the separation from the world of decisions and consequences. While the ivory tower exists for good reason, to allow researchers and scholars to reflect at a distance, this distancing can go too far. Glendon (2011: 221) argues that academics should attend to public affairs not only out of civic duty but in order to remain grounded in reality. Academics, she maintains, cannot put aside politics in conducting research, but ought to be close to 'what is going on in the life of the polity' since universities as places for learning and research are not completely unfettered by political agendas. Policy advice-giving by academics is as old as government itself. Policy makers also need to keep in touch with the world of ideas and stay in touch with academics, especially those researchers who produce policy-relevant research outcomes.

Policy makers cannot master everything, but they will usually collect, examine and weigh up all the relevant facts and arguments before making decisions, and academics can assist them in this process, which is evolving ever more rapidly. Glendon (2011: 221) ends her book by quoting from Immanuel Kant's *Perpetual Peace* of 1795, in which he reminds us that academics must not remain silent in the realm of politics but must 'speak openly'. Plato also warned against intellectuals becoming 'prisoners who take refuge in a temple' (*The Republic*: 495a). The function of the academic, Kant says, is to assist with the 'enlightenment of the business of government' – to provide advice and good counsel based on their expert knowledge, or what Aristotle calls practical wisdom. Glendon (2011: XII) discusses the tensions, challenges and opportunities in the relationship between researchers and policy makers, noting in the end that 'the optimal confluence of gifts, favourable conditions and plain luck will always be elusive'. Her historical survey of figures such as Cicero, Burke and de Tocqueville demonstrates the fertile ground for a stronger relationship between politics and the academy based on a normative understanding of the uses of expert or research-based knowledge. However, it was Russell Kirk (quoted in Birzer, 2015: 246) who reminded us that:

> If the scholar deserts his realm of scholarly competence for the agora, he is liable to attain neither wisdom nor the public good. The man who has been an able professor may become an able politician ... Very few persons, nevertheless, can be competent simultaneously in quite different vocations. For better or worse, the scholar turned politician must give up pure scholarship. If one has a taste for the hustings, one ought to abandon the pose of speaking authoritatively from a chaste, impartial love of pure learning.

Kirk (in Birzer, 2015: 247) goes on to add that if an academic speaks on political matters then he should do so as an 'observer' and not as a 'participant'. Following the model of Socrates, he notes that the scholar must know 'that the lover of wisdom must not drink from the cup of power'. Kirk did not wish to exclude academic involvement in politics or policy making, but he did wish to caution us.

It is worth reminding ourselves that Aristotle was himself both an intellectual and a policy adviser, most notably to Alexander the Great. Aristotle did not separate politics from the academy and indeed embraced practical politics in his own life. However, it was Aristotle's teacher, Plato, in the pages of his *Republic*, who first advanced the ideal of a state ruled by intellectuals (philosopher-rulers) who possessed comprehensive knowledge along with the practical ability and wisdom to apply it to concrete public policy issues. In Plato's view, philosopher-rulers do not derive their authority solely from their expert knowledge, but also from their practice of justice and their moral insight: making political decisions requires good judgement and a certain level of competence. In practice, few intellectuals have such comprehensive knowledge; contemporary academics tend to be disciplinary specialists, and fewer still have the range of capacities or practical wisdom needed to resolve policy issues. This is why academics rarely enter professional politics, and also why they are seldom publicly blamed for the actual implementation of their policy ideas. The scholarly reputation of the academic is priority number one, and if policy advice is given from their 'expert' position in academe, it is often easily challenged by other academics with conflicting world views who say they are out of touch, have outdated views, or simply that their research is flawed. The incentives to get involved in policy advice are few, and academics are naturally wary of such involvement.

It was Harold Laswell, the father of 'Policy Studies', in his 1951 paper *The Policy Orientation,* who first called for the study of the role of 'knowledge in and of the policy process'. This process consisted of a series of rational stages for policy formulation and implementation – a stage or phase process theory that would comprehensively cover every aspect of how a policy is made. He also envisaged an applied and multidisciplinary social science that could help guide the political decision-making process. This new applied social science, he thought, would act as a mediator between academics and policy makers and would have an explicitly normative orientation based on human values – particularly the emphasis on human dignity (see Fischer, 2003: 4–5). It would involve two broad objectives: studying the policy-making process itself and addressing the research needs of policy makers. However, as Fischer (2003: 16) outlines, the field became dominated by a neo-positivist and empiricist methodology that prevailed in the social sciences. This meant that the practices that have defined policy makers, through the lens of the social sciences, were 'narrowly empiricist, rationalist and technocratic'. Fischer (2003: 14) believes that the relationship between research and policy followed this constricted vision that ignored normativity and instead emphasised the technical and scientific nature of research focusing on 'questions of efficiency, performance and predictability'. In other words, the human dimension and the role of social values in policy making were diminished through the de-politicisation of policy by rationalist – and by implication instrumentalist – approaches (see Torgerson, 2007). The community's attainment of the good life requires policy makers to design public policy that can actualise the good society.

Carol Weiss (1979) and other academics in the field began a modest challenge to this dominant positivist approach in the social sciences by reformulating the goals of policy analysis in terms of the 'public enlightenment' function of research-based knowledge. This Kantian idea encourages intellectuals to assist with the 'enlightenment of the business of government' already mentioned above. Laswell opposed the instrumentalist approach in the production and use of policy-relevant knowledge or what might be called the attempt to managerialise or instrumentalise knowledge production and its utilisation. He believed that policy makers need to use their discretion in the making of policy, which means that they needed to combine research-based knowledge with complex social and political realities. This is why Fischer and Forrester (1993) believe policy making is essentially about arguments relating to the discursive construction of policy and the normative role of such discourse where values are all-pervasive.

Lindblom (1959) had already advanced this idea as early as 1959, saying that research-based knowledge depends on the effective articulation of arguments to key decision makers. He believed the role of research-based knowledge was limited in the policy process and that we simply 'muddled through' via incremental changes aimed at agreed-upon policies. He believed this to be a more accurate description of the policy process than Laswell had outlined. There is clearly an inescapable normative character about educational policy, hence Bridges and Watts (2009: 50) argue that policy cannot be free of ideology, and must by definition have a normative foundation. As they say, 'this normative framing may be discovered in the intentions of whoever promotes the policy; it may lie in an evaluation of the observable consequences of the policy; it may be discovered in the various readings of the policy that different stakeholders can provide. In other words, the "normative framework" is open to interpretation, construction and reconstruction.' Policy formulation is effectively designed against such a normative backdrop, but researchers and policy makers do not always clarify their normative assumptions in research and policy-making processes.

There is certainly a role for ideas, beliefs, world views, culture and tradition in understanding policy making. Making decisions about what kind of public policies we should adopt, therefore, involves taking positions on value-laden issues. This decision-making process places an emphasis on the values that underlie policy choices and constitutes a normative approach in the sense that every policy presupposes an underlying moral argument by way of justification. For example, 'Why ought we to use the powers of government to do A rather than B?' From the perspective of moral philosophy or ethics, the term normative refers to the attempt to convince people that a certain course of action ought to be adopted on the basis of relevant facts and values that revolve around policy. These become normative arguments about the shared values and goals that we might support within particular contexts, which make it a debate about the greater good. Research-based knowledge is not sufficient on its own, since normative arguments will justify and promote one set of policy ideas over another. We can distinguish between the two senses of normativity as *evaluating* X as better than Y and *normativity* as prescribing X over Y. For example, we can evaluate a certain educational policy as better than Y, yet refrain from actually *prescribing* it for some practical or pragmatic reason, e.g. it would face too much opposition, be too costly, etc. Normative approaches will ask *how* we should behave, while positive approaches simply ask what the behaviour *is*. Teachers who value a particular ideal in education will take it to provide reasons for their action and it will guide their deliberation about how to teach and interact with students. In the end, it says something about the good life.

Another way of looking at this is to consider 'what is good or bad about what is' in the light of 'what one ought to do'. Policy is formulated within a context of conflict and purpose, asking what the right thing to do *should* be? In policy deliberation, there is an on-going struggle over ideas of what the public interest *ought* to be – a debate about the greater good. These normative ideas about values, attitudes, beliefs and identity lie behind policy debates and they influence policy makers by providing reasons and arguments for their decision making. This normative approach cannot simply rely on unconscious values or unsupported instinct, since these often take for granted the very assumptions, beliefs and values that influence and affect the positions adopted by both policy makers and researchers.

It is useful to understand the two different normative models of society underlying the use of research-based knowledge in policy that were originally proposed by Lindblom (1977), but which have been much extended here. It can be argued that there are two normative models of public policy making which are concerned with the basic beliefs, world views and implicit theories that citizens, including academics and policy makers, may hold. Certain values and interests (norms) are implicit in these world views and are embodied in specific social, cultural and historical situations. Hence, a country that historically and geographically shares a set of traditions (laws, institutions, language and common practices) is inescapably bound to particular understandings and interpretations of policy making. These beliefs serve as a standard or guide to people's thinking and provide reasons to think and act – they are the characteristic expression of a given society.

The first model, which I call the Technological Model, can be characterised by viewing society as ordered by reason and materialistic determinism, informed by the optimistic assumption that people have the capacity to act reasonably and will do so. In this model, there is a belief in the unlimited progress of society. This kind of society is run by professional elites (including academics and politicians) who define public issues and decide what is best for society from the available scientific research and data. It is generally assumed that this data and research, produced by the professional elites, has the public's confidence and trust and that it is accepted as fact. In this model, facts and values are separated, and the emphasis is on efficiency and effectiveness together with a belief in the pre-eminence of scientific-based decision making. It is a society regulated only by government authorities and there is a desire for continued policy change. Policy documents within this model remain aloof from any substantive statements about the importance of values, and there is little struggle over ideology in formulating policy. The approach is largely empirical and focuses on what works in practice. Rationalism is the operational mode of thought in this essentially reductionist model of policy making. It breaks problems into discrete parts, and values the kind of functional and quantifiable knowledge that can be expressed in words and numbers over other kinds of knowledge that cannot be articulated in this way. It seeks abstract rules and principles that can be applied across all contexts, but correspondingly undervalues or even rejects the importance of particular contexts and local traditions. What counts are demonstrable outcomes that can be recorded and measured, but, as Einstein put it, not everything that counts can be counted.

The second model, which I call the Humanist Model, views the human intellect as limited, so scientific knowledge is always incomplete. Conflict of ideas and human diversity are valued and decision making is de-centralised. In this model, policy making is not independent of the political culture and values in a society. As Lindblom (1959: 84) says, 'limits on human intellectual capacities and on available information set definite limits to man's capacity to be comprehensive'; accordingly, you cannot consider policy making as an exclusively rational process. Uniformity and utilitarian aims for public policy are discouraged because of a distrust of abstract designs, calculation and sophistry. Political problems are essentially seen as moral problems, so free association and deliberation among citizens is prioritised through interconnection and interdependence while speedy political reform in policy is not: policy makers are expected to demonstrate prudence or practical wisdom gained through experience. This is why values, judgements and ideology can be more important than research evidence and why Lindblom (1959: 86) believes 'a wise policy maker consequently expects that his policies will achieve only part of what he hopes and at the same time will produce unanticipated consequences he would have preferred to avoid'. Making policy is, in this model, a rough and ready process, and the policy maker will often feel more confident when 'flying by the seat of his pants' than following the advice of academic experts. However, this approach can result in confirmation bias – discounting evidence that is not consistent with prior beliefs. Then it can become more a question of power, world views and competing ideologies than research evidence. The citizens in a democracy, within this model, have a role to play in examining public policy announcements and act as a critical resource for the legitimisation of these policies. There is a focus on what is desirable in terms of the common good and where we are going as a society. There is a combination of facts and values which are offered as good reasons for a particular policy. Significantly, this model *does not reject* the empirical, but rather places it within a larger set of normative concerns that give meaning to research-based knowledge (see Fischer, 1998: 139).

These are not the only normative models that one could employ in understanding the background and context for policy making, and Dror (2003: 131ff.) provides many others. Educationalists have been debating the normative basis of education for centuries and it would seem that it is unlikely that they will reach a consensus any time soon. Bell and Stevenson (2006: 8) identify a normative, four-stage policy process in education that begins by:

> recognising the importance of the wider socio-political environment in shaping the discourse within which policy debate is conducted. From within this discourse, a strategic direction develops in which specific educational policies become more clearly defined, and success criteria are established. As policy texts emerge with greater clarity, this in turn shapes the organisational principles, and ultimately the operational practices, that shape the experience of policy at an institutional level.

While they recognise that policy is about the power to determine what gets done, they also acknowledge that policy embodies an expression of values – statements of what ought to happen – and that this results from a particular context and discourse as well as from a process of negotiation and compromise. Everyone in education, they claim, has the potential to influence policy development, and people should not see themselves as simply 'passive implementers' of policy. Educational researchers are always 'entrepreneurs' in the sense that they are in the business of creating new ways of thinking and new ways of seeing the world through the creation of new knowledge in solving problems and transforming lives. Nevertheless, while teachers will make technical judgements about the most effective means to obtain particular educational gaols, they will inevitably make normative judgements about the acceptability of the means they employ. They will make a normative claim about what is right and worthy of passing on to the next generation.

This text is intended to build the confidence and skills of education academics in securing greater policy impact for their work. The text – intended to be informative across all disciplines – is aimed at educationalists who are building impact case studies, as well as those seeking to influence educational institutions, practitioners and policy makers with their research outcomes. Research outcomes, or findings, refer broadly to the knowledge produced by academic researchers who generally, but not always, have an academic institutional affiliation and appropriate academic qualifications that give them the status of 'expert' in a particular field. These academic researchers will normally follow disciplinary procedures, conventions, methodologies and conceptual understandings which confer authority on their research activity and findings. Today, universities around the world seek to recruit academics who have an eye for the impact of their work; people who can engage policy makers and influence or benefit society with their research. As early as 1984, Husen and Maurice Kogan held what was perhaps the first symposium on 'Researchers and Policy Makers in Education: How Do They Relate?' in Sweden, which debated the impact of educational research on policy making. They concluded that the impact of research on policy making was not direct, but rather that research influenced policy in more subtle ways. Research findings in education were often inconclusive, from the policy makers' and researchers' points of view. Today, there is a greater focus on the use and influence of research in public policy, and this text examines the phenomenon through the lens of policy entrepreneurship.

Influence is the ability to steer others to act, think or feel as you intend. Influencing the policy process can mean anything from minor reforms of existing policies to the creation and adoption of new policies. Research impact is an 'auditable occasion' of influence, which takes place either within a university or external to a university, through the impact on society or the economy. Demonstrating impact through policy entrepreneurship is now an important element in gaining research grants, and this book seeks to assist educational researchers by outlining the necessary kinds of skills for academics to acquire. The opportunities for academics to contribute to educational policy formulation are varied. Educational researchers can contribute to this process through identifying issues, assessing benefits and harms attached to proposed solutions, estimating costs and consequences, and participating in the policy process itself. The text is specifically written for the field of education, and for academics who wish to see their work have more policy impact. It employs examples both nationally and internationally to illustrate the insights into policy entrepreneurship activities that advance impact. It combines theory and practice, putting a practical emphasis in some chapters on how to *do* policy entrepreneurship in education. The book has both theoretical and practical dimensions, and recommends that readers choose appropriate techniques, devices or methods they can employ to advance the impact of their own research.

Chapter outline

Chapter 1 examines the academic/policy maker interface and considers the influence and impact that academic researchers have on public policy. It recognises that the distinctions between policy impact, policy discourse, policy analysis, policy evaluation, policy transfer, policy advice and policy making are blurred, both in practice and in the literature. It considers the role of universities in a time of declining impact on policy from higher education. The chapter considers the nature of evidence-informed policy and looks at how education policy is implemented, giving some examples of successful policy entrepreneurship in the education field.

Chapter 2 defines policy entrepreneurship and evaluates the idea of policy entrepreneurship as a driver of educational policy changes. While 'entrepreneur' may be a key concept used to explain the timing and extent of policy innovations, we need to be clear about how we use the term, and also consider its misuse. Who are the entrepreneurs? What is their role? What skills do they possess? Do entrepreneurs sell ideas or services? Do they benefit from policy outcomes that favour their beliefs, or from material outcomes? This chapter looks at how to build coalitions: identifying issues and problems, developing expert knowledge, gaining insights, accessing decision makers, winning support for ideas and networking in policy circles. This chapter identifies the main characteristics of a policy entrepreneur in practical terms. This involves identifying and engaging with stakeholders and developing networks – making connections between different people and different groups. Relationships build the trust necessary to bridge the gap between research-based knowledge and action. The area is a vastly complex, inter-related web of structural, bureaucratic and personal factors. It cannot be entirely grasped in rational terms, and it is difficult to quantify or measure the success of policy change. It requires long-term engagement demanding in-depth knowledge of personalities and structures. It is important to be familiar with the issues involved; this means the goals, policy entrepreneur supporters and the opposite position on the issues.

Chapter 3 looks at the practice of policy entrepreneurship, showing how the concept manifests in real life, while Chapter 4 considers how policy entrepreneurs introduce, translate and implement new ideas into public policy through an examination of three contrasting case studies in recent UK education policy. Chapter 5 considers the Jubilee Centre for Character and Virtues in action. Extensive use will be made of the successful impact strategies employed by the Jubilee Centre together with the author's own entrepreneurial actions. This chapter attempts to 'put some flesh on the bones' by providing a detailed case study of the Jubilee Centre. Some readers may want to read this case study as a stand-alone contribution, since it considers policy entrepreneurship in the context of the emergence and establishment of the Jubilee Centre. The chapter chronicles the evolution of the Jubilee Centre and identifies precipitating events and significant points of time in the Centre's emergence and influence. Chapter 6 concludes the text with some final commentary on policy entrepreneurship.

1

THE INFLUENCE AND IMPACT OF ACADEMICS ON POLICY MAKING

> Our most direct and urgent message must be to the [researchers] themselves: learn to communicate with the public, be willing to do so and consider it your duty to do so.
>
> *Royal Society, London,* The Public Understanding of Science, *1985*

Introduction

The President of the John Templeton Foundation, Dr. Jack Templeton, first used the word 'entrepreneurial' in relation to research at a discussion with me over breakfast in London's Royal Over-Seas League Club in May 2005. It was not a word that I had ever imagined would be used in the context of research, and at the time I did not understand the extent of his implications. Was he asking me to start a new business? Did I have the set of personal characteristics to pursue such entrepreneurship? I was especially surprised that Jack used the term, given that his background was in medicine. He was an eminent paediatric surgeon in Philadelphia but had retired from his medical practice in 1995 to manage the charitable foundation created in 1987 by his father, Sir John Templeton, the pioneer global investor and philanthropist. His use of 'entrepreneurial', I later discovered, was concerned with encouraging researchers to think outside the box, to reflect on what they called the 'big questions' and to consider what difference their research would actually make. He was using the word 'entrepreneurship' in its original French sense to characterise someone who undertakes a significant project or activity over a period of time. Dr. Templeton knew that issues of policy in the public realm can take many years to resolve and that knowledge acquisition and network building need considerable time and effort.

His use of 'entrepreneurial' still shared some similarities with a business plan, but it was distinct in that it had the goal of mission-related impact. It was concerned with making the world a better place – the creation of the 'good society'. He believed that if a researcher discovered something worthwhile in their research, then they should share it; they should make it accessible to the public and to policy makers. He made me think more clearly about the purpose of my research and about its policy implications in terms of communicating the outcomes to a wider audience. I could see that his use of 'entrepreneurship' could have radical potential in that it could challenge traditional ways of doing things. It was not about quick fixes or immediate solutions to problems. I had first met Dr. Templeton at the invitation of Dr. Arthur Schwartz, Executive Vice President of the John Templeton Foundation (JTF). The intention of the meeting was to brief Dr. Templeton on a character research project funded by the JTF that I was then directing in collaboration with the University of Bristol.

This was unusual in that few grantees ever get to meet and brief the President of the JTF. It was a privilege, and initiated a lasting friendship with Dr. Templeton. He effectively became a mentor to me up to the time of his death in 2015. He taught me about 'entrepreneurship' and 'impact' within research contexts long before research impact became a requirement in the UK Research Excellence Framework of 2014. He was wise enough to know that new knowledge gained through research does not necessarily result in attitude or behaviour change, but he believed that excellent research can achieve impact and benefit society. Importantly, he believed that research focused on application or addressing societies' strategic needs is as valuable and important as fundamental research. Like Marshall McLuhan, the Canadian philosopher and public intellectual, he regarded some researchers as people who know more and more about less and less until they know everything about nothing! His warning here was that we should be careful to see both the wood and the trees together. He would often ask 'So what?' and 'What next?' when it came to funding research projects.

I understand policy entrepreneurship as a process by which research, policy and practice become more closely connected. It is also about making a contribution to policy agenda setting through the production of new ideas that emerge from research which is then made accessible and intelligible to the public, professionals and policy makers. It is essentially about maintaining research integrity while maximising impact, and many methods towards this end are detailed in this text. Dr. Templeton had introduced me to the concept of being 'entrepreneurial' in the use of research outcomes, and I have become a kind of 'policy entrepreneur' – this did not happen overnight, but took many years of experience, experimentation and exploration. We talked about theories of change and understanding the context, the different actors involved, and the events leading to the final impact being achieved. Policy entrepreneurship is not a concept that most educationalists will have encountered, but I believe that exploring its meaning and application in education has the potential to enhance our understanding of how to develop and promote solutions to issues within educational policy and practice. It involves a mixed methods approach to research, including descriptive, evaluative, prescriptive and exploratory methodologies.

Research methodologies are much contested in the social sciences, but are generally characterised by a proliferation of divergent philosophies and techniques. Essentially, policy entrepreneurship, when applied to academia, is a specialised academic or research role for someone engaged in applied research and who is establishing contacts and networks as well as their own external visibility as an academic in promoting their research findings.

It should also be noted that I recognised from the outset that all public policies are contestable and that policy work is not neutral in that I was adopting a point of view – namely that character education matters. As a contested area, this brings to mind the work of Briggle *et al.* (2015: 1), who noted that 'we do not need to tell the authorities what they want to hear, but we do have an obligation to address questions that they think are important'. I knew that working in this area would be uncertain and that any influence would be unpredictable and ultimately beyond my control. Policy entrepreneurship has many risks and is normally open-ended; it does not end with policy adoption, but rather with policy implementation. As Crowley (2003: 9) notes, 'there must be a true mission, a true passion, and a true higher aim. No one can wake up one day and decide to move a policy mountain. Brief interludes with the power structure simply do not qualify. Policy entrepreneurs must be in the game for the long run.' This summed up what I set out to do, but I was not entirely aware of all aspects of the process, and tried to prepare for surprises and the unexpected. I also recognised that the word 'entrepreneurial' is often used rather loosely, and that sometimes little effort is made to explain the use of this market-based metaphor.

Academic influence and impact on public policy

It is an accepted tenet of a thriving democracy that people and organisations are allowed some degree of influence on policy makers and hence on policy formulation. The range of people and organisations that seek to influence public policy is wide and includes politicians, civil servants, local government, courts, interest groups, associations and foundations, trade unions, think tanks, policy networks, the media and universities. Increasingly, these organisations will conduct research to influence practice and policy, which gives them an apparently solid base for their advocacy. Think tanks and many other organisations with research capabilities compete with academics in universities in creating new ideas and shaping the ideas that inform public discourse. These differing types of researchers and research-oriented organisations have very varied abilities to access policy makers at different levels. Many are already convinced by their own policy position and simply go out to gather in the evidence to try to get their policy recommendation to the top of the political agenda. There is a strong rhetoric for policy making rooted in a robust evidence base – variously termed evidence-based or evidence-informed policy (Nutley *et al.*, 2007). The rhetoric of evidence-based or evidence-informed policy decisions has permeated all areas of UK public policy making since the 1990s.

It is often assumed that the relationship between research evidence and policy making is linear – a problem is identified, and research provides the policy options or answers. Lomas (2000: 140) has suggested that this way of thinking is viewed as 'a retail store in which researchers are busy filling shelves of a shop-front with a comprehensive set of all possible relevant studies that a decision maker might some day drop by to purchase'. There is little agreement on what the term 'evidence-informed' policy actually means in practice. It is, therefore, important to look at the nature of evidence, influence and impact in policy making, but also to recognise that policy making is inherently political. Politics is always integral to policy making, and Perry (Perry *et al.*, 2010: 27) found a common theme in his interviews with policy makers which was 'evidence can do little in politically charged areas'. A number of other scholars in the public policy literature reiterate this point with Beeson and Stone (2013: 2) remarking, 'When the political context is not conducive, even possession of what are widely accepted to be "the facts" may not prove sufficient to win the policy debate' (see also Sebba, 2013; Brown, 2011). Hallsworth *et al.* (2011: 12) observe that:

> When politics is mentioned, it is presented as something external to the policy process, a 'context' that must be 'understood' or 'managed'. Such an attitude grows out of a long tradition of believing that the application of 'higher' scientific criteria can answer the questions currently mired in the rather distasteful realm of politics. Such a treatment of politics is: Unrealistic: in reality, policy making can never be extricated from politics; Undesirable: politics adds value to policy making; and Flawed: evidence and analysis is never 'pure' or above politics.

They conclude that the exemption of Ministers in government from studies in policy making is perhaps the biggest flaw in attempts to improve policy making. However, there is no shortage of failures among those seeking to turn ideas and research knowledge into policy.

Bowen and Zwi (2005: 600) propose that an 'evidence-informed policy and practice pathway' can help both researchers and policy makers navigate the use of evidence. They outline a new pathway to 'evidence-informed' policy and practice by describing three stages of progression that are influenced by the policy context. The three stages are (a) sourcing the evidence, (b) using the evidence, and (c) implementing the evidence. The pathway also involves decision-making factors through a process which they describe as a cycle of 'adopt, adapt, and act'. Once adopted, evidence about implementation is usually adapted or changed before use in the policy context. Policy makers and practitioners need to understand and decide how best this evidence should be acted upon in each circumstance. Each stage in this pathway is underpinned by a variety of individual, organisational and system-level values. Fundamental to the transfer of evidence into policy and practice is diffusion, the process by which an innovation is communicated over time. As Bowen and Zwi (2005: 605) say: 'Evidence is usually sought to show effectiveness ("it works"), show the need for policy action ("it solves a problem"), guide effective implementation ("it can be done"), and show cost effectiveness ("it is feasible and may even save money").'

Kothari *et al.* (2009: 38) have detailed how a number of different kinds of information are associated with 'policy-related/policy-relevant' research, including:

- Research that informs all stages of the policy cycle, from agenda setting or defining the critical questions to evaluation and implementation;
- Research that helps to explain or describe the policy decision-making process;
- Research undertaken in response to specific questions by policy makers;
- Research informing organisational issues such as guidelines affecting individuals or policies within institutions;
- Research informing macro issues involving legislative changes and government regulations;
- Research with implications for change in large systems or groups in society.

It takes time for researchers to build relationships with policy makers, and there are often challenges, including the unrealistic time frames of government – politicians, who are often not in office for long, want something today, which makes it difficult for academics to respond at short notice. As Glendon (2011: xi) notes, 'scholars can debate endlessly about the wisdom, justice, and advantages of a course of action, but statesmen must make decisions and take responsibility for them'. They often make these decisions with imperfect or partial information to hand.

Policy makers increasingly like to present their policy positions from an 'evidence base' rather than simply from their political intuition or belief. They sometimes seek greater technical legitimacy for their policy by using evidence, but this 'evidence base', whatever the quality, can also be used as a mask to support existing political beliefs. Research evidence is not the sole active ingredient in policy articulation – it is one among a number of competing factors. Policy makers will consider costs, statistics, consultations, evaluations, public opinion and a number of other factors in their deliberations. Given the number of other factors under consideration, why should academics engage in public and political debates? The reality is that they do make contributions through various activities, including assisting government agencies, serving on advisory boards, collaborating with community organisations, serving as expert witnesses, consulting for government and non-profit organisations, giving media interviews, blogging for academic work – the list goes on. Cohn (2006: 8) believes that 'academics have an obligation to become involved in public life by participating in the policy process and to ensure that the knowledge they create serves the public good'. Judy Sebba, one of the most eminent scholars on evidence-informed policy in the UK, has also written on the economic, moral and academic imperatives in the use of academic research findings in education policy (2013: 394–395). However, researchers can sometimes be politically naïve, with a poor understanding of the links between evidence and policy making and unrealistic expectations about what research can achieve. Policy makers will of course value other types of evidence based on their personal experience, information from the press or advice from trusted friends. Indeed, policy making is shaped by the multiple factors already mentioned, and has to be viewed through competing values and perspectives – a point that is also strongly made by Whitty (2016).

Nevertheless, there are also many academics who promote themselves as 'experts' in particular public policy areas, and they continue to advise and hold strategic positions on government boards and councils (see Griffiths, 2010). Academics, who claim expert knowledge, frequently get their voices heard above many others in society, but their influence on policy is often indirect. Our understanding about how educational research can influence policy and practice remains at a relatively low level. However, there is the on-going question of how much difference research has made in public policy. The orthodox view is that educationalists have hitherto failed to translate their research into potential solutions for the many problems facing schools and education, partly as a result of pressures to publish in high-ranking specialist education journals. Educational research itself necessarily competes for the attention of policy audiences within an open market of research-based knowledge sources.

It is within this context that many educationalists in universities set themselves the goal of encouraging knowledge exchange, supporting use of research and strengthening its impact, albeit within a context where it is difficult to see when and how decisions about policy are made. The issue of why many educationalists are failing to connect with society's deepest interests and its most pressing concerns in schooling raises the additional question of where academic leadership in education is coming from. As Ball (2010: 153) says: 'There is a sense that academics remain unhelpfully out of touch with real and practical policy problems; that they are detached, cynical and more concerned with peer review … and spending time *thinking* than with getting on and *doing*.' There is a disconnect between academic research and the practice of non-academic organisations and practitioners (see Bartunek *et al.*, 2001). Teachers and policy makers are encouraged to make use of the latest research and information about best practice, and to ensure that decisions are rooted in this knowledge. However, this can be a difficult challenge given the large amounts of information generated by educational studies and research that may be biased and methodologically flawed; in addition, they may reach conflicting conclusions and that can be misinterpreted and misrepresented. It is not always clear which results are the most reliable, or which should be used as a basis for practice and policy making. Researchers often have to jockey for a position of influence within the policy-making process and their research is often not conclusive enough to be taken seriously. It is, therefore, not surprising that some academics believe that policy making is, for the most part, about 'muddling through' rather than the social sciences having an influential part to play in the process (Parsons, 2002).

Supporting research use within a policy context is effectively encouraging 'evidence-based policy' or 'evidence-informed policy', which are not in fact neutral terms or activities. Indeed, it has often become a highly charged and polarising idea. As highlighted in the previous chapter, emphasis on such a 'technological model' of policy making has a number of normative implications, even if they remain implicit. Nevertheless, there is a democratic principle at stake here as Willinsky (2000) reminds us that 'going public with our knowledge, for all of the challenges it poses, is about better equipping people to participate in a civil society and democratic society, to steer a steady course through the current state of information glut and knowledge fragmentation … it seems absurd that so little is done to ensure that the knowledge [social sciences have] to offer is a source of greater control for people.'

Geoff Mulgan (2003: 15), who was Director of the Prime Minister's Strategy Unit until 2004 and founder of the think tank DEMOS, recognised the 'rather non-ideological climate' in which policy is being made, and he notes that there is 'a great deal of fertility and experimentation' on the fringes or 'at the margins' from which good policy innovation emerges. Academic researchers are recognised by Mulgan as some of these policy innovators at the margins, and he suggests that most governments are simply interested in 'what works' rather than what makes ideological sense, and 'that means that there is likely to be a greater willingness to see practice rather than theory as the best source of ideas'. This emphasis on practical real-life evidence has become a central feature of what policy makers appear to want. Policy makers and practitioners often lack the time, patience or expertise to read through research reports. Ball (2010: 153) observes there is a movement 'away from academic expertise and towards simple messages that can be understood by politicians, policy makers and the public'. However, alongside politicians and civil servants, Mulgan, as a political adviser, must be seen as a former policy maker. The questions he raises about whose evidence, whose practice, what constitutes good evidence, who determines what information is considered to be evidence and practice, and how it should be used, are all contested areas in the literature.

Chris Brown is another former education policy adviser in the 10 Downing Street Policy Unit who has turned academic. Brown (2013) argues that policy will never be 'evidence-informed', nor will initiatives be truly successful in the long term, unless both researchers (as storytellers) and policy makers (as audiences) understand and play their part in the 'evidence-informed' process. He believes that research serves to enhance policy development by allowing policy makers to make sense of the social world and to anticipate the likely reaction to policy initiatives. He has noted a trend in evidence use within education policy-making contexts, in that policy makers require 'policy-ready' evidence. Here, policy makers seek more than just presentations of research findings; rather, they are looking for advice and recommendations on how research findings might be implemented as well as the implications of doing so. Brown (2015: 155) concludes that: 'Policy-ready outputs … result from the research acting more as a pseudo policy maker than simply being able to communicate their research effectively.'

Extending the economic metaphors, research outputs are treated as commodities, with policy makers acting as consumers, whether the research has been commissioned by government or not. Politicians enter the crowded market of policy ideas and solutions where they select and consume or ignore what they will. Brown clearly sees benefit in partnerships between researchers and policy makers for the improvement of future policy development, but the researcher needs to know that politicians will sometimes follow their political convictions irrespective of the research evidence; they can dismiss evidence for purely ideological reasons, which means there are limits to a technocratic approach to policy making. Academics can bring policy ideas to the table, but these ideas will be combined with the tacit knowledge of politicians so any policy outcomes will occur over an extended period of time.

More evidence, less ideology

The use of evidence in government policy making is not a new phenomenon, as can be seen in Haldane's (1918) report which noted that 'in the sphere of civil government, the duty of investigation and thought, as preliminary to action, might with great advantage be more definitely recognised'. The modern accent on 'what works' has led to an emphasis on data and metrics rather than on political beliefs. This can be misleading because focusing exclusively on the objective and 'neutral' language of policy making merely hides the political nature of policy making. As Patrick Diamond, another former Number 10 policy adviser turned academic has highlighted, this 'depoliticisation' is, somewhat paradoxically, an 'intrinsically *political* process' (2015: 431). The movement away from ideology was evident in the 1999 White Paper *Modernising Government* (Cabinet Office, 1999) which sought policy that is evidence-based, properly evaluated and based on best practice; it noted that government must 'produce policies that really deal with problems; that are forward-looking and shaped by evidence'. Pawson (2006: 175) is critical of this position and believes that 'much of the recent governmental head-nodding to evidence-based policy is mere lip service'. A report from the Cabinet Office Strategic Policy Making Team on Policy Making for the Professional Twenty-First Century also noted that 'policy making must be soundly based on evidence of what works' and that 'government departments must improve their capacity to make use of evidence' (1999: 40).

With respect to education policy, Michael Gove as Secretary of State for Education gave a speech entitled *Seizing Success* at the National College for School Leadership in 2010 in which he said:

> Indeed, I want to see more data generated by the profession to show what works, clearer information about teaching techniques that get results, more rigorous, scientifically-robust research about pedagogies which succeed and proper independent evaluations of interventions which have run their course. We need more evidence-based policy making, and for that to work we need more evidence.

The rhetoric of evidence-based policy making thus reached new heights, but the Labour Secretary of State for Education, David Blunkett (1999), in an address to the Confederation of British Industry (CBI), had already pushed matters forward when he said 'some researchers are so obsessed with "critique", so out of touch with reality that they churn out findings which no one with the slightest common sense could take seriously'. Blunkett's (2000) speech to the Economic and Social Research Council called for a new relationship between social science and government, one that would end the 'irrelevance' of social science research to the policy-making process. He asked that social scientists 'tell [the government] what works and why and what types of policy initiatives are likely to be most effective' and argued that:

> We're not interested in worthless correlations based on small samples from which it is impossible to draw generalisable conclusions. We welcome studies which combine large scale, quantitative information on effect sizes which allow us to generalise, with in-depth case studies which provide insights into how processes work.

The view espoused here by Blunkett and Gove is simplistic, as there are of course other factors than simply 'what works' that ultimately influence policy making. Indeed, I would go so far to say that it is simply impossible to investigate 'what works' unless you are guided by a paradigm of 'what matters', which is often based on political or philosophical ideology. As highlighted above, the role of values, beliefs and political ideology are usually strong driving forces along with the experience, expertise and judgements of individual policy makers. Hallsworth *et al.* (2011: 82) see that evidence can only ever form part of the solution to a policy issue and that 'policy making always involves personalities, negotiation, and complexity, with competing objectives and motivations: these things cannot simply be seen as inconvenient "noise" that disrupts an ideal policy process'. Indeed, evidence suggests that research in education is more often than not ignored by policy makers and, according to one surprising study, of 70,000 research projects undertaken in education, only 70 had a significant influence on education policy and practice (Molas *et al.*, 2000). Ultimately, evidence only provides a basis upon which decision making can make informed judgements.

Where research evidence is incomplete, ambiguous or contradictory, policy decisions still have to be made. Steve Hilton (2015: 31), former political adviser to then Prime Minister David Cameron, has cautioned against over-reliance on data because he believes it is dangerous to make assumptions based on data sets. He advocates a more human approach to policy making which involves politicians speaking to those affected by the policies they make. It is easy to see how research and decisions by both academics and policy makers could be out of touch with people's real lives. There are also risks of enlisting educational research in the cause of government policy making. Munn (2005: 24) argues that 'where research spills over into advocacy, an important boundary has been crossed', and she is opposed to researchers 'arguing for the desirable' – in other words for normative positions. It would be worth exploring further the boundary between policy and political strategy, which is sometimes conflated with the boundary between the uses of research knowledge and public policy.

As Weiss (1982: 620) says, 'cases of immediate and direct influence of research findings on specific policy decisions are not frequent' and 'rarely does research supply an "answer" that policy actors employ to solve a policy problem. Rather, research provides a background of data, empirical generalisations, and ideas that affect the way that policy makers think about a problem.' In other words, the main value of research findings is to help policy makers improve their conceptualisation of the issue and widen the range of options that they consider (see Davies, 2012). Davies (2015) outlines that there are many other factors than evidence that influence policy making and that evidence does not tell policy makers what to do or how to act. He argues, along similar lines to Weiss, that evidence provides a basis upon which policy makers can make informed decisions about the likely effect or impact of a particular policy intervention. Munn (2005) summarises the circumstances in which evidence might directly influence policy: (a) when the research is timely, the evidence is clear and relevant, and the methodology is relatively uncontested; (b) when the results support existing ideologies which are convenient and uncontentious to the powerful; (c) when policy makers believe in evidence as an important counterbalance to expert opinion; (d) when research users are partners in the generation of evidence; (e) when the results are robust in terms of implementation and (f) when implementation is reversible if need be.

Academic models of how policy is actually made in government can be unrealistic in practice, as they often follow a distinct stage theory. There is a general assumption that the politician is elected with some ideas, and these ideas are translated within government into plans for action which are then implemented by officials. There is an inherent logical flow here between discrete stages, or a series of sequential steps to the final policy. However, this is an oversimplification since policy development is frequently more indirect and diffuse, and takes time to appear. It is often a result of the cumulative impact of many different initiatives, or may even be determined by sudden events. While there is an extensive literature on research utilisation, Weiss *et al.* (2008: 30) suggest – rather discouragingly – that even when research is conducted in the most favourable conditions for policy implementation, 'most studies seem to be used in selective bits, reinterpreted to fit existing preferences or ignored'. This suggests that policy makers are subject to confirmation bias and will focus on evidence supportive of shaping the policy while ignoring what is not supportive.

Policy makers in government often commission research that can help validate their policy choices, and even advertise government concern and activity for a particular emerging policy (see 'Models of Research Utilisation' in Chapter 2). Decision making involves consideration of a wide range of factors, not least political priorities, the availability of resources, other contextual factors and information such as academic research. As Hallsworth *et al.* (2011: 12) note, 'good policies emerge from a combination of the political (mobilising support and managing opposition, presenting a vision, setting strategic objectives) and the technocratic (evidence of what works, robust policy design, realistic implementation plans)'.

Bates (2002: 403) draws attention to the use of educational research: 'the ways in which educational research is typically produced and utilised is as part of a complex conversation about a diversity of purposes, effects and judgements, rather than a more technically orientated implementation of "what works".' It is true that research findings can be used in more subtle and indirect ways to bring about changes in understanding or shifts in perceptions and attitudes that can potentially alter the ways in which policy makers and practitioners think about ideas and what they do with them. However, for academics to state baldly that their research ideas are imperceptibly changing the face of education policy and practice is insufficient in the impact-orientated climate of the Research Excellence Framework (REF). Social science research outcomes are not as predictable as those in the natural sciences and often simply offer general principles to be considered.

In contrast, Tom Bennett, the founder of ResearchEd, wrote that 'there are few things that educational science has brought to the classroom that could not already have been discerned by a competent teacher intent on teaching well after a few years of practice. If that sounds like a sad indictment of educational research, it is. I am astounded by the amount of research I come across that is either (a) demonstrably untrue or (b) patently obvious … here's what I believe; this informs everything I have learned in teaching after a decade: experience trumps theory every time' (Bennett, 2013: 57–59). There have always been concerns about the utility and value of educational research, and it is advisable to use the term 'research evidence' in a broad sense when applying it to educational policy formation. There is an uneven coverage of areas of education on the research agenda, as well as much of the research being short-term and small-scale, which is, of course, not unique to educational research. There are not enough educational researchers with experience working with large data sets, and too many are simply concerned with communicating with each other in refereed journals in order to advance their careers in the academy. There is a need to strengthen the impact and value of educational research on policy formation, but the modest resources available for research in education make this goal a dream. Whitty (2007) argues that all types of educational research should be promoted, but with the proviso that it must be high-quality research.

While it is important to acknowledge difficulties, both in the lack of socially relevant research and in the various barriers they may face in securing influence, academics should aim to inform policy debates as scholars and not as party political advocates. When asked for advice and research findings they need to offer what they know and not what they wish for. Given the onus presently placed on 'what works' and evidence-based policy, it is important to consider political scientist Jack Walker's (1981: 92) point:

To the extent that scientific criteria are introduced for policy determination … agencies that seem to be ignoring valid scientific knowledge or whose policies are administered with bias will be in constant danger of losing their legitimacy.

Academics are not usually the authors of particular policies, as they often fail to translate their research into language accessible to audiences that lack familiarity with their disciplinary discourses. Many academics do not wish to work with the media, and some think that such engagement activity diminishes them in the eyes of colleagues. It is understandable that some academics do not feel that they have the skills to appear on a media platform, but engaging with the public can improve communication skills, influencing skills, confidence. In this way, academics can raise their own academic profile and develop important networks, which can in turn enhance their careers. Although this careerist mentality may appear selfish in isolation, there are realistic, individual benefits for engaging successfully with policy makers. Educationalists should be concerned about examining the impact of their research on informing policy, and that of research and policy on practice. Many are indeed committed to influencing societal development, with government and schools as their primary audience. Hence, a greater interaction between decision makers and researchers would be beneficial in better understanding each other's goals, influencing each other's work, forging new partnerships and promoting the use of research-based evidence in decision making. An enormous amount of research is published each year – and most of it will not be known to or taken up by policy makers or practitioners. Policy makers will also take advice from a variety of other sources, so educationalists need to be aware of the policy environment in which their knowledge competes. Policy entrepreneurs are risk takers; they have a vision that gives them direction and are able to tell a compelling story. They have the ability to collaborate and build a consensus with others in a process that is part political and part managerial. Yet it is important to understand that policy entrepreneurship is not equivalent to the application of private sector techniques to civil society.

This book addresses activities within one of these organisations that attempt to influence policy making – namely universities – and in particular looks at how educational research is and can be employed to advance particular policy options through 'policy entrepreneurship'. It is therefore important to consider the place of the university in society, and in influencing the policy-making process in particular.

The role of the university

The identity and purpose of universities is changing rapidly, contrasting sharply with traditional missions of a university. Although the ideas of the 'entrepreneurial university' (Etzkowitz, 1997) and 'academic capitalism' (Slaughter and Leslie, 1997) have been discussed for some years, it is not an easy task to conceptualise the current role of universities within policy entrepreneurship. Jeroslav Pelikan (1992: 16–17), echoing Newman in his *The Idea of a University*, offers a vision of the traditional university when he wrote:

> The advancement of knowledge through research, the transmission of knowledge through teaching, the preservation of knowledge in scholarly collections, and the diffusion of research based knowledge through publishing are the four legs of the University table, no one of which can stand for very long unless all are strong.

There is no mention here of engagement, influence or impact, but Pelikan and Newman would have recognised that universities often reflect on their place in the larger society and do demonstrate benefits to society and the wider economy – in other words, it is the impact of the university on society and the economy that is some justification of its continued public funding and support. Indeed, many of the new universities established in the nineteenth century were motivated by a more applied and practical orientation (Arthur *et al.*, 2016; Bond and Paterson, 2005: 332). Pelikan has a chapter on the 'Duty of the University to Society' which recognises that academics have always contributed to and engaged with society – hence, he adds the additional dimension of service to society to his conception of the role of a university. Universities are expected to be accountable and clearly useful to their societies while retaining their academic autonomy. In his study of academics, Watermeyer (2011: 407) writes that engagement might assist academics and improve the quality of knowledge in 'ways that do not harm, jeopardise or diminish the integrity of the expert'. Entrepreneurial academics can help bridge the gap between the worlds of academia and politics through their engagement. There has been a shift in higher education from universities seen as 'ivory towers' to universities as transparent public institutions, with governments viewing university research as a resource to be utilised. As Scott (1990: 40) argues, to 'retain their vitality even the most academic disciplines must be associated in some sense with a wider culture; to maintain that association they must satisfy criteria of relevance, even utility, that transcend their private scholarly values'. Since the public pays for universities, they should be able to understand what comes out of them.

There appears to have been a shift of power and influence on policy makers from the university to think tanks and lobbying agents. If this is the case, then we are witnessing the decline of universities as sources of policy ideas, knowledge and influence. In a review of the reasons why university researchers often fail to have an impact on public policy, Hammersley (2005: 319–320) outlines how researchers (a) are not focused enough on the concerns of policy makers and practitioners, (b) fail to produce research findings in time, (c) produce conflicting and confusing evidence, (d) can sometimes produce evidence that sits uneasily with common sense or what is 'known' by policy makers, which raises doubts about the validity of the research, and (e) prepare conclusions that are buried in obscure journals or are jargon ridden. Another reason is that researchers do not always possess the range of skills necessary to advocate, communicate and translate research outcomes into policy ideas, and many others lack project management skills. However, as a brief survey of UK university websites will reveal, this has not stopped them from claiming credit for policy making even where the research involved constituted perhaps a small element of a complex pattern of wider influences.

Universities have faced criticism about the insufficient impact of their work from a variety of sources. In 2014, universities in the UK were expected, through the Research Excellence Framework (REF), both to engage with communities outside higher education and give consideration to the impact of their research on society and the economy. This movement to demonstrate the impact of research on external audiences has swiftly become a permanent feature of university life – the need to articulate the impact of one's research beyond the academy. This emphasis has changed the way some academics think about their research as they consider who their research reaches, rather than where it is published. They now seek to ensure that their research gets to those in practice or policy with the power to make use of it. Such academics believe that the relevance of their research is as important as its quality. They seek to promote capacity for solutions to societal or economic issues. However, this way of thinking about the academic role is not universally agreed, and many academics feel that they cannot be an academic while simultaneously practising impact. They argue that others, perhaps 'middlemen', should translate their research into impact as it involves a different language and methodology, as well as different concerns. They claim that they are motivated in their research to enquire and discover, but leave change in society to others. Some researchers clearly do not identify any policy implications in their research, and it is against this background that some argue that there should be no public funding of research without some kind of public benefit.

In 2012, the Russell Group, representing 24 leading UK universities, produced a paper 'The Social Impact of Research Conducted in the Russell Group Universities', which attempted to connect the worlds of the policy maker, practitioner and researcher. It demonstrates that universities provide research facilities that support specific issues. We read that at Newcastle University, 'pioneering academics strive for excellence with impact', and that at Manchester, 'The University of Manchester's research has a positive impact on societies, businesses and individuals across the globe.' There is no shortage of claims to engagement, influence and impact from all universities, but universities are not often very precise or clear what they mean by these terms. Academics today require many more skills and qualities to succeed than simply a good PhD or prestigious university appointment. Research Councils UK has also published 'Inspiration to Engage', which outlines how academics can enhance their engagement activities. The document encourages academics to engage effectively with non-academic audiences. Government is increasingly setting strategic priorities for research through Research Councils UK.

Universities have certainly been obliged to become more entrepreneurial, sometimes in response to reductions in income, but just as often because they wish to acquire more resources. We even have the annual *Times Higher Education*

Entrepreneurial University of the Year Award, which encourages universities to become more entrepreneurial, including their academics impacting public policy. Indeed, few funding bodies now accept proposals that do not require researchers to identify the steps they will take to disseminate their work and to generate engagement and impact. Funders now expect a degree of applicability and utility in research.

Challenges and critiques of research projects directed towards impact have come from a number of angles. Thomas Molnar (1994) in his *The Decline of the Intellectual* has claimed that some academics have lost their way by collapsing their sense of intellectual vision into political activism, social engineering and cultural manipulation. In a series of critical articles, Stanley Fish (2003) argues that civic engagement as a goal of universities is misguided, if not immoral. He argues that academics should not take a stand on any political issue, and that attempts at engagement and influence of policy makers involves academics taking such a stand. However, accountability criteria, such as the impact element of the REF, require universities to deliver benefits from their research to society. Gordon *et al.* (1997) identify several types of policy research, each of which fall within a continuum which they characterise as either analysis *for* policy or analysis *of* policy. At one end of the continuum we have policy advocacy where the aim of the research conducted is to promote and advance either a single specific policy or a set of related policies. This can result in policy advocates arguing from their findings towards a particular conclusion, which is then offered as a recommendation. Other researchers may begin with a strong commitment to a particular course of action which predates the research, so their analysis is designed, consciously or not, to support the case to be argued. At the other end of the continuum is analysis of policy content where research is conducted for academic interest rather than impact; this is sometimes referred to as 'blue sky' research. This is more popular among educational researchers than the *for* policy variety and is certainly more critical in its approach. In between we have research conducted to inform policy makers with new information and advice. Policy monitoring and evaluation is also a popular form of policy studies which involves assessing impact, but evaluations can also influence the development of policy. The relationship between educational research and policy in education is often vague and undisciplined, and impacts policy in odd and unexpected ways. Most research is also government sponsored, with few independent sources of funding. It is also the case that the nature of the research itself is only one factor that might influence whether or not it is taken up by policy makers (see Brown, 2013). The credibility of the researcher is another such factor.

In 1999, the Economic and Social Research Council (ESRC) established the Evidence-Based Policy and Practice Initiative, a collaborative network of seven research units aiming to bring social science research much nearer to the policy-making process. The ESRC guidance (2009: 10–11) on social science research offers three goals for the training of competent social scientists which speak directly to the need to facilitate greater impact. First, the guidelines say that new social scientists should be trained to appreciate the potential use and impact of their research within and beyond academia; second, that they should develop the ability to engage with relevant users at all points in the research process; and third, they ought to have the ability to communicate their research findings effectively to a wide range of audiences. These three training goals will involve researchers participating in user networks such as subject associations and policy conferences and seminars, and may even extend to working with teams of professionals in practice. The content of training courses, based on these goals, will take into account the context for public engagement and will typically cover purposes and audiences, practical steps on how to engage, making use of partnerships, evidencing impact and turning plans into action. The ESRC is concerned that researchers are appropriately trained in a range of what might be termed 'entrepreneurial' skills.

Implications for the educational researcher

So, where does this leave the educationalist in the university? While educational research can be both pure and applied, many of its concerns are practical since the issues and problems it seeks to address are normally practical. As Winch (2001: 449ff) observes, the general public and policy makers' perception of education is that it is of practical relevance and ought therefore to be judged on its ability to say something relevant. Educational researchers, therefore, work on the assumption that educational research informs debates and decision making in education policy. Nevertheless, there is often a loose interaction between researcher, policy makers and practitioners in education. Policy makers would normally use research in two ways: to clarify policy goals and provide evidence. There has also been considerable discussion of what counts as educational research as opposed to any other kind of research. However, it is hard for educational research to claim neutrality since political commitment is apparent as soon as researchers espouse the promotion of justice or democracy in relation to their advocacy and engagement. As highlighted in the Introduction, research aimed at the promotion of such concepts – even if implicit and presented in technocratic language – has an expressly normative dimension.

It remains the case that some educationalists take an overtly ideological stance, however. Bertram Bruce and Mustafa Yunus Eryaman (2016: 1) in their *International Handbook of Progressive Education* outline the kinds of research projects conducted by progressive educationalists, who aim to 'develop self-actualising individuals who can take charge of their own lives and participate fully in the creation of a greater public good'. While the *Handbook* offers no single definition of progressive education, because efforts vary greatly, the chapters clearly indicate that progressive educationalists are often activists who engage in activist academic work to promote their versions of social justice. Monzo and McLaren (2016: 664), two *Handbook* contributors, in a provocatively titled chapter 'The Future is Marx', state that 'we advocate the advancement of a revolutionary Marxist critical pedagogy'. They also say, in an almost self-satisfied way for academics, that: 'Our love and devotion to the other, to the immiserated and oppressed, spawns our willingness to suffer and struggle alongside them.' It can be difficult to discern whether their research outcomes are the cause of their activism, or whether these outcomes merely serve to reinforce their pre-existing beliefs and feelings. Education policy making has become highly politicised, so the way researchers interpret their raw research data can be subject to bias. Researchers will ascribe significance to their findings, leading them to recommend policy ideas – so it is important to ensure that the research itself is of the highest quality; however, as we have seen, even this does not ensure take-up by policy makers. Many conservative politicians are suspicious of university research and often disparage qualitative educational research, particularly if it is derived from an academic approach grounded in sociological or cultural studies (Bastow *et al.*, 2014: 144).

Ball (1998: 76) comments that the 'idea that human sciences like educational studies stand outside or above the political agenda of the management of the population or somehow have a neutral status embodied in a free-floating progressive rationalism are dangerous and debilitating conceits'. Miles and Huberman (1994: 19) argue that there are no educational issues that are devoid of partisan interests, and that researchers are usually powerless to affect political debates. Academic researchers ought to have a sense of public duty which must not be confused with their own particular interests. An academic's private interest, which includes holding and actively promoting an ideology, could make it difficult for them to consider policy questions objectively. These ideological conflicts often result in conflicts of interest, but it is also difficult to distinguish them from policy disagreements. Ideological conflicts of interest are unavoidable in educational studies, which means that both academics and policy makers need to be able to identify and manage perceived conflicts of interest when considering the use of evidence in policy making. Morwenna Griffiths (1998: 3) in her *Educational Research for Social Justice: Getting Off the Fence* is explicit that educational researchers are justified in 'using research for working towards justice' and 'it is about taking sides and getting change'. She calls this 'committed research' and rejects the idea that having a position makes your research biased and suspect – you simply have to acknowledge the position adopted. After all, it is ideology that primarily prefers ideas of social justice in education.

However, some policy makers may look upon such research intentions as subversive activity. This can generate mutual distrust, where policy makers and practitioners are unfamiliar with researchers and lack an understanding of research principles. One of the most challenging aspects of becoming a successful policy entrepreneur is the creation of an 'apolitical shield' which protects them and allows their continuing mission to flourish. This shield, as Lewis (1980: 17) notes, 'serves to obscure what otherwise might be widely understood as political acts. If the entrepreneur is to succeed, he must make and sustain a public image of his actions and his organisation that appears to be free of partisanship, greed, self-interest and personal self-aggrandisement'. However, the reality is that setting the goals for education is a political and value-laden issue and it is not always possible to reach consensus. Beliefs drive political action much more than facts or research evidence, so research itself is seldom the final arbiter of political decision making. There is a strong case for academics to drop the veneer of impartiality and allow themselves to participate in partisan discussions and work in partisan organisations such as think tanks and policy-orientated organisations such as charities.

Education policy is often ideologically driven (Ozga, 2004: 1) and contrasting evidence-based policy with opinion-based policy is not always helpful, since it assumes that ideologically-based policy development is untested and only makes selective use of evidence. The reality is that policy makers need to consider more than research evidence – they need to consider the impact of new policy ideas on various interest groups and ask: Who benefits? Who feels threatened? Who loses? What would make the policy more desirable to all? Can we afford the policy? The policy maker as politician needs to link with the culture and socio-economic structure of society; hence, research-informed policy is not sufficient by itself – decisions in policy making cannot be strictly technical, but remain essentially political.

Many educationalists examine educational policy against normative criteria, such as their advocacy of social justice and student empowerment. In the field of critical policy studies in education, it is common to reject the assumption that analysis can be neutral or entirely uncommitted. Educational research is not removed from interests and values and there is always a connection between educational research, practice and policy. Thinking about educational issues is always ideologically laden, and to claim otherwise is simply to be unaware of its influence. Pure research in education is not simply about a concern with what works, but must also consider what is educationally desirable. John Elliot (2009) has argued that applied research in education is best characterised by the intention to link research with action in a form that generates actionable knowledge. It is for practitioners and policy makers, he says, to determine whether or not this is actionable. However, simply presenting research to policy makers and practitioners and expecting them to put the evidence into practice is unlikely to work, for the reasons already stated above.

Educational research has suffered considerable criticism, ranging from the inaccessibility of research outcomes to the perceived irrelevance of educational research itself. David Hargreaves (1996) questioned the quality of educational research, as did the Hillage Report (Hillage et al. 1998) and Tooley and Darby (1998). The perception that educational research is of low quality has been difficult to shift. Tooley and Darby (1998: 6) claim that much educational research is going 'unnoticed and unheeded by anyone else', that it is ignored by practitioners and criticised by policy makers. Even with published articles in refereed journals, it is the case that most researchers are not even cited, which means the charge of enduring mediocrity continues. If the purpose of educational research is to identify solutions and provide options for policy makers and practitioners, then much of it has clearly failed.

Hargreaves, in a lecture at the Teacher Training Agency in 1996 criticising educational research, concluded that 'what would come to an end is the frankly second-rate educational research which does not make a serious contribution to fundamental theory or knowledge; which is irrelevant to practice; which is uncoordinated with any preceding or follow-up research; and which clutters up academic journals that nobody reads'. Much of this criticism applies across all the social science disciplines, as in a 2003 Report from the Commission on the Social Sciences that highlighted the continuing poor quality and inaccessibility of much social science research. The view in government, according to the report, was that 'too much of the research and analysis produced by academic social scientists is at best unexciting, at worst simply not up to standard' (Commission on the Social Sciences, 2003: 72). Education policy is only one area of public policy, and academic policy research is only one element in a complex process. Criticism of the research findings of social scientists is not new − Banfield (1980: 18) states, 'It is a dangerous delusion to think that the policy scientist can supplement successfully the politician … what the political leader requires is not policy science but good judgement − or, better, the union of virtue and wisdom that the ancients called prudence.' In other words, we cannot do away with politics and replace it with experts.

There is also a natural tension between researchers and policy makers, as they see things differently, have different time frames, and interpret research outcomes differently. This tension has been termed elsewhere the 'Two Cultures Thesis' (more often used to refer to the Science–Humanities gap), and outlines the various cultural and contextual differences between academics and policy makers (see the Ginsburg and Gorostiaga, 2001, framework discussed in depth in Chapter 2). Policy makers often regard educational research − indeed all social science research − as ambiguous, conflicting and even biased. They can be confused by the nature of evidence, especially as there is no shortage of it, and researchers often do not rate highly the type of evidence prioritised by policy makers. Policy makers often seek out research which pragmatically addresses the issues on their agenda, while researchers are less constrained in what they explore. By no means do all researchers wish to shoulder any responsibility for the use that others might make of their insights − they can be indifferent about whether or how their knowledge generation is applied in the world. Among basic differences are that researchers prioritise theory and methodology, while policy makers prioritise benefit and relevance. Researchers can be highly technical and use inaccessible language, while policy makers want short issue briefs. Hence the need to bring researchers and decision makers closer together so that they can understand and influence each other, especially as government is far more active in the making of education policy than ever before. In order to achieve this goal, researchers must make their research more accessible and more intelligible, as well as making connections with decision makers. The agenda cannot be simply about disseminating research to fellow academics, but rather the translation of research findings, where appropriate, into policy options. This ought not, however, be reduced to some technical or instrumentalist process, as academics recognise the danger of conceptualising new knowledge that is gained from research as mere 'product'. Without a certain relationship to truth, this kind of knowledge seen as product has no intrinsic meaning. Kirst (2000) argues that we need to translate research into plain English, make it accessible, and maintain links with policy networks as well as synthesise research findings from wide a range of sources. This will involve building relationships and agreement around research evidence.

While educational researchers encounter many difficulties when aiming to influence policy – as outlined above – the potential for them to bring about changes in education policy remains. Education researchers need to be concerned with real-world applications of their research findings – they need to be policy-minded. Davies *et al.* (2000: 2) argue that:

> this rise in the role of evidence in policy and practice is the result of a number of factors, which include the growth of an increasingly well-educated and well-informed public; the explosion of the availability of data of all types…; the growth in size and capabilities of the research community; an increasing emphasis on productivity and international competitiveness; and an increasing emphasis on scrutiny and accountability in the government.

Indeed, some of those at the forefront of the evidence-based policy movement saw this as a great opportunity and a very positive development. Geoff Mulgan has suggested that it led to 'a remarkably successful relationship between social science and policy in the UK', encouraging the 'systematic use and mobilisation of social science' (Mulgan, 2011, cited in Diamond, 2015: 445). In theory, this onus on research evidence ought to lead to more informed policy and better decisions that improve practice and outcomes. However, claims that are made about the quality of research do not have a direct relationship on the willingness of policy makers to adopt such research outcomes. As we have seen, policy makers are subject to a great number of other pressures, so an ability to understand and accommodate the influence of political context is, therefore, crucial, as is overcoming any scepticism about the research outcomes.

There are many real-life, practical examples of academic departments demonstrating impact in policy circles. For example, the University of Cardiff Education Policy Analysis Research Group 'has created productive relationships with policy makers, professionals and publics in Wales, the UK and internationally'. In relation to practice, the Education Endowment Foundation (EEF), founded by the education charity the Sutton Trust, received a founding grant of £125m from the Department for Education (DfE) to support the use of evidence-based practice. These bodies have ensured that their research findings have an audience through on-going communication with policy makers and practitioners along with face-to-face meetings, best practice demonstrations, workshops and seminars. They have encouraged researchers to provide relevant and useful evidence.

One of the most important examples in the UK of an impactful research project was the Teaching and Learning Research Programme (TLRP), initiated in 2000 and ended in 2011, directed by Andrew Pollard. This was a project of major national significance that led the way in how educational research can impact policy and practice. Pollard used the discursive spaces in society to debate and resolve policy issues as well as pursuing transformation from research into policy. TLRP's Communication and Impact Plan began strongly with a clear definition of impact:

> We conceive impact not as a simple linear flow (of research followed by transformation, dissemination of findings and adoption), but as a much more collaborative process: *interactive, iterative, constructive, distributed and transformative.* ... for us, impact therefore includes increasing awareness of new ideas and openness to change as well as direct influence on practice and policy. Working for impact is embedded in everything we do.
>
> *(Pollard, 2008, emphasis in original)*

This was the UK's largest education research initiative, which started out facing somewhat unknown terrain, and has tackled it with principled pragmatism. The Programme has enjoyed a great deal of support and good fortune and has benefited from strong alliances and partnerships. The Effective Preschool and Primary Education research project has also been successful in its impact because the researchers knew when to engage with civil servants and politicians as findings emerged from their research. It is also a very longstanding project, and has published reports and findings over a significant period of time, raising its profile and gaining further credibility with each report. Another key national project that has developed an understanding of evidence-informed public policy is the Evidence for Policy and Practice, Information and Coordinating (EPPI) Centre based at the Institute of Education, then a self-governing college of the University of London. Established as early as 1993, EPPI supported systematic reviews of social science research relevant to different areas of public policy and raised the awareness of the educational academic community about the importance of effectively communicating research to practitioners and policy makers. Although the project was focused on relevance and quality, it is often the case that evidence is sought after a policy initiative has been announced. One example of this is the major Social and Emotional Aspects of Learning (SEAL) policy, launched in 2005, and detailed in this text. Another is the introduction of citizenship education into the National Curriculum in England, an initiative that did not rely on research evidence to justify its provision.

In 2002, the Organisation for Economic Cooperation and Development (OECD) noted that research in education is typically funded at below 1 per cent of total education expenditure. In the UK, expenditure on educational research by government departments through universities has dramatically declined between 2002 and 2012 (Bastow *et al.*, 2014: 160). In comparison with health and science research, educational research expenditure in the UK is exceptionally low. Nevertheless, the then British government made efforts to enhance evidence-based policy through the establishment of the National Education Research Forum to increase awareness around research–practice links. Three new research centres were created through government funding between 1999 and 2000: the Centre for the Economics of Education, the Centre for the Wider Benefits of Learning, and the EPPI Centre already cited above. The ESRC also established the Centre for Evidence Based Policy and Practice to improve the accessibility, quality and usefulness of research in the social sciences. The ESRC aimed to encourage research findings to have strong advocates. There is, in actual fact, an array of educational organisations and centres that sponsor greater use of research-based knowledge in policy making. These include the Coalition for Evidenced Based Education and the Institute for Effective Education, both based at the University of York. There is the Evidence Based Education resource at the University of Durham as well as the Education Evidence Portal. There is also the Centre for the Use of Research and Evidence in Education and the Knowledge Network for Applied Educational Research. The British Educational Research Association (BERA) established the Strategic Forum for Research in Education, which brought together researchers and policy makers. All of this activity and the various alliances to advance research-based knowledge in policy making represent many different voices on what evidence-based policy might mean.

Many educationalists will challenge the assumption that entrepreneurial activity has the potential to improve education because they deem the entrepreneurial premise counterproductive and misguided. They suggest that the potential benefits of entrepreneurial activity are outweighed by its risks, and they often prefer policy reform to be channelled through the civil service that draws upon the guidance of professional and academic experts. The mistake is, perhaps, to conflate entrepreneurship in education generally with the specific pursuit of Free Schools, even if those who establish such schools are often the best known educational entrepreneurs. It may be easy to assume that those who support Free Schools are in favour of a kind of entrepreneurship, but that involves a fundamental misunderstanding of entrepreneurship in the sense used in this text. This book is about academic policy entrepreneurs, not the activities of policy entrepreneurs from outside the university. It should also be noted that there is no one single model that comprehensively and satisfactorily explains policy entrepreneurship.

Policy making

Policy making in Britain takes places within the context of a liberal democracy and can be initiated by government Ministers, parliamentarians, civil servants, local officials and sometimes those outside the machinery of government, such as the media and pressure groups. At elections, both national and local, the people are presented with a choice of policies from political parties from which they are entitled to choose. They elect a representative and give them the mandate to try to implement their policies. This democratic process encourages a constant and unending flow of new policy initiatives which can even include policy changes that are unnecessary to those that make the current situation worse. As Davis *et al.*

(1993: 4) observe: 'Any definition of public policy ... risks separating the policy process from its context. For values, interests and resources do not float free, waiting to link together in an ever changing array of combinations'. Research 'evidence' in a liberal democracy is largely produced by universities and think tanks which are given a degree of legitimacy and recognition in the policy-making process, but are not the final decision makers. Any research evidence they supply is considered against the backdrop of the mandate that a politician has received from the electorate. Therefore, researchers, no matter what evidence they find, cannot always expect to influence the very political nature of policy making.

There has been an upsurge of interest in evidence-informed policy and practice in the UK since the election of a New Labour government in 1997, with its anti-ideological stance. The period since 1997 has seen repeated efforts to define and rationalise policy making. The connection between policy making and the use of evidence is complex and involves both direct and indirect processes. Many have attempted to create models and theories of these complex sets of relationships, but have not succeeded in producing a model that works in practice. Policy making is the first step in any planning cycle, so when we consider this we need to understand who does it (actors) and how (the process). A broad view of who can be considered as policy makers is adopted here, while recognising that some politicians may reject the idea that they are policy makers at all, that they are advocates for certain positions and that they attempt to influence someone higher up; they see government as the real policy maker. We also need to remember that policy making is not conducted in a vacuum, but is inherently political, despite the apparent move towards 'what works'. Education is everyone's business, and it is the policy maker who attempts to balance these contradictory demands when making policy.

The link between research evidence and policy making took a utilitarian turn with 'what works' as the buzz phrase. There are now demands on researchers not only to produce useful research findings, but usable ones. This is why the then Labour government established the Centre for Management of Policy Studies in 1999 within the Cabinet Office, so as to ensure that government departments made better use of research evidence. Boswell (2009: 4) notes that by the early 2000s, civil service spending on policy-related research rose to £1.4 billion per year; and the National Audit Office report of 2003 highlighted that this increase in expenditure on research was in line with other countries, demonstrating 'increased awareness and activity to make these strategies and priorities a more integral part of policy-making'.

Hammersley (2001) saw this view of policy informed by research evidence as a good fit with 'a progressivist philosophy in which evidence-based practice is seen as opposing the "forces of conservatism" in the public sector; forces which are taken to represent entrenched interests'. New Labour was clearly suspicious of vested interests in policy making and sought to open up policy ideas to outsiders for 'external validation' (see Diamond, 2015: 437). This provided academics with an opportunity to influence and impact policy developments. However, Nutley et al. (2002: 2) warn that evidence is used in various ways by different people in the policy process, and so academics need to make modest claims for influence. They suggest that it is more realistic to speak of 'evidence-influenced' or 'evidence-aware' policy. Hammersley (2001) also reminds us that in education, 'evidence-based' cannot supply 'highly reliable answers to questions about what "works" and what does not'. Solesbury (2001) also argues that 'what works' is not all that matters and that we need 'an evidence base to policy in all stages of the policy cycle – in shaping agendas, in defining issues, identifying options, in making choices of action, in delivering them and in monitoring their impact and outcomes'.

The UK Audit Office, in its *Modern Policy-Making: Ensuring Policies Deliver Value for Money* (2001: 1), made it clear that policy is the 'translation of government's political priorities and principles into programmes and courses of action to deliver desired changes'. In other words, policy is government action or inaction in response to public issues and concerns. Policy making requires us to have a broad understanding of a range of inter-related processes. The classic way to understand policy making is to break it down into stages. The 'policy cycle' model provides a number of stages to understand how a particular policy emerges and includes six distinct stages: (a) agenda setting – identifying problems, (b) policy formulation – setting objectives and choosing solutions, (c) legitimation – gathering support for the solution, (d) implementation – policy accepted, (e) evaluation – assess the policy and (f) policy maintenance, succession or termination – continue, modify or discontinue policy. This policy cycle was once popular as a simple and understandable tool to understand how policy emerges and had the advantage of coming at the issue from multiple perspectives. Today, however, it is recognised that this scheme is perhaps overly complex and that the stages do not always run in this order.

Professionalising policy making

Ministers in government cannot pay attention to all of the research ideas that are available at any particular time, and so they focus and promote a small number while ignoring the others. In addition, many policy decisions are also not shaped in detail by political policy makers, but are rather devolved to administrative policy makers in the civil service. Politicians see many of the decisions in policy making as too complex and time consuming for them to make directly, but it is often said that the bureaucracy at the heart of government can be resistant to change and oppose any drive for policy innovation. Mulgan (2006: 147) observes that 'the civil service is viewed as inert, bureaucratic, conformist and poorly designed for original thought' given its size. However, civil servants are policy makers and in *Twelve Acts to Professionalise Policy Making: A Report of the Policy Professions Board of the Civil Service* (2013) it is made clear that policy officials are concerned with developing implementable policy. The three major concerns are: first, securing sound evidence; second, understanding and managing the political context; and third, planning from the outset how the policy will be delivered. The report uses the work of Hallsworth and Rutter (2011: 14) and describes five policy tests that policy officials, including those in the DfE, consider with respect to each initiative in policy development. These are:

PURPOSE – Are you absolutely clear what the government wants to achieve? Do you have a very clear idea of the high-level outcomes and outputs that the government would like to see?

ROLE – Are you absolutely clear what the role of the government is? Is there definitely a problem here that can only be fixed through some form of government intervention?

EVIDENCE – Are you confident that you are providing world-leading policy advice based on the very latest thinking?

CREATIVITY – Are you confident that you have explored the most radical and creative ideas available in this policy space ... including doing nothing?

DELIVERY – Are you confident that your preferred approach can be delivered?

These tests provide policy officials with significant influence on policy formation and make them co-policy makers. Civil servants are expected to build on 'best practice' and consider 'what works' by asking 'what is the point?' before leaping to deliver a solution. The idea is that they consult with practitioners as well as experts to ensure that their policy advice is based on the latest expert thinking before policy reaches the implementation stage. The DfE also seeks an Open Policy Maker strategy, with the aim of understanding what excellence looks like and who the experts are; understanding the user perspective and that of relevant networks; and actively going where the debate is in order to generate a better understanding of the nature of the problem, better insights and ideas and to broaden the dialogue outside Whitehall. This is a plan to interact with experts, practitioners and academics. The Public Administration Committee (January 2014) stated that:

> The Civil Service does not have a monopoly on policy making, but civil servants are well placed to act as the guardians of the policy process, ensuring representation, analysing, moderating and support.

It is often said that civil servants and politicians do not take sufficient account of academic and expert opinion, but in the Cabinet Office's *Modernising Government* (1999) it is explicitly stated that policy should be 'shaped by the evidence rather than a response to short term pressures'. Advisory panels are being set up by departments in government so that more civil servants feel able to ask how government could do something differently and then tap into advice from academics on relevant research in a given area.

The Cabinet Office's Behavioural Insights Team, sometimes called 'the nudge unit', is a good example of how policy officials in the civil service can act as innovators of policy ideas, drawing on insights from academic research in behavioural economics and psychology and applying them to policy making. The Unit has undoubted skills in forming alliances as well as the ability to form good relationships and partnerships with the academy. The purpose of the Unit is to come up with new ideas in government to encourage pro-social behaviours and allow citizens to make better choices in their lives. It was created in June 2010 as a unit within the Cabinet Office and consists of a small team of policy officials who consult with academic experts; it also has an academic advisory panel. It acts as a policy change agent by promoting innovation and new policy ideas, and is an excellent example of how academics and policy officials interact to improve policy formulation by using the best available evidence from a range of sources. Brown (2015: 158) has consistently recommended that academics ought to work with civil servants to establish policy-learning communities that develop expertise in relation to policy use. He believes that these learning communities can be points of knowledge creation. These communities can also assist civil servants in mediating effectively between academic researchers and politicians.

Bastow *et al.* (2014: 164–165; for further empirical evidence also see Brown, 2011) conducted research with policy advisers in the civil service and have noted that civil servants often perceive academics as long on diagnosis but short on solutions. One senior Whitehall official commented that academics who show a 'willingness and ability to help us think through what our response should be, get invited back'. Other policy officials commented that 'it is really about the translation role. Unless we can distil that evidence down, boil it down into key messages that really have political traction, then we are not going to have much impact' and 'it may be great research, but unless you can do that translation job ... and often that is the role of my colleagues to say: "The key thing in this research is X" ... it does take particular skills to do that. And researchers who can do that are going to develop more trust.' Civil servants are eager to identify worthwhile knowledge gained through research evidence that helps build traction on a particular policy issue. Civil servants can also be entrepreneurial, and there have been calls for civil servants to be more entrepreneurial, with David Cameron speaking in January 2012 about 'liberating the hidden army of public service entrepreneurs' (see Cahn and Clemance, 2011: 11).

Mulgan (2007) identifies three policy fields and groups them into three types: stable policy fields, policy fields in flux, and inherently novel fields. Stable policy fields are 'composed of areas where knowledge is settled; governments broadly know what works; there is a strong evidence base; and the most that can be expected is some incremental improvement'. Academics and professionals in these stable fields can be relied upon to give good advice. In the area of policy flux 'most people recognise that things need to change; that policies which once worked are no longer working'. He says that professionals in these areas of flux are often as much a part of the problem as the solution and that their networks 'may be the last to recognise the need for change'. The role of academics is not specified, perhaps because academics often support the professionals. The third type of policy field – inherently novel fields – are seen as fields where 'no one knows for sure what works or what doesn't because these are virgin territories – the experts will only be just ahead of the amateurs'. His description throws up many questions, not least how politicians make good decisions. Should these decisions be evidenced-based? What counts as evidence? With evidence to back them up, politicians may expect to command greater public support. However, Lasswell (1951) would have asked more sophisticated questions in terms of what works for who, when and how. What kind of evidence works for what kind of problem/policy, in what context, and for whom?

It is worth mentioning briefly that Stephen Ball along with Richard Bowe and Anne Gold (Bowe *et al.*, 1992) developed the concept of the 'Policy Cycle' in which they considered the key question of the extent to which the state determines the policy-making process and, as a consequence, the room available for other actors, especially those involved in implementation to re-interpret the policy text in practice. In their analysis both the process and the extent to which the state determines policy content is key. Bowe *et al.* (1992: 10) have argued that the state-controlled models of policy making are too simple because they neglect the agency of anything other than the institutions of the state. They focus on the detachment of the policy generation from implementation and believe that:

> The image implicit in the conception of distinct and disconnected sets of policy makers and policy implementers actually serves the powerful ideological purpose of reinforcing a linear conception of policy in which theory and practice are separate and the former is privileged. The language of "implementation" strongly implies that there is within policy, an unequivocal governmental position that will filter down through quasi-state bodies and into the schools.

They argue 'that it is not simply a matter of implementers following a fixed policy text'. They therefore reject models of education policy which separate the generation and implementation phases of policy. The notion of a policy cycle is, therefore, about where and how policy is made and remade in different contexts. They outline a number of contexts in which the struggle for policy is enacted, for example the context of influence, of text production and of practice. Ball (1994) later extended these contexts to include contexts of outcomes and political strategy.

Conclusion

Many authors, particularly those who have worked in government, appear to frame evidence-informed policy making as an antidote for ideology-driven decision making. They also confuse 'evidence' with 'proof', which can lead to an undue sense of certainty in decision making, as there is no certainty in using any kind of research evidence. It is hard to say how realistic this approach is when it is clear that policy making is carried out within a normative context, with multiple interpretations of evidence, together with multiple sources of research knowledge. A busy research engagement schedule alone does not necessarily provide for impact on policy. Policy making is multi-faceted and covers a wide range of processes, and government has become much more technocratic since Tony Blair referred to the 'post-ideological' approach to policy making (quoted in Boswell, 2009: 4). As the activity and scale of government action expands, particularly with centralisation and bureaucratisation, the perceived need and rhetoric that advances and produces technical policy solutions appears to increase. And yet Perry *et al.* (2010: 39) observes that 'the distance between evidence and policy seems to grow, the longer a government is in power' and (2010: 40) that 'many of our interviewees perceived a reduction in the use of experts and academic educationalists, and an increase in the power of political advisers'. This, of course, has not prevented intellectuals and social activists pursuing an ever-increasing array of policy initiatives.

It is also the case that the greater the quantity of research knowledge produced, the harder it is for a policy maker to see what the recommendations are. Academics can contribute by helping generate policy options or ideas which they can help evaluate with policy makers so that the policy maker can make a better policy decision. The idea that research is directly useful in the policy-making process has been disputed in this chapter. Even the idea that there is such a thing as 'evidence' that speaks for itself and is waiting in the wings of academe to be shaped effortlessly into policy is highly problematic. In the context of the perceived declining policy influence of universities, there is a renewed emphasis on the direct, instrumental use of research, in which evidence of what works in a particular area has become the apparently predominant concern of policy makers and practitioners. Despite New Labour's proclaimed belief in evidence-based policy, the reality was that many policy announcements were made without any research being involved. Research from universities is increasingly judged by economic criteria, with judgements of quality based upon numerical data. Only those activities subject to numerical calculations are noticed and valued – a point well made by Whitty (2016).

There is a problem when many education articles in academic journals appear to have the same opening mantra – the subject matter is contested, it is complex and problematic, the research is in progress, and the research outcomes are unclear and contradictory, being presented in a language almost deliberately inaccessible to practitioners and policy makers. This is perhaps why David Blunkett (November 2002) was so critical of educational research knowledge. Yet, in his contemporaneous diaries he recorded the following: 'I am making a lot of judgements by instinct, just by feeling in my guts whether the information being given to me stands up. Much of politics is like this. People expect it to be scientific and clinical, but it isn't.' There is a research–policy/practice gap with the general assumption that what works is not always translated into practice. The main way to improve the uptake of evidence in both policy and practice is to develop on-going interaction between academics and users of research evidence, but this may raise concerns about independence and impartiality. It also raises questions about how accessible policy makers are, and whether such access and evidence increases policy legitimacy. Educational policy entrepreneurs may help us re-define our sense of what is possible as they seek to instigate change. The term can be used to describe a wide variety of phenomena and we need to explore this in more depth. There is also the question of dealing with those who oppose your policy ideas, and on this Taylor (2005: 750) offers us some wise advice:

> The researcher's strategy needs to differentiate clearly between those people who can be persuaded, those people who cannot be persuaded, those people with whom it is possible to compromise and deal with, and, sometimes, those people who need to be isolated and simply defeated, because they are going to stand up against change.

2

POLICY ENTREPRENEURSHIP

Start by doing what is necessary, then do what's possible, and suddenly you are doing the impossible.

St. Francis of Assisi

Introduction

The previous chapter set out to examine the relationship between academic research and the policy-making process. It was suggested that this is a particularly pressing issue given the fact that social scientists have struggled to understand fully how policies establish their place on the public agenda. This chapter will present the outstanding literature on policy entrepreneurship in detail, showing how the framework can help academics to tackle the obstacles in securing policy impact for their work.

The phrase 'policy entrepreneur' is open to multiple definitions and interpretations. Policy entrepreneurship is essentially about influencing society with persuasive arguments made to decision makers. It demands vision and a sustained commitment combined with sound administration and good operational management. It is essential to have the ability to communicate complex ideas in jargon-free language to policy makers and practitioners who are seeking usability and ask demanding questions of researchers. It is important to note that not all educationalists will have the capacity or inclination to involve themselves in these pursuits. There are also significant tensions between new knowledge and engagement with policy take-up, and within the academy there are changes in the way that success is being measured. There is a fixation with quantification and measurement, and the growing impact agenda will shorten the time from ideas to implementation – in other words, there is an increasing emphasis on the short-term imperative and opportunism.

The diverse conceptual literature on policy entrepreneurship lacks clear definition and is dominated by American and Australian academics Kingdon (1984; 2003), Mintrom (2000), Roberts and King (1991). While the concept has developed largely within an American context, it has wide application and scope in terms of describing and explaining the agenda-setting process within public policy elsewhere. In the US, the political system has allowed the growth of policy entrepreneurship activities and Baumgartner *et al.* (2006: 965) have suggested that 'the less central role which political parties play in American politics is clearly reflected in the tendency of the American agenda-setting literature to emphasise interest groups, think-tanks and policy entrepreneurs rather than political parties'. Young and Connelly (1981: 163) were the first British academics to employ the term when they placed emphasis on the entrepreneurial activities of select individuals in the formulating of local government policies in England. They stressed that: 'Change does not occur as the result of the operation of an "invisible hand" of organisation dynamics. It arises from the activities of policy entrepreneurs who act (sometimes covertly) as advocates of change and who are the prime movers in development.'

It is a useful starting point to describe what a policy entrepreneur might look like, what they do in practice and in what context, but it is difficult to distil this down into one definition or template. Since the 1980s, various scholars have tried to develop a range of models of how this works and have been concerned with the question: What are the defining characteristics of a policy entrepreneur? We need to consider the motivations of policy entrepreneurs and their interaction with their contexts – their specific environment. The motivating factor for politicians to involve experts in the process of policy making is the prospect of a more cooperative public – to secure public acceptance of policy change ideas before they are implemented. This is why policy makers must consider how the public might react to new policy ideas. How do contextual factors constrain and shape their actions? We also need to understand their limitations: policy entrepreneurs are not responsible for all changes in policy direction, and Mintrom and Norman (2009: 651) have long argued that the contextual factors must be studied further so as to understand policy entrepreneurs within their context and how this shapes their actions. There has been increasing interest in the literature in models of the policy-making process, particularly on how policy changes emerge.

It is also interesting to note, given the definitional ambiguity surrounding the concept, that there is no single unifying theory with respect to public policy, and that policy making is an elusive and moving target. Indeed, it could be suggested that the literature on policy entrepreneurship lacks definitional clarity precisely because of the 'organised anarchy' of the policy-making process (see Cohen *et al.*, 1972). As Jobert (1989: 376) observes:

> For two decades the arguments about the impossibility of making sense of the policy making processes have been piling up. The complexity of the data to be mastered by decision-makers seems boundless. Political choice has to

take into account different scales of values, different dimensions of knowledge, different social groups, and there are no obvious clues about how to combine them.

In attempting to ascertain how a particular policy decision is made, researchers need to look at the role of individual actors, groups, institutions and contexts, among others, because there are multiple policy processes at play, which are often complex and messy. It is not exactly clear why a policy entrepreneur may be successful in having an impact on one issue and fail in another. Sabatier (2007: 4) observes that 'understanding the policy process requires knowledge of the goals and perceptions of hundreds of actors ... involving possibly very technical scientific and legal issues over periods of a decade or more while most of those actors are actively seeking to propagate their specific "spin" on events'. This complexity and unpredictability make it difficult to measure policy impact, and of course there is always more than one way to interpret the significance of any policy initiative from the research evidence gathered. As academics appraise and review the policy process they normally combine and fuse different theoretical models as well as significantly change the meaning of different aspects of the policy process. Taylor (2005: 750) argues that it is vital that the researcher understands the policy process and:

> not just the process of getting the idea in, and not just the process of the policy documents being written. We need, in effect, an understanding of what happens after that: the process of the idea and documents going to the politicians, the process of how it turns into policy advice, and then the process by which it goes from policy advice at the centre and out to those people who need to implement it at street level.

The concept of *entrepreneurship* is not a neutral word in the academy and is often regarded with suspicion, but it has nevertheless diffused into scholarly discourse that deals with public policy and management. Since the 1980s, a variety of studies – predominantly American – have used this idea to explain different case studies and policy results, but few exist in the field of UK education. There is an increasing tendency to use economic and market analogies to discuss the role of government in public policy formulation. There is a need for closer study of the motivations and strategies used by policy entrepreneurs in education, and also for more study of the interactions between policy entrepreneurs and their specific policy contexts. The UK REF requires submissions to demonstrate the impact of research on society and the economy. Policy entrepreneurship capacity is increasingly required by university hiring panels for senior professorial staff, and requires a rare blend of skills. Impact is defined as exploring who could potentially benefit from the work of researchers as well as looking at how they can increase the chances of potential beneficiaries benefiting from their research. Policy entrepreneurship by academics can make a significant contribution to impact, but it is challenging to study because of the great variation in policy outcomes.

Conceptions of policy entrepreneurship

There has been a significant proliferation in the use of the term 'entrepreneur' in the academy over the last 30 years. Historically, the term has been interpreted as having a specific meaning bound up with what may be termed capitalist activity. The word originates from a thirteenth-century French verb, *entreprendre*, meaning 'to do something' or 'to undertake'. It was Richard Cantillan, an Irish economist, who introduced the word entrepreneur into economic theory in the mid-1750s. However, it was the French economist Jean-Baptiste Say (1767–1832) who popularised the term and identified the entrepreneur as an exceptionally talented and motivated individual. For Say, an entrepreneur initiates, organises and manages a business activity as well as assuring the risk for the venture. It is interesting that the term entrepreneur is absent from *The Wealth of Nations,* with Adam Smith preferring to use the words 'employer', 'capitalist' or 'enterpriser', which are similar concepts. Say certainly thought that Smith had failed to specify the full meaning of 'entrepreneur' in his work, but it is possible that Smith was thinking more in terms of leadership of an organisation or business. Building on Say's understandings of 'entrepreneur', the Austrian economist Joseph Schumpeter (1883–1950) saw the entrepreneur as an innovator and change-maker. All of these economists link entrepreneurship to different forms of economic growth within a capitalist market. In this view, the entrepreneur is a person who is driven by the search for profit and wealth and is focused on taking risks and pursuing opportunities.

This association of the term with capitalism has the power to offend many within the academy, particularly within political science where the concept of policy entrepreneurship usually sits. 'Capitalist entrepreneurship' is regarded as an essentially amoral practice, while by contrast the 'academic' policy entrepreneur is often driven by an explicit moral good or normative argument. They are normally individuals who want, like social or 'civic' (see Leadbeater and Goss, 1998) entrepreneurs, to make the world a better place through some vision of the good. Nevertheless, the moral character of the entrepreneur is ambiguous, and Llewellyn *et al.* (2007: 255) draw attention to Weber's description of the ethical character of the entrepreneur as rooted in protestant temperance, reliability, shrewdness and devotion to business; in current usage, it is often associated with danger and risk taking. When discussed in relation to public services, it is also often linked to questionable deals and anti-democratic activities. In current parlance, therefore, entrepreneurship is understood as referring primarily to an economic function carried out by an individual.

Early ideas of *policy* entrepreneurship begin with Bardach (1972), who saw it simply as a form of political skill in advancing a particular idea in the public realm. Weissert (1991) views policy entrepreneurship as pushing ideas into the political space, including a range of different meanings, such as being skilled in the art of argument, persuasion or manipulation as part of this political skill. According to Lewis (1980: 17), policy entrepreneurs need to exploit the contradictions found in the political milieus which contain a mix of values. Walker (1981: 85) saw it as individuals causing 'new departures in policy' and noted that when a 'body of research emerges providing clear justification for the use of a given solution ... an opportunity exists to break traditional patterns with a dramatic proposal for change'. Bardach (1972: 10) believed that a policy entrepreneur needs to 'identify the number and type of interests that will support his proposal; policy entrepreneurs must engage in ascertaining the disposition of the various interests who might support them; assessing how weighty their views are among the relevant authorities'. Consequently, accessing the network of professional and political contacts is a vital resource for the policy entrepreneur. Schon (1971: 123–127) spoke about 'ideas in the air' and 'ideas in good currency'. Even if they amount to slogans, he believed that they can be exploited by policy entrepreneurs to advance a particular position. All of these scholars understand policy entrepreneurs as change agents and see them as influential individuals who promote and influence policy changes. They are involved in various stages of the policy process, and Majone (1992) makes it clear that persuasion, along with effectively presenting the appropriate evidence at the right time in the policy argument, are the keys to success in policy adoption and implementation. He seems to suggest that a policy entrepreneur ought to develop the important skills of gathering evidence, preparing arguments, and using persuasion to acquire influence on policy formation – rather like a barrister.

The reality is that traits attributed to policy entrepreneurs are wide-ranging and have been variously attributed to 'policy intellectuals' (Wilson, 1981), 'policy champions' (Van de Ven, 2007), 'bureaucratic entrepreneurs', 'executive entrepreneurs', 'academic entrepreneurs', 'civic entrepreneurs', 'public entrepreneurs', and 'political entrepreneurs' (see Catney and Henneberry, 2015: 15, footnote 2). There are also social entrepreneurs and moral entrepreneurs, often discussed in similar terms. All of these different conceptions of the entrepreneur intersect with each other, but they also clash and do not form a unified whole. There is a tendency in the literature to use 'policy' interchangeably with 'public', 'political' and 'bureaucratic', so these categories need to be differentiated. All of these different labels for different expressions of policy entrepreneurship introduce and translate ideas into policy options, and they often have a 'symbiotic relationship' with politicians (see Roberts and King, 1991: 148). Their function is to act as a kind of 'coupler' in a complex policy process. As Weissert (1991: 214) says of policy entrepreneurs, they are 'persons willing to use their own personal resources of expertise, persistence, and skill to achieve certain policies they favour'. Indeed, it is the right combination of persistence and opportunism that is needed to win an argument in promoting a policy idea.

Some of the later prominent theorists of policy entrepreneurship have expanded on the concept theoretically, with many tackling the definitional confusion. Roberts and King attempt to distinguish between four different types of 'public entrepreneur', suggesting the following typology:

> Political entrepreneurs, who hold elected leadership positions in government; executive entrepreneurs, who hold appointed leadership positions in

government; bureaucratic entrepreneurs, who hold formal positions in government, although not leadership positions; and *policy* entrepreneurs, *who work from outside the formal governmental system to introduce, translate, and implement innovative ideas into public sector practice.*

(1991: 152, emphasis in original)

This typology is particularly useful as it distinguishes 'policy' entrepreneurs from other types of 'public' entrepreneur through the fact that they are *'outside the formal government system'*. This is acutely relevant with regard to those attempting to influence policy from within academia. Elsewhere, Mintrom (2000: 131) highlights the necessity for policy entrepreneurs to attach problems to solutions, in order to 'carefully explain the nature of the problem as he or she sees it and, having done this, suggest the kind of innovation that might address the problem'. Jones and Baumgartner (1993: 26) discuss how the policy issues are understood and emphasise the policy entrepreneur's ability in 'image making', which is the modification of the perception of an issue in order to reframe it within the political and public context. This theme of 'image making' or 'problem framing' is also reflected in the work of public policy and policy change theorist John Kingdon (1984, 2003). Aside from his hugely influential 'multiple streams framework' (see later in this chapter), Kingdon (1993) also suggests that policy entrepreneurs are required to 'hook solutions to problems'. He highlights (2003: 181) how they need to be in a state of policy readiness and that proposals need to be developed well in advance of any potential opportunities to influence policy. However, it is important to repeat that we cannot assume that knowledge directly affects policy formulation. As highlighted in Chapter 1, there is no simple, linear movement from cause to effect.

Moving away from public policy theory, David (2015: 166) introduces the concept to security studies, and sets out three skills that he believes are essential for a policy entrepreneur: (a) contextual skills in which opportunities are sought, (b) ideational skills in which ideas are promoted and (c) organisational skills in which networks influence policy change. He believes that the policy entrepreneur 'should be endowed with qualities and strengths such as charisma, reputation, knowledge, conviction, connections, motivations, experience, and drive' (173). Others, such as Mackenzie (2004: 321), list credibility, strategic sense, networks and bargaining skills as necessary qualities, while Mintrom and Vergari (1996: 424) give emphasis to intellectual ability, reputation and tenacity. David (2015: 165) recognised that these individuals may not be the designers of any particular policy but that 'they are alert to opportunities, they frame the agenda (define the problem and the solution), they organise and lead coalition-building, they influence the public and private debate, and they act and appear to have a flair for the right ideas'. As Mintrom and Norman (2009: 650) say, 'policy entrepreneurs distinguish themselves through the desire to significantly change current ways of doing things in their area of interest'. Individuals may invest huge amounts of time and energy into securing policy influence, but as a number of scholars point out, 'their real strength comes through their ability to work effectively with others' (Mintrom and Norman, 2009: 653; see also Roberts and King, 1996).

The market rhetoric of entrepreneur to describe non-economic areas of human activity raises one question: Why is the word used at all in relation to policy ideas and lobbying? This is probably why most of the writers in the area of policy entrepreneurship do not draw on the theories of capitalist entrepreneurship. Any form of entrepreneurship has the potential to be used in misleading ways outside the capitalist context and suffers from a good deal of fragmentation. Mintrom (2000: 5–6) acknowledges that importing a concept from one world to another is never easy, but he believes that 'thinking carefully about what entrepreneurs do in markets generates significant insights for those who seek to explain the emergence to prominence of ideas in the policymaking process'. He contrasts the use of 'entrepreneur' in the market with its use in politics. Those who produce a product and manage to sell it in the marketplace for a profit are deemed successful, while individuals who 'come up with a corpus of ideas for policy innovation and then take the steps necessary to secure their desired policy change' are also deemed successful. Policy entrepreneurs may be motivated by non-business aims, but this does not mean that all of their initiatives are necessarily seen as benign or are free from controversy. Policy entrepreneurs can aim to disrupt belief systems by using the media to initiate the public into controversial areas.

The political arena is not always receptive to new ideas, which is why 'new policies will emerge only when a prominent problem can be linked to a viable policy consistent with national mood at a time when elected officials can make a decision' (Beeson and Stone, 2013: 3). The ideas generated by policy entrepreneurs need to chime with and give intellectual credibility to ideas that are already circulating in the UK and internationally. The political context should, therefore, be conducive, with a permissive political environment and national mood to help cultivate the rhetoric of consensus around ideas. It is not simply about being in the right place at the right time. Kingdon (2003: 224) understood policy making as a 'complex adaptive process' in which agents need to react to the changing environment. Change comes from the ability of these ideas to adapt, and from the abilities and qualities of entrepreneurs to engage in active policy promotion shaped by the political environment in which they operate. As Mintrom (2000: 126) notes, 'a well-developed set of social and professional contacts can make the difference between success and failure in the launch of an innovation'. This timing can also be crucial. Bardach (1972: 273) makes the observation that 'a proposal in its incubation period is unusually vulnerable to attack by its opponents', so he suggests keeping it secret in the early stages of development.

Entrepreneurial thinking

Stephen Ball (1998: 74ff) has made reference to 'policy entrepreneurship', claiming that we need to recognise its role in educational studies. Ball, while acknowledging that it has a variety of meanings, proceeds to a narrow definition of the term without much reference to the literature. He argues that it 'rests on the proselytising, and in some cases the sale of "technically correct answers" around the globe'. He skilfully uses examples from the school effectiveness movement to justify his argument and concludes with the view that policy entrepreneurship is 'problem-solving technicism' in which policy becomes de-politicised and technicised. The work of Frederick Hess and others in the US (2007, 2015, 2016) illustrates what Ball is referring to: for-profit ventures in public education, the marketplace approach with an emphasis on delivery; engaging the private sector in schooling and exploiting opportunities for grants, subsidies and other resources from the public education sector. As Hess and McShane (2016: 6) say, 'entrepreneurs will only create the things that they are encouraged and rewarded for creating', which seems to suggest a profit-centred ideology. They are spurred on by competition and are expected to improve performance in education for the promise of financial reward.

These American entrepreneurs have certain common characteristics: they are generally young, have attended elite universities, are business-minded, are distrustful of public institutions, have no educational or teaching qualifications, and view themselves as entrepreneurs who seek to drive up quality in schools. Research evidence is not their first port of call and they approach public education with the intention to cause disruptive change with an 'always a better way' mind-set. This kind of capitalist entrepreneurship has little connection with the kind of academic policy entrepreneurship that this book is concerned with advancing. Education is not just another business like making cars or manufacturing shoes for sale in the market – such an approach is at odds with the democratic values and public nature of education. The normative model of policy entrepreneurship I am concerned with emphasises the intrinsic values and beliefs of teachers (teaching as a vocation and noble calling) and not extrinsic profit motivation. The latter is derived from economic theories of the utility-maximising individual and a positivist conception of valuation. Nevertheless, there has been a conceptual shift in the use of the term 'entrepreneur' from the 1960s when it was first incorporated into business discourse, and then in the 1980s into the public services discourse.

While recognising that policy entrepreneurs are often pressured to commercialise their ideas and present them in a technical way to policy makers, this need not serve as their principal aim or motivation. They may not be driven by the profit motive, but rather by educational and social goals of the good. Only rarely are schools driven by the profit motive; they are more typically motivated by many social and political goals, which are often difficult to quantify. In their definition of policy entrepreneurship, Boyett and Finley (1993) identify head teachers as the first within the schooling sector in England to act in an entrepreneurial way in education. Leadbeater and Goss also identify the example of head teacher Norma Redfearn in their *Civic Entrepreneurship* (1998), and her awareness that results would only improve in her school if the life-chances of those children and the outside community in which they lived also improved (1998: 21–26). There is always a need to consider normative and political questions about what is educationally desirable. In England, it is commonly thought that the public sector is a poor environment for the kind of American 'educational entrepreneurship' and the reasons given are that English state-funded schools have too many rules, procedures and policies and strict hierarchies; that they have inflexible and restrictive recruitment and dismissal processes; that they lack sufficient autonomy to be creative or innovative and that they are too risk averse.

As Bernier (2014: 259) argues, these schools have multiple goals generated by social and political considerations, and they are subject to public scrutiny as well as regular political interference, which means that state schools are less exposed to the market. There are clearly many structures in place which suppress public sector entrepreneurialism, but these are designed to prevent individuals from acting unilaterally with public money. So why would for-profit entrepreneurs even try to get involved? It is perhaps ironic that as the government attempts to free schools from these procedures and local controls it simultaneously increases centralisation and adds new supervisory controls, including regulations that require detailed permissions for anything from changing the length of the school day to altering the religious education curriculum. Bernier (2014: 260) notes that 'centralisation is an inhibitor of entrepreneurship' and Boyett and Finley (1997: 90) observe: 'Entrepreneurship occurs in the public sector where there is an uncertain environment, devolution of power, and at the same time re-allocation of resource ownership, to unit management level.' American forms of entrepreneurship in schools operate within a different context with fewer central controls and political pressures. Cahn and Clemance (2011: 11) distinguish between public and private sector entrepreneurs by offering four key points of difference: 'Firstly, in their conceptualisations of profit; secondly their levels of acceptable risk taking; thirdly their capacity to act proactively; and fourthly and importantly, in their approach to innovation.' They quote Bason (2010) who says: 'In the private sector, the innovation challenge is largely about opportunities: how to identify them and leverage them for competitive advantage … in the public sector, the innovation challenge is much more about problems: how to define them, what to do about them, and how to know whether they are being fixed or not.'

If academic policy entrepreneurs were simply selling their ideas for profit, then this would be disreputable as academics would be reduced to mere calculating individuals. Ball employs the concept of entrepreneur as a rather loose metaphor as someone who is very alert and sees a market opportunity and takes advantage by earning profits. There is no effort here to clarify the extent to which entrepreneurship in the public sector is really analogous to entrepreneurship in the private sector. His argument is to present the underlying 'capitalist' characteristics of policy entrepreneurship as being at odds with the values of democratic politics and administration. Indeed, an exclusively business or economic concept of entrepreneurship would be problematic within the public education policy realm. There is often a blurring between non-profit and for-profit ventures in this type of entrepreneurial approach. For-profit ventures are a form of entrepreneurship that is designed to serve a social purpose and make a profit – creating value for a community or school by having a social impact while simultaneously creating economic value. It has dual social and economic objectives, two different and sometimes divergent objectives, and these objectives can easily be compromised through pressure. Non-profit entrepreneurship, on the other hand, is motivated by ideas and not financial gain.

Business entrepreneurs are concerned with achieving competitive advantage, and their success is ultimately measured by sales and profits. Entrepreneurial profit cannot be easily equated with the policy entrepreneur as it is possible to have an altruistic or civic-orientated form of policy entrepreneurship that focuses on the benefits to society from the introduction of innovative policy ideas. As with the examples provided in Leadbeater and Goss (1998), Schneider *et al.* (1995) identify entrepreneurs not as 'heroic, larger than life figures. Many are ordinary citizens who entered the vortex of local politics because of a single issue about which they cared, often with a passion.' We need to make a distinction between other-regarding and narrowly self-interested entrepreneurs. Social entrepreneurs are usually individuals who start a non-profit organisation and bring market-style ideas to charitable work. This can often mean employing business accountability methods and adopting business best practice in a charity context. It often involves a focus on resourceful, dynamic and innovative leaders acting as chief executives who lead these charities and who have an expert grasp of metrics. However, their motives and tactics can concern people as they could be seen as manipulating the public with goals that are questionable. They can be greedy, self-interested and opportunistic, and it is why Ball (1998) is suspicious of the term.

However, in this text 'entrepreneurship' is employed to signify the generation of innovative ideas that are seen through to policy ideas which inform policy formation. As Benz (2009: 23) argues, entrepreneurial activity has substantial non-monetary benefits, including the ability to pursue one's own ideas. These may be called 'non-market entrepreneurs' (see Osborn and Gaebler, 2000). An outstanding example of this kind of academic entrepreneurship is Dr. Ralf Dahrendorf who, as a sociologist, was variously director of the London School of Economics, Parliamentary Secretary of State in Germany's Ministry of Foreign Affairs and a member of the British House of Lords. He wrote and advocated for many issues and can be considered an exemplary policy entrepreneur, combining as he did the will to improve society evident in many examples of civic entrepreneurship with the innovation and proactive aspects of entrepreneurship as generally defined.

In the literature on policy entrepreneurship, a similar example of this kind is Professor Ara Darzi and his work on healthcare reform across London (see Oborn *et al.*, 2011). Professor Darzi, an experienced surgeon, was asked by the government to develop 'a joint strategy for health services' across the London region. While the subject of Darzi's policy reform perhaps involved more science than social science, his role was to reform public services while attempting to bring together a number of conflicting interests to make this happen. As highlighted elsewhere, this work entailed the coordination of a 'coalition of entrepreneurs', and the presentation of research evidence to add credibility (2011: 328–335). Ultimately, to ensure success, Darzi:

re-defined (new and existing) problems, enlisted stakeholder support, and enrolled critical actors. In order to mobilise resources and groups, he articulated a vision supported by strong allies to render it more compelling.

(Oborn et al., 2011: 339)

While a number of contextual differences might suggest that this example is far removed from cases of policy entrepreneurship within education, many of the skills Darzi exhibited in achieving success are transferable to other contexts (as the examples in Chapter 4 will also highlight). Crucially, Darzi combined the entrepreneurial traits of proactivity, brokerage and leadership with a social vision and conscience informed by notions of fairness and accountability. In this sense, the example could be said to bridge the gap between the 'technological model' – in that evidence was provided to add credibility to the policy, and the 'humanist model' – as a normative vision could be said to guide the work.

The term entrepreneur has usually been associated with the efforts of one individual who, regardless of his or her chances of success, manages to transform a vague vision into a great success. Morris and Jones (1999) have proposed viewing entrepreneurship as a process in which an agent is involved in an entrepreneurial event. Ideas are central in their role of bringing the event to fruition. Trying to understand the entrepreneur through their psychological make-up does not assist us in clarifying how some are successful and others not. Leadership is also key, as entrepreneurs must believe in what they are advocating; that it is important and valuable in its own right. The entrepreneur needs to exhibit a greater desire for change than others. They must care about what they are advocating if they are to develop an entrepreneurial mind-set. Longstanding public issues in social policy questions do not respond to quick fixes or easy answers. Opportunities for policy action are uncertain and they need to be patient – the policy entrepreneur cannot be purely opportunistic as they need to be firmly linked to an issue over time if they wish to be more effective.

In order to increase the probability of success, policy entrepreneurs must be alert to new opportunities, persist in advocating their ideas and frame ideas in novel ways. They will portray the issue in simplified and favourable terms to non-specialists. There is agreement in the literature regarding the importance of policy entrepreneurs as agents of change in the policy innovation process (Baumgartner and Jones, 1993; Kingdon, 1984, 2003; Schneider *et al.*, 1995), but actually understanding entrepreneurial activity is often carried out descriptively in *post hoc* fashion. Nevertheless, policy entrepreneurship needs to be understood within more encompassing conceptualisations of policy change, policy streams, advocacy coalitions, research utilisation and policy images. Next we turn to Kingdon's policy, political and problem streams.

Multiple streams framework

Kingdon (2003) believes that at any given time there are many policy ideas that policy framers can apply to a particular problem, and that solutions look for problems. McComb (2004) offers three ways in which the work of policy entrepreneurs comes to the attention of policy makers. The first is through *indicators* – where metric data and information defines the shape of a problem, such as unemployment rates going up or down. The second is through a current *event* (such as riots in London). The third is through *feedback* – the evaluation of current government policy initiatives – findings that indicate the policy is not working or has unintended consequences. Kingdon has provided an extremely influential model which he calls the Multiple Streams Framework to understand policy making. He sees three streams in any policy formulation: problem stream, policy stream and political stream. The problem stream is simply a current issue that needs to be addressed. The choice of which problem needs addressing is based on how the problem is defined by those involved in the policy process. Kingdon (1984: 95, 120) believes that policy makers 'could attend to a long list of problems' but that they pay attention to only a fraction of them. This is because the policy agenda is congested; hence, successfully raising a problem into the political arena is a major accomplishment.

The policy stream concerns the ideas or solutions floating around at any given time; these take time to develop, especially as the public often do not know what they want on the menu of ideas. Kingdon (1984: 129–130) uses an evolutionary metaphor to describe the time and effort it takes for a policy solution to emerge: in the 'policy primeval soup' ideas and solutions to problems evolve and mutate with policy participants changing, modifying and re-articulating the ideas of others. The ideas can come from anywhere, including from civil servants, academics and charities, but Kingdon maintains that there is no way of tracking the source of the ideas or tracing the dominant players since, he says, 'nobody really controls the information system' (1984: 78). Only some ideas 'survive and prosper' (131) as a result of public acceptability and a 'reasonable chance for receptivity among elected decision makers' (138). Consequently, some ideas survive intact, others are combined, while still others disappear. If the idea is perceived to be difficult to implement or does not correspond well to a politician's values, then they are unlikely to survive the soup. Nevertheless, as Moore (1988: 78) said, 'ideas matter because they establish the contexts within which policy debates are conducted, organisational activities are rendered coherent and meaningful, and people's actions are animated and directed'.

The political stream concerns the influence of the national mood, or of organised political forces and pressure groups. It is concerned with how receptive people are to certain ideas and solutions at particular times. It depends on swings in national mood and changes in government. Politicians will be conscious of opinion polls and try to assess whether a particular policy issue is important at any given point in the political cycle. Civil servants will also be alert to issues that gain public attention and will ensure they are included on the agenda for Ministers. All three streams need to be aligned simultaneously to make policy change possible. The conditions have to be right, which is why Kingdon's theory stipulates a 'window of opportunity' where all these forces come together and interact before change is possible. The three streams may influence the selection, definition, development, sorting and matching of problems to policies. As he says (1984: 174), the window of opportunity for major policy change opens when:

> separate streams come together at critical times. A problem is recognised, a solution is developed and available in the policy community, a political change makes it the right time for policy change, and potential constraints are not severe ... these policy windows, the opportunities for action on given initiatives, present themselves and stay open for only short periods.

Therefore, the point at which the streams join is called a window, and when it opens the policy entrepreneur takes the opportunity to initiate action. Different participants play differing roles in each of the three streams, but since politicians lack the time for detailed policy work they delegate this work to civil servants who consult think tanks and academics to consider ideas and produce solutions. Kingdon believes that politicians do not 'discover issues', they 'elevate issues'. This provides an emphasis on 'solutions chasing problems' with the assistance of policy entrepreneurs who help frame the issues.

Policy entrepreneurs attempt to couple all three streams, and they are more successful at this when they have access to policy makers. Kingdon spoke of the 'softening process' that policy entrepreneurs performed, allowing policy ideas to become viable for consideration (2003: 128). Exworthy and Powell (2004: 263ff) have adapted Kingdon's model by emphasising the status, reputation and power of the policy entrepreneur as well as developing a more expansive interpretation of Kingdon's streams. In this respect, policy entrepreneurs are not simply advocates of ideas, but are power brokers and manipulators of policy ideas within all three streams. Success depends on how ideas are received by politicians, and what resources, money, time and energy the individual policy entrepreneur can use to push the policy idea as well as how they can manipulate the ideas in order to engage all three streams.

Policy entrepreneurs have the potential to motivate a range of coordinated activities that, in their absence, would not have been started – they create persuasive narratives that help others 'connect the dots' between specific actions and desirable outcomes. For Kingdon, all three of his streams need to converge with the policy entrepreneur for policy windows to open up.

Kingdon (2003: 181) believes policy entrepreneurs wait for their opportunity and need to be ready and flexible when the window opens – as he says, they 'do more than push for their proposal – they lie in wait'. Policy players who get along well with others and are well connected in the local policy context tend to achieve more success in securing policy change than do others. As Weissert (1991: 262) said, 'the importance of policy entrepreneurs [is] in bringing issues to the fore and moving them from incubation to enactment'. Skill, expertise and persistence are also recognised as important in the policy entrepreneur. Weissert (1991: 264) believes that expert knowledge gives credibility and standing and, therefore, a degree of control over the issues, while Stone (2007: 274) says 'the role rests on a delicate phroenetic blend of "softening-up" actors in the political and policy stream through the use of personal contacts, networking, media strategies and the creation of powerful policy narratives that simplify technical issues into manageable items of public policy'. Policy entrepreneurs become brokers and advocates of policy innovations and they operate both inside and outside the policy process to push their policies through the window of opportunity.

'Policy entrepreneur' is used by Kingdon (1984: 21, 104) to describe actors who use their knowledge of the process to further their own policy ends. He says:

> We have spoken of advocates for proposals or for the prominence of an idea. Let us label these advocates policy entrepreneurs. The entrepreneurs are not necessarily found in any one location in the policy community. They could be in or out of government, in elected or appointed positions, in interest groups or research organisations. But their defining characteristic, much as in the case of a business entrepreneur is their willingness to invest their resources – time, energy, reputation, and sometimes money – in the hope of a future return. That return might come to them in the form of policies of which they approve, satisfaction from participation, or even personal aggrandisement in the form of job security or career promotion.
>
> *(2003: 122–123)*

According to Kingdon, policy entrepreneurs are usually people with the knowledge, power, tenacity and luck to be capable of exploiting windows of opportunity and heightened levels of attention to policy problems to promote their particular solutions to policy makers. *Displaying social acuity* means that the entrepreneurs are well-versed in the social-political context in which they are interacting and demonstrate high levels of social acuity in understanding others and engaging in policy conversations. Thus, the policy entrepreneur can identify 'windows of opportunity' for introducing innovative policy within the existing social order. They use relevant information from their 'policy networks' as well as the thoughts, ideas, motives and concerns of others in their local policy context, and are therefore able to respond effectively. The advantage of Kingdon's approach to policy entrepreneurship is that he does not focus on any one area of policy change, but allows the operation and coordination of each element according to the context and skill-base of the policy entrepreneur in question. Kingdon also portrays a chaotic policy process in which policy making is confused, fragmented and emphatically not composed of discrete stages. He uses the 'garbage can' model to explain this, which is the best-known statement of the idea that policy change is chaotic – or 'organised anarchy' (Cohen *et al.*, 1972).

The six keys to policy entrepreneurship

Michael Mintrom (2000) has written extensively on the theory of policy entrepreneurship, and in attempting to clarify a distinct framework, his 'Six Keys' model is outlined here (see also Mintrom's 'Four Elements' model: Mintrom and Luetjens, 2014; Mintrom and Norman, 2009). Mintrom argues that policy entrepreneurs have succeeded in shifting the public education debate away from a focus on resources and their equitable distribution and towards issues of leadership, management and accountability. As a result, citizens have been cast in the role of consumers. Mintrom's intention is not to judge the overall merits of the use of the market in the design of public policy, but rather to understand the nature of policy change and the role of policy entrepreneurs in this process. He argues that policy entrepreneurs are noted for their efforts to bring policy ideas into 'good currency' and that they must achieve a degree of credibility with politicians by showing that their ideas are prudent. They must demonstrate 'the workability of their ideas and convince politicians that if their ideas are implemented, they will yield greater social benefits than current policy settings' (2000: 253) and that their innovations put in place a decidedly new way of doing things. Mintrom offers six keys to policy entrepreneurship that are worth detailing, which he sees as starting points for thinking about how policy entrepreneurs might improve their chances of success. These keys are inter-related; success in one activity affects success in the others. By following these keys, Mintrom (60, 113ff, 152–153, 275ff) argues that the policy entrepreneur will have a better chance of seeing their policy ideas accepted or adopted.

These six characteristics of successful entrepreneurship begin with the idea that policy entrepreneurs must be *creative and insightful*. This first step revolves around the policy entrepreneur seeing how particular policy innovations alter the nature of policy debates. Indeed, introducing innovations to the policy debate is a distinguishing characteristic of the policy entrepreneur, and these innovations 'represent changes that are deliberately designed to lead or force people to break out of particular routine behaviours and come to new understandings of their environment' (114). The object here is to place a new issue on the policy agenda and have their innovation adopted. This means framing the issue in such an appealing way that it is considered a plausible solution to a perceived problem. It means thinking creatively about how to formulate arguments that bring other people to agree that a problem exists and that it requires action or is worthy of government attention. Taylor (2005: 749) offers advice in this respect by recommending the avoidance of two mistakes: 'the first mistake ... is to complete a piece of research, place it in the newspapers, see that people are excited about it – and then wander off, because the research funding runs out or the researcher loses interest. So the idea, having got half-way through the door, never gets pushed any further ... the other mistake is to keep making the argument in exactly the same terms over a long period of time. Researchers need the opportunism to recognise that arguments can be adapted to take advantage of the political *zeitgeist*.'

Policy entrepreneurs work in the world of ideas, and their policy ideas are essentially abstractions until they are taken up as contributions to workable policies. Agenda setting is the way that problems and solutions to policy issues gain or lose public and policy maker attention.

The second key states that policy entrepreneurs must be *socially perceptive* and, therefore, able to see problems and issues from a range of perspectives so that they can propose policy ideas that will attract broad appeal. Communication of ideas is central here, as is the ability to listen to others and identify their needs in such a way as to produce new ideas and understandings of how these needs might be met. Mintrom (2000: 153) believes that policy entrepreneurs need to achieve some critical distance from any given social setting and see things in unconventional ways.

The third key declares that policy entrepreneurs must be *able to mix in a variety of social and political settings*, so that they can readily acquire valuable information and use their contacts to advantage in pursuit of policy change. Clearly, social and professional contacts will represent a huge resource for policy entrepreneurs and may even make the difference between success and failure in the launch of an innovation. The key challenge here is to 'establish sound connections and relationships of mutual trust' and 'minimise points of difference and disagreement between themselves and those around them' (127). It is also important to form broad associations of policy specialists and advocates – join with people of a similar policy mind-set. As Mintrom (2000: 129) says, it is in 'rubbing shoulders with both the potential supporters and enemies of policy change, that policy entrepreneurs can gain many insights into particular policy problems and come to an understanding of the sort of policy solutions that might address those problems'. Talking with others who have different views helps formulate arguments for the opposite view. For this reason, policy entrepreneurs need to understand their opponents and find creative ways to counter their arguments or neutralise their opposition. Essentially they need to mix in unfamiliar circles, and as Mintrom (2000: 272) says, 'by working with a range of people who initially perceive themselves as having little in common, policy entrepreneurs can come to develop coalitions of support that can aid them in multiple ways as they strive to prompt policy change'.

This leads us to the fourth key which is that policy entrepreneurs are able to *argue persuasively,* which includes using different arguments for different groups while keeping the overall story consistent. Policy entrepreneurs need to advance conceptual arguments supported by concrete examples and transform these arguments into compelling proposals for policy change. They need to have a specific audience in mind when making arguments and adjust how they frame a problem for each group of potential supporters. The greater the extent of the policy entrepreneur's social perceptiveness and social connectedness, the greater the likelihood that they can put forward arguments that appeal to a broader range of people. The truth is not enough: it needs high-quality packaging and presentation.

The fifth key concerns policy entrepreneurs being *strategic team builders* who are able to determine the type and organisation of coalitions best able to support their pursuit of policy change. As Mintrom (2000: 138) says, 'they must engage in activities such as devising strategies, working the system, organising others, and providing leadership'. They need to pay attention to timing and setting and closely work with the many others who are inevitably involved in the policy process. Policy entrepreneurs know that policy change is complex, so they find other people to work with in pursuit of policy goals. They need to demonstrate that their policy ideas enjoy broad interest and support and convey their own integrity and seriousness to policy makers. Choosing who to work with as partners is vital, as is thinking about what kind of partnerships make strategic sense. It is also important to have close connections with formal policy makers such as politicians and civil servants without relying on them alone to ensure policy adoption. We need to be close enough to government to have impact, while also maintaining independence. Connections with established pressure groups will also be a factor as well as creating newer coalitions. Policy entrepreneurs need to remember that there is a limit to what they can achieve on their own. As Mintrom (2000: 211) says, 'a policy network consists of a group of actors who share an interest in some policy area and who are linked by their direct and indirect contacts with one another'.

The final key is being *prepared to lead by example*, to create 'prefigurative forms' of the policy innovations they seek to introduce. They need to convince others that their vision of the future is believable. They need to demonstrate personal commitment and show social and political dexterity. They need to coordinate others in indicating what it might look like in the future. Finally, policy entrepreneurs must be able to translate their ideas into actions: they must exemplify the ability to lead by example and to translate an abstract idea into something concrete and believable. There is considerable attention to political process in Mintrom's keys, but little attention to concrete actions or to research. How knowledge is acquired and applied will shape how we identify and understand policy issues, and expert knowledge or research itself must be open to political debate. Since policy is all too often thought of as having a solid research evidence base – research evidence that has been systematically collected and presented in a coherent research report – it is worth looking at the utilisation of research knowledge.

Models of research utilisation

There are a number of research utilisation models in the literature, a cross-section of which are outlined here. The three main ways in which research is used in policy making are instrumental, symbolic and conceptual. 'Instrumental' use of research is where research simply feeds into decision making for policy and practice. This produces research outcomes that are of immediate use to policy makers because they have sought the research in response to a policy issue and may have indeed commissioned the research itself. It is true, however, that even when policy makers commission research or carry it out in-house, it does not ensure take-up (see Nutley *et al.*, 2007: 18). There are other occasions when the policy maker is not interested in the research itself, either its content or nature, but uses the research as ammunition to back particular points of view – where research results may be used to legitimate and lend credibility to pre-determined decisions. This is 'symbolic use' of research where the focus of attention is not the research *per se*, but the policy and arguments gleaned from research that supports the policy. Finally, the conceptual or enlightenment model (Weiss 1979: 428) of research use emphasises the indirect and subtle impacts of research on policy development. In this model, the concepts and theoretical perspectives derived from research 'permeate and creep' into the policy-making process. As previously highlighted, it is important to remember that the transfer of research into policy is very rarely a simple, linear process. Policy makers must take account of ideological positions, the values that particular research outcomes support and the possible effects of policy ideas – in short, they have to take account of more factors than any single research study, not least the views of the electorate.

Knott and Wildavsky's (1980) seven stages of research utilisation are also worth describing, especially as studies such as Landry *et al.* (2003) have validated the scale:

Reception utilisation takes place when the user has received the policy relevant information.
Cognition utilisation takes places when the user has read, digested and understood the information.
Reference utilisation takes place when the information has altered the frame of reference of the user – the way the user sees things.
Effort utilisation takes place when an effort is made to adopt the information.
Adoption utilisation takes place when the information is adopted as part of policy.
Implementation utilisation takes place when the adopted policy becomes practice, i.e. when it is implemented.
Impact utilisation takes place when the policy yields tangible benefits to the citizens.

This model is helpful in describing what the impact agenda might be for university research outputs, but another model by Meagher *et al.* (2008) outlines five categories of impactful research that include (a) *instrumental* – practical solutions for policy makers, (b) *conceptual* – generation of policy ideas for use by policy makers in argumentation, (c) *capacity building* – forming collaborations for policy advancement, (d) *cultural change* – academics acting as ambassadors for the value of research to policy makers (e) *connectivity* – putting together and creating networks through engagement that assists policy makers. This is why Pettigrew (2011) has called for more 'Scholarship with Impact', which would involve research becoming an instrument of persuasion – the act of research in itself can be used as a political tool to legitimate a course of action or inaction. This is an instrumental use of research to support decisions already made.

Boswell (2009: 7) challenges the instrumentalist accounts of knowledge utilisation by exploring policy makers' motivations in using research. She says that policy makers value research highly, and that research and expert knowledge still play a crucial role in policy making and political argumentation, but mainly through symbolic use. The first of these symbolic uses she calls a *legitimising* function by which the very process of drawing on expert knowledge creates confidence in the decisions of a government department or politicians. It gives them what has been called 'epistemic authority' and, therefore, a degree of credibility as a person or organisation having access to 'reliable, relevant and detailed knowledge' that bolsters their decision-making credibility. The second symbolic function she calls the *substantiating* function by which 'it is not so much the content of knowledge that is being valued, as the signal it conveys about the credibility of an organisation or its policies'.

This second function is concerned with the way expert knowledge can lend authority to particular policy positions. Boswell (2009: 250) concludes that research is a symbolic resource for legitimising policy makers or substantiating their policy preferences. She makes it clear that policy makers do not draw on research solely or predominantly to improve policy, but rather make use of various types of knowledge to establish their authority in contentious areas of policy. According to Weiss (1999: 146), relevant research or knowledge provides policy makers with the 'background of ideas, concepts and information that increased their understanding of the policy terrain'. Her enlightenment model has established a new understanding of the process through which knowledge influences policy choices. Previous research on instrumental knowledge use was largely associated with the direct effects of information on policy choices, while the enlightenment model describes policy dynamics that work 'in the long term' (Weiss *et al.*, 2005: 14). She observes (1993: 98): 'Perhaps it takes 5 or 10 years or more before decision makers respond to the accumulation of consistent evidence.' Weiss (1999: 471–472) introduced the term 'knowledge creep' to explain how ideas 'seep into people's consciousness and alter the way that issues are framed and alternatives designed' and this 'creep' describes a 'slow trickle' that produces 'slow results'.

In summary, with respect to research-based knowledge there appear to be three types of use: instrumental, conceptual and symbolic. Instrumental use is the application of knowledge to a specific problem in a direct way. Conceptual use involves using research knowledge for general enlightenment of an issue, and symbolic use is using research to legitimate a predetermined position on the part of the policy maker. It may be the case that when critics of educational research speak of its irrelevance they have in mind the instrumental and symbolic uses of research and ignore the conceptual, which is always difficult to measure. It has also been noted by Beyer and Trice (1982: 608) that: 'The most persistent observation in the literature on utilisation is that researchers and users belong to separate communities with very different values and ideologies and that these differences impede utilisation.' Beyer (1997) concludes that in the final analysis, policy making is more about interpretation, argumentation and persuasion than it is about utilisation of research knowledge. Or as Weiss (1979: 429) accurately states: 'Rarely will policy makers be able to cite the findings of a specific study that informed their decisions, but they have a sense that social science research has given them a backdrop of ideas and orientations that has had important consequences.'

Use-inspired research and the policy entrepreneur

Roberts and King (1996: 3) provide a number of categorisations which assist in understanding the role of the policy entrepreneur. They begin with a definition of *policy intellectuals,* who they say generate ideas without engaging in design of policies. Design of policy entails deliberate and purposive planning in which innovative ideas play a central role. Design is about coming up with solutions and a strategy that is likely to achieve the desired outcome. Roberts and King believe that while any strategy for policy change will be 'bounded, constrained, and limited', it is possible to make a difference – we can maximise leverage for policy change through interventions. *Policy intellectuals* are really ideas advocates rather than proposal advocates, and they provide the conceptual language for those who make changes happen. They are concerned with thoughts and analysis, not action, so many academics might see themselves in this category. *Policy advocates* in the academy, in contrast, extend their work into the design phase and 'mould an idea into a proposal and press for its acceptance'. They are action orientated and their goal is to initiate a new policy rather than theorise about it. They do not implement policy; they are its proponents. Roberts and King (1996: 13) also refer to *policy champions* who comprise elected officials and civil servants who champion an innovative idea and translate it into a concrete form for implementation. They go on to acknowledge different types of entrepreneur in the policy process, recognising that there are sometimes crossovers between *advocates* and *intellectuals* outside government, and *champions* within it.

Roberts and King also describe a four-stage process with respect to innovative ideas. First, the creation stage, which is the emergence and development of an innovative idea. Second, the design stage, which translates innovative ideas into a concrete form. Third, the implementation stage, which brings the innovative idea into actual practice. Fourth, the institutionalisation stage, which marks the movement of the idea into the realm of accepted practice. Roberts and King (1996: 8) believe that conceptualising the innovation process in these terms has some advantage and that 'it makes clear that an innovation is more than a new idea. It is a new idea that has been turned into a prototype, taken into the field for experimentation and evaluation, tested and successfully implemented, and accepted into common practice.' Not every new idea is an 'innovation' and, as Wilson (1981: 227) observes, there are as many poor ideas as good ones – 'innovation is not inevitably good'. In relation to the impact of educational research, Figgis et al. (2000: 366) examined four case studies and concluded that 'it is now recognised that complex networks bridge the divide between research/practitioner and policy maker and that neither policy making nor school practice is so straightforward and logical an enterprise, that research findings can simply be slipped into the mix and automatically find themselves absorbed into the ongoing activity'. It is also the case that the usefulness of research findings is rarely self-evident to policy makers and practitioners, but rather varies according to the context in which it is received.

There is a perceived underutilisation of research in policy making. Lindblom and Cohen (1979: 126) were clear that this resulted from a lack of communication, which is a disconnect between researchers and policy makers despite mutual needs and interests. They comment that: 'In public policy making, many suppliers and users of social science research are dissatisfied, the former because they are not listened to, the latter because they do not hear much they want to listen to' (1979: 1). There are many other reasons why research might be ignored by policy makers, which can range from electoral pressures that trump research expertise, the lack of policy relevance in the research itself, or simply its inaccessibility. It should be understood that the average length of time an education Minister spends in government in England is under two years (see Perry *et al.* 2010: 21, and Cleary and Reeves, 2009: 7 indicate that it is as low as 1.3 years) and that this short period in office militates against the use of research knowledge. It also encourages a short-term approach to policy making. Bogenschneider and Corbett (2011: 113), following and building on the work of Holzner *et al.* (1983: 9), see two distinct cultures at play here. This explains this underutilisation of research, which they describe as 'community dissonance theory' in which two different worlds operate each with different beliefs, values, dispositions and perceptions, thus effectively impeding communication. Ginsburg and Gorostiaga (2001) had previously termed it the 'Two Cultures Thesis' – the differences between the contexts or cultures in which research is produced and in which policy is made. Their theory certainly challenges the instrumentalist account of knowledge utilisation. Using these insights from multiple authors, we can summarise these numerous differences and tensions between researchers and policy makers in the following table. Since researchers can include staff in think tanks and charities, and policy makers can include civil servants who have different motivations and operate under different rules, I have focused here only on university researchers and national politicians.

Two Cultures

Researchers (university academics)	Policy makers (politicians)
Operate within longer time frame	Operate with shorter time frame
Slow movement and pace	Fast-moving environment
Focus on objectivity	Focus on partisan values
Exploratory	Outcomes orientated
Outcomes narrow	Outcomes diverse
Epistemic	Experiential
Ask questions	Look for answers
Detailed or narrow focus on topics	Comprehensive overview of topics
Statistical data and generalisations	Comparative data
Sceptical, cautious and reflective	Respond quickly to rapid change
Ambiguity, nuance and complexity	Clarity, simplicity and intelligibility

Focus on methodology	Little interest in methodology
Use of disciplinary vocabulary	Use of concise and jargon-free information
Concerned with building theory	Concerned with pragmatic/social application
Answerable to other academics	Answerable to the electorate
Homogeneous	Heterogeneous
Research is often retrospective	Little interest in the history of ideas
Producer of research	User of research
Politically naïve	Politically shrewd
Have long tenure and attention span	Have short tenure and attention span
Emphasis on thought and reflection	Emphasis on action and engagement
Hypothesis and testing	Facts and decision making

From this table, it could be concluded that researchers are from Mars and policy makers are from Venus, so is it possible to bridge the gap in a realistic fashion? Boswell (2009: 33) calls this the 'divergence of values, ideologies or decision making styles between research and policy communities'. The table suggests deep-rooted and hard to change cultural differences. There does appear to be an excessive cultural, professional and organisational distance between these two communities. The time frames alone that both work within can exaggerate this disconnect, and politicians often have to act without really knowing what will or will not work. Researchers are often wary of policy makers who seek out evidence to support pre-determined agendas, while policy makers are sometimes wary of researchers who advocate normative or value-laden policy ideas. Policy makers accuse researchers of failing to respond to their policy priorities, while researchers accuse policy makers of not being able to distinguish between 'good' and 'bad' research. Policy makers can also accuse academics of being in 'ivory towers' far removed from the reality of policy in the real world.

Both groups have different mentalities, different career paths and differing perceptions of time; crucially, with shifting interpretations, there is a lack of consensus on what counts as research evidence. Policy makers lack the time and skills to conduct major research projects, and Boswell (2009: 25) notes that 'the boundaries dividing expert and non-expert knowledge are blurred, fluid and frequently contested'. The constraints on an academic come from within their own profession. Weiss (1977: 25) notes: 'Professional social scientists are products of the Enlightenment, and they tend to define their role not in terms of profit, as might an entrepreneur, or higher wages, as might a manual worker, but rather in terms of knowledge in the abstract. The enlightenment of society leads to a more knowledgeable society; this is assumed to be *ipso facto* a better society. The utilisation of such knowledge is not a principal concern of a social scientist, as it is for someone trained in the law and practising as a lawyer, or trained in medicine and practising as a physician.' So what counts as research will be contingent on who uses it – on their beliefs and interests – and, therefore, what counts as research knowledge will be relatively fluid. The simple distinctions between those who produce (researchers) and those who use (policy makers) research is also not credible as an argument in policy making. In short, translating academic research to application to particular situations is not a straightforward exercise.

It can be the case that some of these contrasting positions between researchers and policy makers may overlap or coincide at times. Although they are fundamentally different, policy-minded researchers and research-minded policy makers can bridge this sometimes huge gap. The relationship dimension between researchers and policy makers is vital for creating capacity for evidence-informed policy. They work best when there is discussion, problem-solving and joint development, and sometimes there is overlap in membership between these two groups. Henry Kissinger (2007: 233) once occupied both roles and compared the differences in saying:

> I have been a policy maker, and I have been a professor and I have therefore experienced the different perspectives ... As a professor I could choose my subjects. And I could work on them for as long as I chose. As a policy maker, I was pressed for time, and I had to make decisions in a finite time frame. As a professor, I was responsible primarily for coming up with the best answer I could divine. As a policy maker, I was also responsible for the worst that could happen. As a professor, the risk was that the important would drive out the urgent. As a policy maker, the risk was that the urgent would drive out the important.

Researchers and policy makers need to understand and interact with each other, which involves discussion of what motivates them, what constrains them and how they operate under different demands. Academic researchers are often focused on academic publications and grant capture while policy makers have much broader concerns, not least public opinion. For this reason, researchers should understand the forces that drive policy makers, especially the objectives that policy makers are pursuing. In the end, the conditions under which and the extent to which policy makers will draw on research will be highly circumscribed by the context, even when both groups are resistant to interacting with each other.

Policy networks and coalitions

Ball (2010: 152, 2009) recognises that there has been a redistribution of policy influence within education policy making towards informal policy networks. This movement emphasises the interconnected nature of policy making as well as the flows of ideas and people in the process. Ball (2008: 747) observes that these networks 'bring new kinds of actors into the policy process, validate new policy discourses and enable new forms of policy influence and enactment'. Mintrom and Norman (2009: 652ff) offer us four elements which they claim are central to understanding policy entrepreneurs: displaying social acuity, defining problems, building teams and leading by example. They do not rank these elements in relative importance, but maintain that policy entrepreneurs will exhibit all of them to various degrees. Displaying social acuity concerns understanding the ideas, concerns and motives of others. It is essentially about getting along with people. Defining the problem is seen as a political act in that the policy entrepreneur identifies the salient features of a message they have created in order to get others to pay attention. They effectively highlight the problem in accessible language. Building teams means that the policy entrepreneur must be a team player. Their real strength comes from their ability to work effectively with other players in the policy arena. In this way, they operate within a tightly-knit team composed of individuals with different knowledge and skills who are able to offer mutual support in the pursuit of change. Policy entrepreneurs operating outside formal positions in government (see Roberts and King, 1991) recognise the importance of developing and working with coalitions to promote policy change. Furthermore, policy entrepreneurs often work to gain support from groups that might appear as unlikely allies for a cause. Used effectively, the composition of a coalition can help deflect the arguments of opponents of change. Policy entrepreneurs also lead by example, and when leading by example – taking an idea and turning it into action themselves – they signal their genuine commitment to improved social outcomes. This is very useful in winning credibility with others, and hence building momentum for change. They can offer a working or practical example of what their policy option would look like if implemented.

Mintrom and Norman's key elements place emphasis on cultivating relationships with those in decision-making positions and involve the policy entrepreneur demonstrating their trustworthiness. These elements also emphasise defining a problem in such a way that maximises opportunities for bringing on board coalition partners they would never originally have considered. In terms of an advocacy coalition, Sabatier (1988: 139) defines it as 'people from a variety of positions (elected and agency officials, interest group leaders, researchers etc.) who share a particular belief system – for example, a set of basic values, causal assumptions, and problem perceptions – and who show a nontrivial degree of coordinated activity over time'. The Advocacy Coalition Framework (ACF) is interesting because it understands the policy process by focusing on actors promoting their beliefs. As Sabatier and Weible (2007: 192) note, 'policy participants hold strong beliefs and are motivated to transfer their beliefs into actual policy'. It is these beliefs that bring people together in advocacy coalitions and policy networks. The model recognises a wider variety of players who learn from each other and continuously adapt to their environment by creating minor changes to their policy offerings in order to remain attractive. This model is more dynamic and addresses the importance of ideas, but policy makers also have to be receptive to an idea, which can sometimes be more important that the idea itself. In this incremental model the rate of changes is slow, one step at a time, but moves the policy objective in the right direction over time.

The 'glue' that Sabatier believes holds the coalition together is the shared beliefs over core policy matters that can be translated into policy directions. Membership of these networks or coalitions give them insights into how people think about the issues, but it also gives the policy entrepreneur visibility and helps build their reputation so that they can more effectively assemble a coalition of support. Forming a coalition of policy elites is perhaps the most powerful way to influence policy. By this means, policy entrepreneurs can attract the attention of policy makers by choosing wisely in advance which issues to push on and how to push on them. Successful policy entrepreneurs, according to Mintrom and Vergari (1996: 422), are embedded in social networks; they cannot be isolated figures. Policy entrepreneurs need and benefit from the different motivations, perspectives, skill sets and knowledge of a shared coalition of interests.

Ball (2010: 154) argues that policy networks are usually tightly bound to include only those strictly on-message and that they are representative of the highly interconnected nature of policy-making activities in the UK. He says that 'ideas gain momentum and support and are disseminated through and beyond networks by repetition, reiteration, re-articulation, quotation, cross-referencing, collaborations and co-authoring, co-publishing and associate memberships' – venues of dialogue and sites of discourse generation are established that have some kind of influence on educational policies. The people in these policy networks 'write, speak and appear on platforms' at each other's events. However, Ball (2009) recognises that there are significant interpretive and analytical problems involved that make it very difficult to map empirically 'the structured relationships of power' within policy networks. He asks, 'How do we access and then "measure" or calculate differential resources and capabilities embedded within the asymmetries in power relations?' Ball believes that there are no existing research methods for addressing these tasks. As he says: 'Among other difficulties, almost by definition, network relations are opaque, consisting in good part of informal social exchanges, negotiations and compromises which go on "behind the scenes".' He argues that they are impossible to map and characterise. There are also the conceptual and empirical problems arising from the '(in)stability and short-term existence of some networks and network relations'.

Policy preferences model

It is important for researchers wishing to influence policy to understand how knowledge adoption functions. Based on his practical experience as civil servant and policy adviser, Brown (2013) provides an interesting perspective on the 'knowledge adoption' process which he defines as an often-complicated process by which policy makers 'take on board' evidence. This is interesting because he employs the lens of Social Activity Method to illustrate how the successful adoption of knowledge can be taken to represent the result of a relationship or alliance between policy makers and researchers. This 'alliance' can comprise either a direct relationship between policy maker and researcher or an indirect relationship between policy makers and the texts or work of the researchers. Knowledge adoption is likely to occur when both the researcher and policy maker actively seek cooperation through engagement with one another. Brown (2013: 460) outlines what he calls *internal* and *external* knowledge adoption factors. *Internal* adoption factors concern the researcher's interest in informing policy, not only through managing their research and interpretation of the data, but also through their strategies relating to the (*internal*) components that affect how they might attempt to communicate their findings to policy makers. The *external* factors concern policy makers, as audiences, and here the factors that affect reception are *external* to any given study, but still impact whether its messages are taken on board by policy makers.

Drawing on a wide range of policy literature, including some policy entrepreneur authors, Brown (2013: 461) summarises the internal and external factors that he believes affect knowledge adoption. The *internal* factors are what a researcher exerts some control over, if they develop an appropriate strategy, and include:

1. *Communication* – policy makers want a clear story together with advice they can understand.
2. *Presentation* – policy makers want the presentation of ideas to be accessible, attractive and appealing.
3. *Efficacy of communication* – policy makers are more likely to respond positively to face-to-face communication as opposed to passive communications (e.g. information simply placed on a website).
4. *Proactivity, contextualisation and tailoring* – policy makers want a full range of evidence-informed policy options which are placed in context with other evidence (for and against) available. Tailoring refers to the content of evidence and how it is tailored to different audiences.

The *external* factors comprise, first, the choice by policy makers of which evidence to employ in their arguments or revising their views on the basis of new evidence that emerges. Second, policy makers will be influenced by the credibility of the researcher. Third, policy makers will be influenced by the perceived quality and status of the research undertaken – who carried it out and from what organisation. Fourth, policy maker engagement in the research process is a factor that helps maintain dialogue and the flow of ideas between policy maker and researcher and can ensure that new policy ideas are at the forefront of the policy maker's thinking. Finally, access to policy makers by researchers is vital, especially in the absence of any active involvement by policy makers in the research project. Limited access will mean that the researcher will need to find other ways of communicating their messages.

Brown (2013: 462) introduces the idea of the 'policy preferences' model and links this to partnership working between researchers and policy makers. This policy preference model is presented as a new way of seeing how researchers can facilitate the take-up of evidence by educational policy makers. First, policy preference will depend on whether 'the research relates to an idea currently favoured by the policy makers' – hence the likelihood of whether or not it will be adopted. Second, 'the strength and nature of the relationships' between researcher and policy makers will also determine whether any policy idea is taken up. There is a myriad of possible relationships between researchers and policy makers. Researchers with stronger ties to policy makers are generally more successful than weakly connected researchers who attempt to introduce unfavoured ideas into the policy-making process. In some cases, researchers can be politically motivated; they can be ideological advocates or openly sympathetic to particular governments or their policies. However, there are also credible, independently respected researchers who manage to establish good working relationships with policy makers. Brown (2013: 462) identifies what he calls 'privileged researchers' who have easy access to policy makers and whose work is favoured by politicians, but this can create an uneasy partnership that can result in the policy maker looking for *an* answer rather than *the* answer. Academic policy entrepreneurs who become part of what they study may also become entwined in power relationships, which will cause some to identify them as political actors. Involvement in politics will influence the research, so this must be taken into account when establishing its validity.

Constructing a policy image

Ideas embody assumptions about how the world works and how we might change it, but they are also multiple and changeable. There are two sides to ideas in policy making – they can generate consensus or they can encourage conflict. Within the political dimension, ideas are always disputed and are in a constant struggle. As Lieberman (2002: 709) observes, 'An idea's time arrives not simply because the idea is compelling on its own terms, but because opportune political circumstances favour it. At those moments when a political idea finds persuasive expression among actors whose institutional position gives them both the motive and the opportunity to translate it into policy – then, and only then, can we say that an idea has found a time.' Schon (1971: 17) identifies 'ideas in good currency' as being a primary determinant of public policy. However, he believes that few ideas attain this status of being shared in the public mind and notes that 'when the ideas are taken up by people already powerful in society this gives them a kind of legitimacy and completes their power to change public policy. After this, the ideas become an integral part of the conceptual dimension of the social system and appear, in retrospect, obvious.' In his model of 'ideas in good currency', Schon focuses on the process of change in public policy based on his conviction that there is room for only a limited number of ideas 'whose time has come' at any given moment. As Kingdon (2003: 72) puts it, 'nobody has a monopoly of ideas. They come from a plethora of different sources.' In other words, 'ideas can come from anywhere'.

Hogan and Feeney (2013) argue that, in order for a policy entrepreneur to challenge existing arrangements, a crisis and policy failure must be identified and widely perceived as such. The policy entrepreneur initiates a debate about the issues or ideas generated, but without a politician acting as a catalyst for the new ideas they will not enter the political arena. Their simple message is that the introduction of new ideas into the policy environment, and the transformation into policy, is due to the activities of 'entrepreneurial networks' of policy entrepreneurs, with politicians at their head. In this explanation, they follow the mainstream in the policy entrepreneur literature. Stone (2000: 211) makes an important observation here that 'ideas by themselves are rarely persuasive but require individuals and organisations to act entrepreneurially'. Ideas are essentially used to legitimise policy actions; they can be about knowledge or about what action we ought to take. Ideas are also closely related to the policy entrepreneurs who carry them, and Sabatier believes that, while world views are hard to change, our causal beliefs and our perceptions of what constitutes feasible action are susceptible to change. Policy entrepreneurs employ ideas to further their interests and develop storylines or narratives to argue compellingly for these policy ideas.

The framing of issues by policy entrepreneurs constitutes another dimension of their activity, and it is sometimes possible to identify a frame that is evoked more often than others – this is usually the one that carries more authority (Jones and Baumgartner, 2009). In this way, one frame attracts attention and becomes dominant in the policy agenda, gaining support on the way up. The precise definition or framing of an issue is, therefore, often assumed to inform subsequent policy. Framing is really a public definition of an issue, and it will inevitably meet competing frames of the same problem in the public space. Michael Mazarr comments on this aspect of policy entrepreneurship from a constructivist perspective when he suggests that 'policy entrepreneurs, then, can be seen as the human embodiment of the social construction of policy, the personification of the stories that policy communities tell' (2007: 16). Research findings from university academics inevitably compete with knowledge produced by think tanks and are, therefore, constantly vying for influence on policies. Definition of a problem looks to the identification of missing knowledge research, analysis and eventually policy change – usually called the Engineering Model (Bulmer, 1982). The danger here lies in the possibility of the researcher tailoring research outputs in an attempt to meet policy makers' and politicians' specific requirements for research evidence. Politicians also sometimes employ a policy of symbolism: making grand policy statements whose objectives cannot be achieved.

While some scholars contend that policy entrepreneurs are generally successful at shaping policy decisions, others have argued that they are rarely influential compared with political actors. Mintrom and Norman have claimed that 'existing explanations of policy change, while acknowledging the role of policy entrepreneurs, fail to integrate the separate concepts of policy and political entrepreneurship into their transformative frameworks' (as cited in Hogan and Feeney, 2013: 4). They distinguish between policy and political entrepreneurs: policy entrepreneurs generate emergent policy ideas while political entrepreneurs pick these ideas up and become their champions. In reality, we are talking about politicians as political entrepreneurs. The political side of the relationship transforms these ideas into new policies, but politicians themselves also have ideas. These are individuals whose creative acts have transformative effects on politics and policies by changing the direction and flow of politics (Schneider and Teske,

1992). The politician benefits from the expertise of policy entrepreneurs, and sometimes their support, while the policy entrepreneur can benefit from the 'patronage' of the politician.

It is also obvious that the more senior and more influential the politician, the greater the potential of the policy entrepreneur's ideas being enacted. Catney and Henneberry (2015) treats policy and public entrepreneurship as interchangeable while Roberts and King (1996: 152) separate the terms, with policy entrepreneurship seen as a sub-set of public entrepreneurship – those working from outside government circles. Klein *et al.* (2010: 12) say that 'public entrepreneurship is a management phenomenon' and that 'entrepreneurial ideas are framed, developed, pursued, institutionalised, and enacted through processes that are both analogous to and intertwined with private entrepreneurship'. Because policy entrepreneurs generally lack formal policy-making authority within the policy systems that they seek to influence, they must employ various strategies of ideational and material influence to alter the beliefs and preferences of policy makers. In sum, policy making refers to promoting policy ideas that address public concerns.

One way that research is thought to influence policy is through its enlightenment function (Weiss, 1982) – providing new ways of understanding the world. This challenges the separation between pure and applied research and points to the contribution which social science knowledge makes to shaping opinion and framing policy agendas. However, there are challenges here, including the perceived problems with social science language which sometimes prevent researchers from interacting with policy makers. The inability of academic researchers to communicate their research often stems from a failure to understand policy making and political contexts. Politicians are looking for 'usability' and they can sometimes spin figures and distort findings. Kirp (1982: 137–138) describes five ways in which a policy issue might be settled. First, the issue is settled by 'professional expertise' – in this event the professional's expert view prevails as outsiders are not qualified to take decisions in a given area. Only the professional is knowledgeable enough to decide. Second, the politician settles the issue through political judgement. Third, legal norms dictate how the issue is to be settled. Fourth, bureaucratic standards are employed to settle the issue; and finally, the determination is left to the market to fix the policy outcome. Only in the market of ideas option does the policy entrepreneur as an agent of change appear in a role to perceive opportunities, advocate innovative ideas and transform the political arena. Here the policy entrepreneur needs rhetorical skills as the establishment of networks and positive relationships is vital to the pursuit of their goals as these networks and relationships magnify the individual's influence. It is interesting that Kingdon (1984: 139) makes clear that these actions of the policy entrepreneur are not simply taken for instrumental reasons, but that the incentives are 'solidary' in that 'they enjoy advocacy, they enjoy being at or near the seat of power, they enjoy being part of the action'. This suggests many non-pecuniary rewards for policy entrepreneurs who take risks for their vision of the future and have the ability to organise networks to pursue that vision.

Knowledge brokers

Policy makers often hear about research outcomes through lobbyists and interest groups who use them to advance their own political or ideological views. Individuals who use knowledge and information that may be useful for decision makers and who then disseminate this information so as to influence or advise decision makers are called 'knowledge brokers', 'intermediaries', 'middlemen', 'opinion leaders', 'champions', 'advocates', or 'change agents' (see Sebba, 2013; Brown, 2011). They are popularisers who effectively bridge the gap between policy makers and researchers and can be found in think tanks and in non-government organisations. It is often the case that non-research evidence is better communicated, presented and managed than evidence from academic research. Nutley *et al.* (2007: 250) identified the role of these knowledge brokers in 'specific government agencies, charitable foundations, think tanks and professional organisations' as well as in 'non-government organisations'. Brokers are 'middlemen' or intermediaries who conduct little original research, but appear to be good at identifying important policy ideas. They can also synthesise and translate (broker) knowledge into policy ideas that already exist in terms of research outcomes, as well as conduct policy analyses. They are able to produce evidence to policy makers at the right time, in the right format and in the right language. However, not all researchers have access to these intermediaries and, therefore, to the influence they can generate in research outcomes.

Knowledge brokers are people who move knowledge and information around and create connections between researchers and their various audiences. As early as 1997, Oldham and McLean proposed three frameworks for thinking about knowledge brokering within the public sector (Oldham and McLean, 1997). The *knowledge system framework* relates to the creation, diffusion and use of knowledge, and sees brokering as a way of facilitating or managing these activities. It is closest to the private sector view of brokers as knowledge managers. In the *transactional framework,* brokering focuses on the interface between the 'creators' and 'users' of knowledge and seeks to foster links between the two. Knowledge brokers manage and collate knowledge from a range of sources and present it as accessible information; they are linking agents in that they bridge the gap between academia and government; and they are capacity builders in that they improve researchers' and end-users' abilities to be effective producers and receivers of knowledge respectively. They can target audiences that might be beyond the reach of a researcher's contact base. Holmes and Clark (2008) suggest that as well as presenting research to policy makers, knowledge brokers are also involved in 'facilitating the development of researchable questions to meet the needs of policy makers and communicating them to researchers'. In this way, engagement with knowledge brokers can bring two advantages to researchers: in the short term it can increase the likelihood of research being utilised in public policy, and in the longer term it can help devise a research direction that can result in relevant and usable research outputs.

Clearly, researchers who establish and maintain contact with knowledge brokers can utilise their skills to advance their policy ideas. Nevertheless, academics are increasingly developing the skills that help them identify the key messages from research evidence for policy and can translate this into non-technical language for policy makers. These academics are policy entrepreneurs or even, as Davies (2015: 399) calls them, 'evidence entrepreneurs'. Coburn (1998) has highlighted the important role of 'policy entrepreneurs' in this process as individuals 'who have sufficient research backgrounds and credentials to understand the culture and methods of university research organisations but who also understand the policy process and can communicate effectively with state policymakers'. Sound argumentation is key at every stage of the policy cycle.

Conclusion

Policy entrepreneurship has received sustained academic study without a settled definition emerging. One reason for this state of affairs is that the policy process itself remains mysterious. However, it is possible to identify a class of actors – policy entrepreneurs – who change how we think about policy ideas and how we address them. Policy entrepreneurs are, in part, political actors who promote policy ideas in the hope of bringing about change. Change occurs because individuals act in particular ways to promote their interests, but these interests are shaped by ideas and the context within which they operate. They are active rather than reactive and are good at re-packaging old ideas and mobilising support for these ideas. The activity involves doing things in a new and better way than before. As Kingdon (1984: 181) notes, 'they push, push and push for their proposals or for their conception of the problem' and have a clear focus and 'excellent antennae' (127) to decide when is the right time to take advantage of a window of opportunity.

While policy entrepreneurs can introduce innovation in public sector policies through 'the generation, translation, and implementation of new ideas', they cannot do so alone (Roberts and King, 1991: 147). The boundaries of policy networks that they establish are relatively open and fluid. New policy actors from the private and charity sectors can influence policy, as can academics from the academy. Academics need sufficient authority and legitimacy to be respected by policy makers. Producing research outcomes in the academy and relying on passive dissemination of information is generally ineffective, as we have seen. It is essential for academic policy entrepreneurs to understand user needs and the use of networks or the formation of alliances or partnerships to help communicate and promote research-based innovations. The role of research in policy change processes is often indirect; research knowledge is but one input among many in decision-making situations. In many cases, it will be difficult to discern the influence of research on policy outcomes because decision processes are seldom entirely rational or linear; in fact, they remain rather opaque. Policy entrepreneurs from the academy may or may not gain credit, support, status and even money by identifying issues, networking in policy circles, helping to shape policy debates and building coalitions in support of policy change.

Mintrom's (2000: 282) work on the role of policy entrepreneurs within an education context suggests that 'they are individuals who, through the skills they develop over time, are able to exercise greater levels of agency than other members of policymaking communities', often through the manipulation and transformation of policy images. Kingdon (1984: 205) reflects that 'an item's chances of moving up on an agenda are enhanced considerably by the presence of a skilful entrepreneur, and dampened considerably if no entrepreneur takes on the cause, pushes it, and makes the critical couplings when policy windows open'. Bryson and Crosby (2005: 156) refer to the role of 'policy entrepreneurship' as 'catalysts of systemic change' that are 'inventive, energetic, and persistent in overcoming systemic barriers'; policy entrepreneurs can be involved at any stage of the policy-change cycle. They manage ideas, frame problem causes and explanations, and they analyse and manage the multiple interests that are often associated with these problems. Critically, policy entrepreneurs are considered to require effective political skills, experience of bargaining and negotiation, and an appreciation of the different demands of the policy process from policy formulation, through delivery to evaluation. Cobb and Elder (1981) consider that policy entrepreneurs depend on an ability to orchestrate the flow of people, problems, solutions and choice opportunities. Mistakes and setbacks are a normal part of the process. It is also the case that policy ideas can remain outside this process at any given point in time despite supporting evidence because they are politically unacceptable to policy makers. One publication by an academic is not going to produce immediate changes to public policy regardless of the context. Academic research is best understood as 'informing' policy making rather than in terms of one research outcome resulting in one policy decision. As Jesse Norman (2010: 170) says, in the end 'entrepreneurship is a necessary, vital, chaotic, unpredictable and creative process'. However, the overuse of the term has drained it of meaning.

In the varying accounts that I have presented in this chapter, the policy entrepreneur can be characterised as what Mackenzie (2004: 369) calls a consensus builder, an 'issue generator', an 'issue broker' – someone who is 'alert' to the opening of 'policy windows'. The policy entrepreneur is skilled in the art of argument and persuasion, and is able to shape how problems and policy issues are defined so as to mould new 'policy images'; they are 'catalysts' and 'change agents', 'innovators' and 'ideas' people who pursue their goals through the many entrepreneurial activities described above. He concludes (2004: 369) that 'they possess a strategic sense when pursuing their policy goals, usually have a wide spectrum of interpersonal contacts and collegial networks and often engage in "bargaining" to achieve their ends, particularly when persuasion fails. In short, policy entrepreneurs are significant agents for change.'

3

WHAT DO POLICY ENTREPRENEURS DO?

Introduction

We now turn to some activities that policy entrepreneurs engage in. What is their key message with reference to policy? Why is it important? Some have referred to the four Ps of being influential, and I apply them to the academic role. They are: (a) *Passion* – the academic must care about the problem, (b) *Position* – the academic should have access to some key people of influence, (c) *Power* – the academic should have status and influence precisely as an academic, and (d) *Persuasiveness* – the academic needs to have credibility and be treated seriously by making a convincing case. In short, the academic policy entrepreneur has to be a good storyteller who communicates ideas with persuasive arguments that justify their recommendations, a networker who can identify and interact with officials, a fixer who can resolve issues effectively, a non-partisan agent who can retain their integrity while using their insight to have political impact and who can get their ideas noticed. This academic policy entrepreneur issues a call to action with value-driven arguments which, though non-partisan, may nevertheless retain an ideological intent. It might also be useful to consider Catford's (2006) five Ps for policy entrepreneurship:

Position	What are you seeking? When do you want action to happen?
Perception	How does this fit within the current context? What are the benefits?
Players	Who are you? What credibility do you have? How united are you?
Power	What resources and influence do you have to influence the agenda?
Persistence	How determined are you? Will you stay the course?

With this in mind and with the theoretical background outlined in Chapter 2, we can look at the various aspects of being an entrepreneur in practice.

Leadership

Success derives from a culture of excellence set by the leader. Leadership has always been a key driver in bringing about change. The leader sets the context, establishes the agenda and creates the expectations for the work to be done. The most important quality of leadership is having a vision – a vision that can be expressed to different audiences. The vision must include a plan to translate the vision into logical and manageable steps. You need to maintain the energy to nurture the plan step by step. You need to have knowledge of the big picture and see how various disciplines can inter-relate with each other. This will involve strategic thinking and a positive view of the future – you should be enthusiastic and positive about change. An ability to cultivate and foster partnerships to achieve your research goals is crucial, which will mean developing effective negotiation skills, including strong inter-personal and communication skills. Indeed, as you start out you need to focus on your own values and goals – these are vital to how you will be perceived and how you will introduce yourself to different audiences. Your personal style will determine whether you can promote your ideas effectively and how connected you will become. You need to ask yourself whether you have values that others relate to, admire and respect. Your early actions and decisions will shape perceptions and you need to be aware that the opinion-forming process starts at the beginning.

Leaders take advantage of windows of opportunity and build teams, they win credibility and demonstrate trustworthiness – small wins take you in the right direction through incremental steps, so do not expect quick victories. Hence, developing some key relationships and identifying opportunities are essential qualities of a leader. You need to be motivated, inspired, have the capacity to identify an opportunity, have self-confidence and a degree of luck. You need to be a good storyteller by synthesising simple compelling stories from the results of your research. Leaders are risk-takers as well as being creative and pioneering, they need to be bold – 'to boldly go…'. Leaders tend to be restless and rule-breakers – they are driven, confident, resourceful and adaptable as well as flexible and resilient. When surrounded by trusted colleagues, sometimes the best decision a leader can make is to not be the one to make a certain decision. A degree of delegation has many benefits, including measuring the decision-making abilities of your managers and empowering your team. By handing over some decision-making responsibilities, leaders are also building a better management team and giving them the confidence they need as their responsibilities increase.

Incubation of ideas and research evidence

Translating research into policy requires ideas to emerge by bringing them into reality. Many policy ideas come from different sources and they need to be ranked in terms of policy usefulness. This process normally begins with an individual who comes up with a concept he or she thinks should be further explored. The individual may bring other associated ideas into the incubation process to make the ideas stronger and more viable. Ideas need time to develop and do not occur within a vacuum. Ideas drive policy – indeed, ideas play a fundamental role in policy formulation. The idea of an academic incubator is that it supports the development and formulation of policy ideas and planning activities. Ideas formulation is key to developing networks and achieving credibility as well as to seeing opportunity. The incubator shelters new ideas and helps them form. Policy entrepreneurs define the problems and produce a formal statement that makes the link between the identified problem or issue and the proposed solutions. So, you need to define and publicise problems as you see them. The way that you define and frame an idea will have implications for the policy solutions that emerge. Different players will produce different and competing frames of a problem in the public realm. One of these frames may become dominant in the press and with policy makers. Framing is about setting an idea within an appropriate context to achieve a desired result. In keeping with Mintrom's sixth key to policy entrepreneurship (2000), part of the implantation process is to begin testing the ideas before they become established practice: to lead by example and translate abstract research ideas into something tangible.

Research evidence must be accessible with clear outcomes, so it needs to be low in complexity and relevant to current practice. We do not always produce the answers desired by policy makers. The balance is to maintain research integrity while maximising impact. Sometimes evidence prevails, sometimes opinion. It is important to stay within your area of expertise to remain a knowledgeable source, but equally to collaborate on an inter-disciplinary level. The communication of research findings to users of research is a key skill that a policy entrepreneur must acquire. Does the research relate to a policy idea that is generally favoured by a politician? Is the idea in currency? What is the extent of your relationships with policy makers? Do you have access to politicians? What alternative strategies do you have for your message to be heard? Although there may be some dissonance between rhetoric and reality, as outlined earlier in this book, governments continually affirm their belief in evidence-based policy making. Senior policy makers and politicians turn to the researchers inside their departments, so you should feed your research to them. Ministers also rely on experts and think tanks, as well as both traditional and social media as important sources for them and their advisers. You need to engage with and influence these groups. Working with them requires trust and time to build relationships – for example, sharing findings before publication. Politicians, and particularly civil servants, are much more open to outside evidence than they were. The key, however, is relevance. No amount of evidence will have any impact unless it chimes with the concerns and priorities of policy makers and politicians. You need to begin by defining how you seek to influence policy. You could be trying to find out what policy should be or simply pushing policy in a given direction. You could be an advocate for funding to address an issue or advocating for or against certain practices or approaches. You could then think about your audience and ask what kind of research evidence they are likely to respond to, but it is also important to remember to use existing evidence.

Setting the agenda

In order to have a chance to become actual policy, an issue or idea must reach the top of the policy agenda, something that occurs neither automatically nor easily. Agenda setting is an on-going competition among policy entrepreneurs and others who propose new policy ideas to gain the attention of the media, the public and policy makers. The way in which issues gain or lose attention in the public mind relates to the policy process broadly conceived. This process provides a platform for ideas and issues and highlights particular policy factors that help set up the decision-making process. Policy entrepreneurs seek acceptance of their ideas, but come to realise that the agenda is ever changing in the political context, so items can easily rise and fall in priority and perceived importance. Only policy issues that receive some media coverage can claim to be public issues. The policy entrepreneur is someone who advocates that attention should be given to a particular policy issue or idea. These ideas are generated from the policy entrepreneur's research and interests. This will include historical ideas from the literature, which builds on a number of traditions. The agenda tells us what issues are important, then there is the question of issue duration as most ideas rise or fall on the political agenda. It concerns the set of issues that are the subject of decision making and debate within a given political context. These ideas will be in competition with each other for a place on the agenda. Agenda setting does not happen in a vacuum and depends largely on the issue itself, the networks that support it, the context and ultimately on random political and social factors. If a policy idea is not perceived to be important by a sufficiently large number of people, it will never attract enough attention to reach the top of the policy agenda. The first aim, therefore, is to get your idea on to the policy agenda.

Patrons, support and advice

It is important to enlist thought leaders to champion your cause, including MPs and important people in public life. It is worth making use of policy networks, such as think tanks, that are accessible and well connected. Where possible, work to cultivate close contact with those who are in decision-making positions or close to political influence in the area in which you are working. Networks lead to entry points into other networks and can influence others so that they help achieve your policy goals. Where possible, establish an advisory board or group to your research project or centre, as this can help foster links between researchers and policy makers. The board can help identify and pursue research funding opportunities as well as become an advocate for the research itself. This will, of course, depend on who is appointed to the board. First, you need to determine the objectives of the advisory board and how long you expect it to last. Second, you need to select the right people, who could be big names or technical experts. You need to brief them continuously and provide them with the highlights of the research findings in advance of any publications. The important thing is that they are independent minds who have an interest in the research. You ought to have flexibility in constructing the advisory board. Remember that the board is not constituted to make decisions, so it will not lead the research or have legal responsibilities. However, the advisers should offer candid advice, which is of course non-binding but respected, as they are there to challenge the research agenda. An advisory board encourages dialogue, open conversations and should be a safe and free place that stimulates debate. This will, in turn, support and strengthen the mission of the research and bring different perspectives.

Strategy, funding and milestones

You should organise members of your team and increase the number of supporters while growing the activities around your research. Maintain the momentum and develop a strategy to fit the political context. Use opinion leaders to help promote and disseminate the research highlights or policy ideas. You need to build an environment that is supportive of change, which means that you need to acquire the skills to become an effective change agent. As highlighted in the previous chapter, the use of other academics and external researchers who have research utilisation skills is part of the strategy. Securing funding for research is becoming increasingly central to successful academic careers. In any grant application, you will need to consider what contribution you are going to make to the debates in your field. Hence, you will need to write persuasively about four key things: (a) clear research questions, (b) a justification for why it is important, (c) how you intend to answer the questions and (d) what impact it will have on society. This means you must consider the dissemination of the research outcomes before you begin the research. Producing an early concept paper outlining the research proposal helps enormously, especially when you have it reviewed by colleagues internally or externally before you apply for research funding. Persistence is also important to grant writing, which means dealing with refusal by building a degree of resilience. Remember that the process of applying for funding will take longer when you collaborate with others, particularly external collaborators.

It is important to develop a timeline identifying important milestones to keep your research on track and for wider research impact. Researchers generally develop timelines and milestones when they apply for funding. In most cases, your funder wants to know in great detail what you plan to do, what you hope to accomplish and how long it will take you to complete your work. If your grant proposal has set out a realistic plan, then you can use it to establish a complete and realistic timeline and milestones for your research team and collaborators. For all research, starting with a clear plan for management, a reasonable timeline, and common milestones all increase your chances of completing your project on time. But remember that your plan should be a working document, which you can update or modify as necessary if ideas change or unexpected complications emerge. You also need to plan what happens at the end of the grant period in order to produce this timeline, even though this may not be easy. It is hard to keep your research on track when you are working by yourself or with your own team. It is even more difficult to keep a project on track when you are managing a team of researchers.

Dissemination, media and campaigns

You need to plan a wide audience for any dissemination strategy, which means newsletters, taught courses, CPD courses, books, articles, position papers, reports, seminars and conferences. Dissemination may give visibility to a research outcome, but it cannot guarantee impact on policy and practice. Dissemination should be considered right from the start of any project. Planning how the research will be shared can help guide the research process and maintain focus on the project's ultimate goal. Depending on the nature of the research, some information may be communicated before the entire project is completed. You need to ask who would find this research valuable. Ultimately, research dissemination is communication, and different audiences require suitable approaches. Good communication considers the practical needs, current knowledge level, and language/terminology preferences of the audience. Focus on goals. The dissemination should reflect the purpose of the research project, whether it be to inform, to motivate or otherwise. Rather than simply reporting what the research uncovered, you should contextualise the information to help the audience understand why the research was done, what makes the results important, and what actions should be taken next in the light of the research findings. Distributing a regular newsletter summarising study findings is an ideal way to update study participants and participating agencies. As outlined in the two cultures thesis, the common audience for a policy brief is more interested in potential solutions based on the new research evidence than in the research/ analysis procedures. Policy briefs should be just that—brief and concise—and should focus on the implications of the new evidence for a particular policy (see DeMarco and Adams Tufts, 2010). Summaries of research findings should identify key issues, including any recommendations or points for action. Producing actionable messages derived from the research is something that ought to be on-going rather than a one-off event. Nevertheless, to attract the media, you should try to relate your findings to current events.

Academics need to make greater use of their university press offices and respond to enquiries as well as react to news stories. This will involve providing training for academics so that they can become more proactive in responding to media enquiries. The media portrayal of issues often influences how they are understood by the public and government and whether or not action is taken on the issue. When the media emphasise a theme, the public receiving the message will consider the topic to be important. It is worth developing a proactive press strategy and training your people. Press releases offer one of the most efficient and effective ways to disseminate information, particularly to the media and other organisations. The speed that issues can gain attention can be rapid in the media. Research in the news gets cited more often – it draws more attention.

Cohen (1963) notes that 'the press may not be successful much of the time in telling people what to think, but it is stunningly successful in telling its readers what to think about'. Stories in the media should never be considered a neutral presentation of the facts.

Media campaigns promote ideas by considering what research evidence you are working with and the message it communicates – it can highlight issues that have been ignored. Place an idea on the agenda. Sometimes we need translators: editors, coaches and communication professionals to help us reach external audiences. Campaigning is about awareness-raising and involves efforts to educate or involve the public by mobilising their support on a particular issue, or to influence or change public attitudes. Although it is often difficult to differentiate between campaigning and advocacy and other forms of political engagement, it is important for academics to engage with politicians and policy makers while preserving party political neutrality.

Policy collaborators and political contacts

When coalitions are formed, there are advantages for both sides in the relationship. The expertise of the policy entrepreneur combined with the patronage of the political entrepreneur can help frame issues, define problems and influence agendas. Agents who are highly interested and aligned should be natural allies and collaborators. They can widen the network of supporters, but you need to be clear about the issues people are coming together to raise or change. The policy process today is more collaborative, but you need to develop membership criteria and mechanisms for including new members into any collaboration. Sometimes it is a rational and orderly process in which good arguments and evidence win. On other occasions, it is a quick and decisive response to a major event. Forge more networks of people doing or potentially interested in doing entrepreneurial work in education. Networks are a hallmark of vibrant entrepreneurial sectors: formal and informal mechanisms for people to meet, share ideas and lessons, and keep their fingers on the pulse of the sector. Networks can be formed formally, by convening people in specific locations and linking them in communications networks. Working with others reinforces what you stand for and provides positive endorsements for your policy ideas, especially when you are working towards similar goals. However, it is important to decide what your collaboration or network will and will not do.

Policy makers are very cautious and they do not rush in with new ideas. It is generally the case that researchers will have more influence at the beginning of the policy process when perceptions are still loosely formed. Contacting politicians without prior research into their interests is not a good tactic. You need to know what drives them – in other words, to understand the politics of the situation and be flexible. Indeed, where possible, you should relate your policy ideas to government policy objectives. You should remember that politicians are constantly asked to do things, stop things, pass things, enact things and so on. You need to get them to act as a bridge between those advocating new policy ideas because they are key: they sit at the centre of the process and choose from the ideas generated by the policy entrepreneur. Ministers are busy and rarely read research reports – they want brief summaries of evidence and 'action points'.

It is interesting to consider why some US academics are more effective at influencing policy in the UK than some UK academics. Politicians want something which looks reasonable and has a clear message – American academics appear to be better at this. There are many examples of this in the UK education sector, even in the area of character education, with the more popular science books and briefs presented by various US academics being cited by UK politicians (see Morgan, 2016). As previously mentioned (Baumgartner *et al.,* 2006: 965), this may well have something to do with the American political system and the greater opportunity for academic policy entrepreneurs to influence the agenda – hence, the honing of associated skills. Although there is a demand for usable knowledge, you should only engage with policy makers if you believe it is a valuable exercise. A great deal of research is produced, but it is difficult for policy makers to read, far less make sense of it. Policy makers have their own information and research evidence needs, so the researcher needs to help them navigate through the territory of research evidence.

Publications and research reports

Publications for an academic audience are normally concerned with articles and books, but you need to diversify your outputs if you wish to have influence and impact on public policy. You need to find ways to present your research evidence or findings in forums and media that are more accessible to a general or specific audience. You cannot stop with an academic paper. Not all outlets are appropriate in particular cases, so you must give careful consideration to genuine and constructive forms of engagement. Researchers are normally rewarded for publications in academic journals that practitioners and policy makers do not read. So if you wish to have enhanced impact, you need to think beyond purely refereed academic publications. The Jubilee Centre has expanded its range of publications so it works to plan publication after the collection of new data sets and other information. It is important to consider a wide range of both academic and non-academic audiences.

The production of specialist yet accessible summaries of research is essential. Reports must not throw up obstacles for practitioner engagement with research findings. Good reports will offer interpretations for policy makers and practitioner audiences while acknowledging the understandings of those at whom the research is directed. Good reports will connect abstract principles with concrete examples and will have a clear and unambiguous purpose. It is key to ensure clear, simple, short and jargon-free writing. No matter what the project, you should have a summary of the research findings. Projects that are meant to produce a formal research paper will have a ready-made document to distribute. Reports or summaries of the report can be shared with other organisations, with government and with members of the academic community.

Public presentations and consultations

You must identify an intended audience and encourage others to coalesce around an issue – promoting one issue or a fairly specific issue exerts most influence. The intention is to inform – your document must not be complicated since your audience should be able to comprehend the subject matter fully. You are seeking to persuade so that your audience willingly accepts your proposals – they may even be roused to action. This involves presentation skills – usually the ability to speak well in public. It involves preparation and practice – presentations, media appearances, interviews, talks, lectures and writing all require communication skills. In publications, especially research reports, it is important to make conclusions and recommendations more specific or more operational. Reports need to be readable and appealing in presentation. A public presentation of research results can range from a press conference to a presentation at a professional conference or other public forum, or even to a rally or public demonstration. You have to create the opportunity to speak directly to people, using appropriate verbal and non-verbal language and cultural sensitivity. In addition, a public forum lets you answer questions, expand on anything people don't understand, as well as generate energy for working on policy change.

You need to become a trusted voice with a strong sense of independence when you are consulted as an expert by a policy maker, as they usually call upon experts before they announce policies. You should consult the public and relevant organisations to help with research questions and to solve problems. Sometimes it is simply about feedback and opinions on a theme from the research – a two-way flow of information between researcher, practitioner and policy maker. This could be a one-stage process or a continuing dialogue. Bring the expertise, perspectives and ideas of others into the discussion – this allows you to consider unintended effects and practical problems at an early stage of development. Then there is informal consultation, which can take the form of phone calls, letters and informal meetings – all designed to collect information from interested parties. There is a kind of continuum from simply informing the public, to consulting them, involving them, collaborating with them and empowering them.

Advocacy, lobbying and engagement

Advocacy is normally about persuasion and influencing people for change whereas lobbying is about a case for political change and is usually directed at politicians. It involves working with policy makers and civil servants who may or may not be sympathetic to your views and means of introducing the new language of your project. You will need to demonstrate relevance to press your case effectively, which means identifying who you advocate to. For those who are interested in what you have to say, but are not aligned at present, you will need to bring them into alignment with your policy ideas. You will need to show a clear need for something or for your proposed intervention. Lobbying involves mounting a concerted campaign and could be difficult for many academics, given other constraints on their time and resources. A policy entrepreneur seeks to mobilise opinion by finding and gaining adherents for their policy ideas. Trying to influence or change public opinion is indirect lobbying. It is about creating general awareness around your ideas. Academics can advocate on behalf of their research outcomes, even though many are reluctant to do so. The research base for lobbying should be nonpartisan and non-aggressive – which means it must give a fair exposition of the facts and allow the reader to form an independent opinion.

Academics should take their research into the realm of public policy and convince the public that a new policy or different approach is valuable. Foster change. Engagement can be seen as a two-way relationship of trust, respect and interdependency, leading to collaboration and even co-production. Public debate plays by different rules than academic debate, so you need to be prepared for unfamiliar tactics and players. Try to be careful not to lose control of the message, although this may be inevitable to some extent. This theme of 'issue ownership' is one that has emerged in other cases of policy entrepreneurship (see Oborn *et al.*, 2011). This was particularly prominent in the case of Professor Darzi in London:

> As ideas and policies develop around networks, they are translated in ways that may not be under the control of those who originally devised or promoted them (Latour, 1987). Ideas may mutate or may misrepresent an initial intent. Indeed, the policy entrepreneur may need to pay this price in order to enrol more actors.
>
> *(2011: 341)*

This mutation of ideas may come unnaturally to many academics, but it can be crucial in securing influence and impact for your research. You will get blowback so you need to be prepared for it. When building an engagement strategy, you should try to build activities on each other so as to achieve the highest possible impact. For example, findings published in an academic journal may at the same time be broadcast in the media, written up in a four-page briefing paper, and launched with an event that is publicised widely through social media, such as Twitter. The ESRC provides some basic details of what good public engagement might look like:

- *Project start-up*: involving stakeholders at this stage of the process can help shape the research agenda. This ensures that the research tackles pertinent issues.
- *Preliminary findings*: sharing preliminary findings with key groups not only increases awareness but can tease out issues, helping shape later stages of research or analysis.

- *Project end*: sharing and testing research findings both with stakeholders and with other groups who might be interested in the research, including the general public. This raises awareness of the research and of social science; it can potentially enable the outputs to be used more widely and have greater impact.
- *Other times*: public engagement activities don't have to be linked to specific projects. For many groups, meeting and working with a researcher is a valued experience and provides a unique opportunity to understand research findings and processes. It may also provide new, unexpected research opportunities.

Policy entrepreneurs must demonstrate high levels of understanding and ability to engage with others. Personal connections between researchers, practitioners and policy makers – that is, the relationships between individuals above and beyond formal working obligations – promote reciprocal awareness and can be beneficial for both parties. You need to develop these personal connections in order to access and become part of informal networks of colleagues. You can disseminate knowledge and understand the concerns of practitioners and what they want. Sometimes the relationship between research and policy is *ad hoc,* and knowledge passed on through these informal channels can be very influential. They can throw up opportunities for collaboration. Policy makers in particular often need to access information quickly and fall back on their informal connections. Chance meetings can instigate academic/policy collaborations and positive human interaction. Building these connections takes time, and the benefits do not appear immediately – a degree of trust is required. Face-to-face engagements with decision makers are more likely to lead to research findings being acted upon.

Civil servants will build a network of experts for a number of uses: information and evidence, invitations to government groups, informal relationships, evidence to select committees. This is predicated on the belief that bringing academics into the policy-making process can help policy be innovative, more robust and based on the most up-to-date knowledge. There is, therefore, a strong argument for making better use of research evidence. Communication channels with civil servants and government advisers should be kept open through regular contact. Proactivity is key here, and having more than one contact is also important.

Selecting the team

You need to recruit, select and retain the best researchers with the highest potential to achieve excellence in your research project. At the same time, you also need to identify skill gaps and provide professional development. You need to consider the mix of people in your team in terms of knowledge, skills and personal chemistry. This means you need high levels of competence, energy, focus and trust, and you need to expect it from your team. Central to a high-performing research team are two essential characteristics. The first is people: this means recruiting and retaining the best. A mix of staff is central and is associated with staff who are research trained, who are senior (professors), and who have international experience. The 'glue' that creates the high-performing research unit is its research culture, underlying values and leadership. You must allow research staff space to get on with their work, partly due to the recognition that their success was attributable to their strong leadership and the research culture of the team. Creating a values framework for the staff should include a sense of public service – in other words being a part of something with a positive influence on society. As a team at the Jubilee Centre, we wanted to find answers that would make a difference, so we had to have high standards and a culture of excellence in which 'only the best will do'; high expectations of performance combined with a supportive environment of mutual value and support. You need to establish a collegial environment where people cooperate and have a strong family identity. You need the right people to create a real intellectual buzz and to regard research as a shared endeavour.

Ideally, the balance and composition of the team in terms of skills, expertise and other contributions will be appropriate to achieve the team's objectives. The research team leader needs to be confident that team members have, or can develop, the necessary skills and knowledge for the research in hand, so you will make recruitment decisions on that basis.

A number of responsibilities are identified in Adair's (1973) action-centred leadership model:

- establish, agree and communicate standards of performance and behaviour;
- establish style, culture, approach of the group – soft skill elements;
- monitor and maintain discipline, ethics, integrity and focus on objectives;
- anticipate and resolve group conflict, struggles or disagreements;
- assess and change as necessary the balance and composition of the group;
- develop team-working, cooperation, morale and team-spirit;
- develop the collective maturity and capability of the group – progressively increase group freedom and authority;
- encourage the team towards objectives and aims – motivate the group and provide a collective sense of purpose;
- identify, develop and agree team- and project-leadership roles within group;
- enable, facilitate and ensure effective internal and external group communications;
- identify and meet group training needs;
- give feedback to the group on overall progress; consult with, and seek feedback and input from the group.

The support staff within the team are just as important.

A good definition of entrepreneurship sees it more as a process in which an agent or entrepreneur is involved in an entrepreneurial event, which Bernier (2014: 257) describes as:

the conceptualisation and realisation of an innovative idea, concept, service, product or activity. The agent is the individual or group that takes on the responsibility of bringing the event to fruition. Of course, the entrepreneurial process involves values, especially a willingness to take risks in order to bring about creative change, and involves behaviour that is traditionally associated with the strategic process: identifying and assessing an opportunity, defining a business strategy or concept, identifying the necessary resources to implement it, acquiring those resources and bringing the project to fruition.

Conclusion

Many of the suggestions and recommendations in this chapter focus precisely on reducing the distance between the research and policy-making communities. Put rather simply, we either defend existing policy, extend existing policy or we innovate with the generation of new policy ideas. Educational policy entrepreneurs should focus both on the problem and the potential solutions in education. A majority of academic educationalists spend too much of their time examining and detailing theoretical problems. While problems must be studied and described, it is important, from a practical standpoint, that the potential solutions are examined as well. This practical activity is often not prioritised by academics, who often value their research above its dissemination. To be effective in the policy-making process, the academic must do both well – they must develop the intellectual and applied aspects of any policy innovation simultaneously. The academic policy entrepreneur must consider both areas and be ready to speak on different ground to different individuals. Intellectual aspects of the policy innovation may include identification of key questions, knowledge of relevant theory, reformulation of theory, empirical evidence and research agenda. Applied aspects of policy innovation include simple and clear statements of the rationale, the general policy strategy, specific policy applications and evaluative data. It is not possible to succeed at policy innovation from the ivory tower; as an academic you cannot simply be content with publishing your work, you need to be prepared to advocate and promote your findings. You need to develop a critical mass of people who are persuaded by your policy ideas as well as a coalition to support some form of take-up and implementation of these ideas. Policy entrepreneurs need to be open to and adapt to changing contexts.

There are two policy points to be made: first, policy thinking will be much better if it is from the ground up, based firmly in the realities of people's lives. Second, the innovator of policy ideas is in a much stronger political position if there is evidence of working with real people. You should appeal to a broad political audience and try to avoid partisanship. The primary allegiance of an academic is to his or her ideas and proposal. The political process is naturally partisan, and political actors will almost automatically attempt to connect any 'policy expert' with their political party. Partisan political activity is a disservice to one's independence as a scholar and to the cause of policy innovation. Once associated with a particular political party, your proposal will be weakened and your objectivity will be suspect. The academic policy entrepreneur must learn to engage vigorously in policy, but never in party politics. You must not work on other people's political agenda, as your allegiance is to a policy idea based on sound scholarship. For this reason, you must never sacrifice academic quality. Above all, the academic policy entrepreneur must undertake sound scholarship, which in the long run is what matters most. Politics and public relations mean little in the absence of a strong academic foundation. Nevertheless, you can identify supporters and opponents of your ideas and between these those who can be persuaded – the 'convincibles'.

4

CASE STUDIES OF ENTREPRENEURSHIP IN EDUCATION

> You must get involved to have an impact.
>
> *Napoleon Hill*

Introduction

It is said that researchers and policy makers speak a different language, that they operate within different time frames and even that they care about different things. Researchers, of course, constantly seek to qualify and problematise their research and research outcomes, while policy makers want immediate answers and press for practical applications and definitions. Policy entrepreneurs who use their research outcomes need to show their relevance to existing public concerns and to synthesise these outcomes in language familiar to policy makers. Policy makers are focused on the human consequences of their policies, while researchers are focused on producing research outcomes that are as objective and as valid as possible. Bullock *et al.* (2001) offer a careful examination of four education case studies that detail the benefits of using evidence in policy making as well as describing the barriers to an evidence-based approach.

This chapter offers practical advice that can be used to develop entrepreneurial skills to enhance research impact. Influence is inevitably linked to impact – that is discernible changes (for better or worse) in policy and practice. It should also be remembered that the most influential research is not necessarily the best. We need to consider what policy entrepreneurs do and how they do it. By what means do they come to have influence and what are their methods? Do they work alone or with others? There is no set toolkit to train policy entrepreneurs, nor is there any complete list of methods used. Educational researchers do not have to remain on the side-lines when it comes to policy development. You can choose to become active in the creation of policy or advocate for change in a policy. Policy may be developed and applied at many levels. You also need to understand the role of government in policy making. You may wish to seek out opportunities to raise the profile of your research in the media, the political arena, the public consciousness and in professional contexts. The poor state of the public discussion on a range of educational issues is, in part, the responsibility of the academic community. The challenge we face is to communicate educational thinking. As I have argued in this text, educational researchers need to become more aware of the government, public sector and civil society as audiences for their research findings.

In considering the procedures, methods, devices and strategies in this chapter you need to monitor and evaluate the progress you are making, which would include asking whether your adoption of these methods has worked as well as what did not work and why? You also need to recognise that these activities take time. You need to expect setbacks and learn from them. You need to develop a management plan with a time frame. You need to update or modify this as constantly as necessary if ideas change or if the unexpected occurs. Not all of us are good communicators and some may lack the skill, time or inclination to play the role of educator to the public and political leaders. Sometimes research is not designed to be relevant to policy ideas. The range of educational issues that the policy entrepreneur may concern themselves with is long.

Pollard (2005) warns us as follows:

> My sense is that [the term 'impact'] valorises what is short term, what is readily visible and easily measurable. My sense is also that it has difficulty comprehending and valuing what is complex and problematic; what is uneven and unpredictable, what requires patience and tenacity. My sense is that it finds difficulty in distinguishing between levels of change, between what is fairly superficial and what is, to coin another over-used, increasingly presumptuous phrase 'transformational' between what, in the management literature, is second-order rather than first-order change.

It is not the intention of this chapter to privilege instrumental uses of research over all others. We do not accept the positivist model of research use which sees it as a predictable linear process that is independent of context (see Lemay and Sá, 2012: 474). Nutley *et al.* (2007), Weiss (1979) and others have classified the manner in which research is used for making policy decisions. In describing these typologies, Nutley *et al.* (2007: 36) and colleagues distinguish between instrumental and conceptual perspectives of evidence use. Instrumental use refers to the specific impact of a piece of research on a particular decision or solution. It 'represents a widely-held view of what research use means'. On the other hand, conceptual use relates to the more indirect influence of research: 'It happens where research changes ways of thinking, alerting policymakers and practitioners to an issue or playing a more "consciousness-raising" role.' Academics need to build impact into grant applications and demonstrate that they have an impact strategy.

Academic policy entrepreneurs can have a real impact on society as well as public policy. However, there are several barriers to policy entrepreneurship in the academy. First, policy entrepreneurs must possess a rare blend of skills – they must have the attributes of traditional academics, including inner drive, rigour and skills, but they must also possess the attributes of traditional entrepreneurs, such as the ability to recognise opportunities and create new ideas, and even sometimes be willing to take risks. However, even for academics with the right set of skills, traditional university culture can be a strong deterrent. The UK Research Councils encourage skill acquisition and provide funding for courses to assist academic staff develop in these areas.

We have seen how policy entrepreneurs use a variety of strategies for successful policy entrepreneurship. A significant part of their efforts is advocacy: they aim to persuade powerful decision makers, using accessible language, that their policy ideas are among the most valuable. They largely enact this advocacy role by adapting to the preferences of targeted stakeholders and decision makers. They also try to capture media attention as well as demonstrate the feasibility of their options, notably through evidence and pilot studies. They can guide debates and discussions towards their own interests and concerns. This activity presupposes that policy entrepreneurs engage in negotiation, compromise and cooperation with other stakeholders, as well as co-option of possible opponents. Policy entrepreneurs must use concrete examples to demonstrate that their arguments are realistic and have to explain these examples in accessible language. To do this, the policy entrepreneur needs to be highly tuned to the current policy rhetoric in education. As mentioned already, according to Mintrom and Norman (Mintrom and Vergari,1996; Mintrom and Norman, 2009), these are 'displaying social acuity' (opportunity seeking and recognising, networking), 'defining problems' (framing, socially perceptive), 'building teams' (coalition building), and 'leading by example' (assertiveness and commitment). According to them, these strategies can be grouped in the following four categories; 'attention and support-seeking strategies', in order to demonstrate the significance of a problem and to convince a wide range of participants about their preferred policy; 'linkage strategies', because policy entrepreneurs are mostly unable to accomplish their objectives alone and therefore link with other parties in coalitions, projects, ideas and policy games; 'relational management strategies', as the relational factor is critical in policy change trajectories; and finally 'arena strategies', to influence the time and the place wherein policy entrepreneurs play their policy game.

Research impact is often seen as those auditable occasions that can be systematically recorded. It is recorded by mapping the 'digital footprint' of the research impact through a record of the active consultations, meetings with policy makers, discussions, citations, referencing or the use of a piece of research. This gives us little information either about the quality of these interventions or their actual impact. We examine in this chapter three short case studies of TLRP and SEL already mentioned, and the case of citizenship education, all of which were established during the New Labour government between 1997 and 2010. The first is a successful demonstration of policy entrepreneurship, the second is largely an example of failure, while the third is a mixture of both success and failure.

The case of the Teaching and Learning Research Programme

The Economic and Social Research Council (ESRC) and the Higher Education Funding Council for England (HEFCE) commissioned and funded the Teaching and Learning Research Programme (TLRP), a ten-year effort from 1999 to 2009 to revitalise educational research in the UK using substantial awards to a range of collaborating investigators. The origins of this initiative grew out of a background in which educational research was criticised for being small-scale, inaccessible and irrelevant to policy and practice. The TLRP was initially a £30 million UK-wide initiative, but James and Pollard (2008) claim that it rose to £40 million and was extended for three more years until 2012. The money was not new money in the sense that it was diverted from general research allocations to education as a discipline in the Research Assessment Exercise. The research project was successful in securing financial contributions from a wide range of UK government bodies, and remains the UK's largest single investment in educational research.

The TLRP was ground-breaking and to some degree experimental, not only in its complexity but in its very existence. Large-scale, multi-year, multi-site research and development efforts had been rare to non-existent on this scale in the UK. The activity supported across the ten-year life of TLRP was substantial in both scope and scale, including numerous major or 'national' projects and awards (involving almost 500 researchers), and many 'themed' projects and research fellowships. The TLRP had a major role from the outset in achieving impact and, therefore, key TLRP outputs have included books, research briefings, commentaries, peer-reviewed journal articles, educational resources, workshops, conferences and conference proceedings booklets and newsletters. It raised the profile and visibility of educational research in the UK to new heights through promoting the idea of the UK Strategic Forum for Research in Education, which sought, among other things, to facilitate 'the organisation, production and use of educational research' (see Pollard and Oancea, 2010: 8).

The Director of TLRP, Andrew Pollard (2005), made clear from the start that the project sought to contribute to information, analysis and insight and was intended to improve understanding and decision making by users. In a newsletter from the project in September 2002, he outlined the mission of the project, which included a contribution to 'the new foundations of evidence-informed policy and practice in education'. Pollard (2005) summarised this approach by noting that:

> educational problems, of practice and policy, are often complex and immediate – but are invariably grounded in more enduring issues which merit both practitioner enquiry and sustained, cumulative, multi-disciplinary, social scientific research. The introduction of evidence can clarify the key

factors and major dilemmas which practitioners and/or policy makers face in decision-making.

Pollard was frustrated by how little educational research and evidence was used in the policy process, so he deliberately set out to directly engage with politicians, civil servants, journalists, practitioners and the public. His approach was highly optimistic. While asserting that the first responsibility of educational researchers is to the quality of the research itself, he does not play down the various strategies that can be employed to transform knowledge into more usable forms as well as the methods required for dissemination so as to enhance the chances of impact. TLRP, therefore, experimented with research briefings and commentaries and established a book series, Learning and Improving Practice, to disseminate its research findings. The project employed journalistic support and advice and also sought to build relationships with key user organisations, such as the General Teaching Council and the National College of Leadership. Pollard was also personally well connected to government departments, which largely supported the initiative. At the same time, Pollard emphasised the independence of TLRP from government or political interference, even though some of the funders required him to share the text of any press releases 24 hours before release. The TLRP was one of the first education research projects to develop an impact strategy, which was essentially a strategic plan for its research.

Pollard (2008) has written more extensively about knowledge transformation and impact, and it is clear that he was familiar with and influenced by some of the policy entrepreneur literature. TLRP had a clear and explicit commitment to 'user engagement' and it began with a 'Communication Audit' in order to identify who were to be the beneficiaries and existing networks of communication and influence. This is why the TLRP developed early both a 'TLRP Strategies for Impact' document and a 'Communication and Impact Plan' (2001). This latter plan set out seven components of the TLRP strategy (Pollard, 2008: 7):

- working with networks of practitioners, learners and others;
- engaging with a wide range of user organisations and other stakeholders;
- contributing to strategic debates about teaching and learning;
- raising the profile of evidence-informed teaching and learning;
- communicating conceptual, methodological and practical ideas;
- supporting capacity building activities, including knowledge transformation;
- facilitating discussion within the programme on transformation and impact.

This plan by Pollard (2008: 7) used and built on the work of Nutley *et al.* (2002, 2007), and he comments that 'the TLRP approach was much stronger on intention than it was on realisation'. Pollard established a 'Publications and Other Outputs Group' and identified different audiences for research distribution, but he ultimately believed that policy makers had to decide on the value of the outputs. Using Figgis *et al.* (2000: 356), Pollard (2008: 10) employed the idea of the 'connecting web'

– 'the specific mechanisms which bring people together to exchange and develop knowledge and understanding' – to develop the TLRP's research outputs in relation to user organisations and policy makers.

An evaluation of the extent to which TLRP has had an impact upon policy and practice in the UK and internationally was conducted by Parsons and Burkey (2011) for Host Policy Research. This report draws on the available evidence and follows an interim report of early observations presented in late November 2010. The evaluation focused specifically on a programme-level assessment of achieved impact on teaching and learning policy and professional practice. The application of TLRP outputs was an important feature of the design and management of the programme and its activities, and of the selection of funded activities across the higher education (HE) sector. The evaluation provides an analysis of the ways in which the TLRP has achieved impact through its dissemination, networking and knowledge-transfer activities and also assesses the value added to policy and practice impact by programme, organisation and management.

Parsons and Burkey (2011), the authors of the report, found that the scholarly impact of the projects was difficult to discern for a number of reasons, which included:

- Many of the projects aimed to improve educational practice, as illustrated by the strong orientation to teaching and pedagogy, rather than focusing on knowledge production itself.
- Publications from these project teams were found in relatively low impact journals, meaning articles published in such journals are on average cited infrequently.
- The vast majority of the projects did not cite non-UK research evidence based on improved methodology.
- Much of the research was conducted in schools and attempted to influence educational practice. Research on educational practice is often not considered as prestigious as research embedded in theory.
- Because most of the TLRP research was conducted in practical settings, some policy makers believed that this research should have been transformed immediately into an applied setting.

Parsons and Burkey (2011) did acknowledge that the TLRP website became well-known internationally and was a source of influence through personal presentations and electronic means. They concluded that the TLRP had international impact, serving as a model for other countries to design research funding programmes. It produced well-written commentaries intended to provide insight into findings but framed for a more general readership. Stakeholders and principal investigators highlighted the TLRP's early adoption of a dissemination strategy that archived all outputs online as a key success factor in influencing change and achieving impact. This included a commitment to building capacity in research and the embedding and sustaining of partnerships forged during the life of the programme. The project tailored research findings to different audiences so as to maximise impact. Two successes were identified as the Scottish Applied Educational Research Scheme and the Pedagogy Strategy for Wales, which it is claimed drew directly on the experience and methodologies of the TLRP in their design and ambition. Pollard (2012) has made a series of claims for the success of TLRP on policy and practice.

Pollard (2012) presented a positive message of the TLRP and engaged in constructive dialogue with policy makers from all three major political parties during the project's life. He was conscious of the many differences in education practice and policy within the UK and was careful and sensitive in the translations and compromises that he made in sharing research findings and practice. Assessing the contributions made by TLRP research to policy development and its implementation is not without difficulties. Even where there was direct engagement between individual projects and policy-making and implementing bodies, stakeholders felt it was uncommon for the engagement to translate directly into policy impact. The case studies (Pollard, 2012: 15) of high-impact projects seem to endorse this, with projects such as the Oxford Brookes–Oxford University review of literacy and numeracy at KS2 demonstrating substantial professional impacts, while acknowledging that they had secured little or no influence on policy developments (Pollard, 2012: 38–39). The report authors stated that 'the extent to which awareness of TLRP has translated into impacts – for policy or practice, has been more variable across the programme' and 'impact on policy formation and implementation has been disappointing'.

The report emphasises the importance of sustained and diverse proactivity aimed at direct engagement with policy-making and influencing groups. The evidence found by the report authors suggests that high-impact projects have had more success when engaging initially not with those directly engaged in shaping policy, but with those influencing policy teams and others either as 'brokers' or evidence mediators. The ease of use and accessibility of research-based project outputs to those in the policy arena also emerges as crucial to securing impact. TLRP produced research briefings which were valued, but other outputs were often not presented in ways which made them digestible by policy audiences. Here, the focus on more traditional 'academic' pathways in project outputs and knowledge exchange at policy level has not served dissemination to policy audiences well. Securing high levels of policy awareness of research findings and, in due course, impact requires outstanding leadership. Seeking to secure and demonstrate impact on policy and practice is a legitimate and desirable expectation of large-scale, research-based programmes such as TLRP:

> We propose that in future programmes of this nature, funding bodies need to determine if impact is a primary or secondary goal, and shape programme focus, timescales, selection, monitoring, dissemination and management accordingly. Where impact is seen as a primary goal for the research investments, programme expectations would need to be sharply focused on measuring 'impact potential'. We propose this will require a change in

current focus away from realised benefits and outcomes measurement towards recording and assessing demonstrable policy relationships and attributed influence as well as practice-related outputs and relationships.

This study may provide a starting point but the weakness of secured policy impacts suggests a need for 'better practice' collaborative research with key departmental agencies, and which can take account of different cultures and emerging traditions in different home countries. Such an approach may also help build more robust bridges between policy teams and academic researchers which currently seem to be either lacking or under-resourced. There is scope also to extend this to include comparative analysis outside the UK to identify transferable processes from other developed economies.

The work of the TLRP can be seen through the lens of policy entrepreneurship as the project members engaged in many activities characteristic of policy entrepreneurs. Pollard was explicit about the goals of TLRP and his policy entrepreneurship included: (a) policy advocacy, (b) translation of research outcomes into applicable policy ideas, (c) creation of networks of influence, alliances, partnerships and coalitions, (d) a concern to use non-technical language and make research accessible, (e) interfacing proactively with policy makers (politicians and civil servants), (f) using the press to advance ideas, and (g) concern to work with users of research outcomes. Pollard and his leadership team understood the context in which they worked and adapted their strategy to enhance their agenda. His status and credibility was high and this, too, was used to influence funding and outcomes. He was a policy entrepreneur, which is illustrated by Pollard's (Pollard *et al.*, 2010: 5ff) own words when he discusses and approves of mediation, brokerage, use and impact in education. Pollard and another prominent member of the TLRP leadership team, Professor Mary James, were asked to become members of an expert panel commissioned to advise the Secretary of State for Education on the National Curriculum in 2011: an ideal position to connect with policy makers and influence educational policy. However, by October 2011 Pollard and James had tendered their resignations and in a joint letter informed the Secretary of State that the changes proposed by his advisory group 'fly in the face of evidence from the UK'. They claimed that a shadow team of advisers was advising the Secretary of State and bypassing the official advisory panel. Like all entrepreneurs, their policy entrepreneurship had its limits when it came to influence.

The case of social and emotional learning: the emotion-friendly zeitgeist

We can learn from the policy ideas that were generated for social and emotional learning in the early part of the twenty-first century in England. New Labour's education policies in the early 2000s had a focus on educating the whole child, which was encapsulated in the Every Child Matters policy of 2004, with the welfare state regarded as crucial for supporting people's psychological well-being. This general policy orientation or shift to a more holistic view of children strongly supported the concept of inclusion, coupled with an emphasis on the affective dimensions of learning, such as 'self-esteem' and 'emotional intelligence'. Compassion, equality, holism and the cooperative principle lay behind much of this New Labour thinking, inspired partly by communitarian ideas imported from the US. It was a kind of new moralism generating a new moral agenda for policies. Lack of well-being and additional needs were linked with pupil 'behavioural difficulties' in schools, which it was believed tended to lead to high levels of exclusion; this in turn was linked with a higher risk of offending. The lack of specialist knowledge and resources was identified as an additional problem. Labour recognised that some of these issues and interconnected circumstances had an impact on the well-being of children, which ranged from basic nutrition in school to confidence and building of self-esteem. This was the favourable background and political context which effectively facilitated the rise of the movement for emotional and social learning in schools.

A number of national pressure groups promoting mental health and well-being in education joined in various networks and coalitions with each other to lobby the government to develop policies in the areas already of interest to Labour policy. Specialist consultancies suddenly arose to campaign for school circle-time and better mental health provision. However, the intent of lobbying initiatives was not always clear, as there were multiple meanings to the values and skills being promoted. In any event, an emotion-friendly *zeitgeist* prevailed, which found expression in the increasing movement towards a 'positive psychology' that explored the sources of happiness, satisfaction, optimism and well-being. SEAL was about fixing weaknesses while positive psychology was about enhancing strengths. This accent on the affective area in education resulted in what Ecclestone and Hayes (2008) noted was a proliferation of interchangeable and ill-defined terms, such as emotional literacy, emotional intelligence, emotional well-being, self-esteem and mental health alongside an ever-expanding list of disorders and syndromes – all at the expense of more traditional learning. There was a high level of receptivity to these vague ideas about holistic education, which effectively reduced or even eliminated resistance to these new policy ideas that were a deliberate break with the old way of doing things in schools. This resulted in the adoption of these policies being made easier, but they were not argued for in any convincing way. The *zeitgeist* was more important than argued-for policy ideas.

The Advisory Group on Citizenship (1998) also recommended that pupils in school should be empowered to feel individually confident, while the reinforcement of personal and social education together with the introduction of citizenship education generated a wide range of skills, values and dispositions in the increasing debate around affective education. These skills, values and dispositions became central components of government policy and action in education and indeed opened a window of opportunity. Even then, I regarded character as the most significant policy idea while sitting on a number of advisory panels at the Department for Education and Skills discussing the future of personal and social education; this included, as a priority, the discussion of social and emotional learning. Civil servants had accepted that social and emotional learning was a priority and progressed this idea through government. They tended to invite academics and teachers who were already advocates of social and emotional learning to sit on panels at the Department of Education, and did not listen to any independent advice.

Against this softened background, Katherine Weare and Gay Grey, educationalists at the Health in Education Unit at the University of Southampton, were invited by the government in 2002 to examine how children's emotional and social competence and well-being could most effectively be developed at national and local levels and to identify the best approaches for schools. Weare and Grey were already strong advocates of emotional learning and seized on this window of opportunity. They produced a report that provided no systematic review of the literature; provided no new empirical evidence; selected the experts to be interviewed by personal recommendations from members of the steering group of their own project, all of whom had been approved by the authors of the report; and borrowed the database for their recommendations from the US context. They cited supporting international evidence, but these interventions were different in design, goals and methodology, which meant that it was nearly impossible to ascertain their possible effectiveness in the UK context. They outlined a number of objectives for social and emotional education throughout their report, but these were mainly proximate outcomes, such as the attainment of certain skills; as a result of assumptions or background theory they believed that these skills would somehow lead, in turn, to enhanced well-being and emotional literacy.

Weare and Grey admitted that there was little empirical evidence for the benefits of social and emotional education in England. Despite these serious limitations, they produced a report that was long on recommendations, chief among which was that emotional learning should be explicitly taught in all schools as part of a national strategy. The recommendations were based on the work of Gardner (1983) on multiple intelligences, which suggested that there were many ways to be 'intelligent', including the idea of being intelligent about one's own emotions as well as the emotions of others. In addition, the report drew on the work of Goleman (1995) who, as the science editor for the *New York Times,* published a book on *Emotional Intelligence* that popularised the term. He wanted children to be more confident, more effective learners and better behaved. However, while he made the idea more accessible, as a journalist he made many unsubstantiated assumptions about intelligence in general. Goleman (1995) claimed that emotional intelligence is a better predictor of success than IQ, but there is no published study to support this claim. The concept of emotional intelligence has been referred to as mere 'pop psychology', while others claim that it doesn't contribute anything more than is already known by psychologists working in the field of personality. Significantly, Goleman (1995) himself refers to emotional intelligence as denoting an individual's 'character' and includes qualities such as optimism, self-control and moral character as part of intelligence.

In their report, Weare and Grey used Goleman's self-help book (it was not an empirical study) to emphasise his five domains, which included forming positive relationships, empathising with others, moderating ourselves, managing our feelings and understanding ourselves. There is no consensus on a definition of social and emotional competence, but Weare and Grey's (2003) description is helpful. It provides some clarity on the wide range of skills and gives clear examples of areas to develop. Their first recommendation was to develop a common language for social and emotional education. The report recommendations were not simply accepted, but warmly embraced by both Ministers and civil servants and Social and Emotional Aspects of Learning (SEAL) was born in 2003. It is difficult to see how research evidence actually informed policy here, but the report (Weare and Grey, 2003: 7) claimed that there was 'clear evidence' for 'teaching behaviour and skills explicitly' in many different school contexts. The government gave official backing to an approach which sought to teach a range of social and emotional skills directly. Pilot versions of this new programme were quickly introduced into primary schools in September 2003 with advice from Weare and Grey claiming that the use of these materials would bring significant benefits to the children. Weare (2004) subsequently wrote a book advising how schools could develop themselves as 'emotionally literate schools'. The skills are described in the DfES guidance as an ability to:

- be effective and successful learners;
- make and sustain friendships;
- deal with and resolve conflict effectively and fairly;
- solve problems with others or by themselves;
- manage strong feelings, such as frustration, anger and anxiety;
- recover from setbacks and persist in the face of difficulties;
- work and play cooperatively;
- compete fairly and win and lose with dignity and respect for competitors;
- recognise and stand up for their rights and the rights of others;
- understand and value the differences between people, respecting the right of others to have beliefs and values different from their own (DfES, 2003: 7).

There was widespread use of the term 'social and emotional learning' by 2007 when SEAL was introduced into secondary schools through the Secondary National Strategy. The teaching and guidance materials were produced centrally by educational advisers and civil servants and were intended to provide a way of promoting the personal and social development as well as the emotional competence of all pupils. Weare and Grey did not define the problem fully, but much was left to the civil servants and advisory groups established during the policy implementation period. The scope of the SEAL programme and the claims made for it included: to stop bullying; reduce violence, drug use and aggression; improve school attendance;

enhance pro-social behaviour; improve academic attainment; and help the excluded or marginalised. No emotion was considered wrong, but acting on them could be inappropriate. Craig (2007: 3) raised early concerns that SEAL would bring about a 'revolution in education and schooling as we know it' without credible supporting evidence or an 'intellectual rationale'. She argued that teaching children calming techniques, in a systematic way, might encourage children to become more anxious and that focusing on the self and feelings might encourage narcissism and self-obsession. She (Craig, 2007: 3) concludes: 'In short, we fear SEAL is encouraging a large-99 scale psychological experiment on young people, which will not just waste time and resources but could actually back-fire and unwittingly.'

The plan was to help children become more resilient to the effects of rapid social change, but the first review of the programme, which took place in 2010 by a team from the University of Manchester (Humphrey *et al.*, 2010), discovered that SEAL had hardly any impact on the mental well-being of children. SEAL's provision suffered from huge variability and many teachers did not understand what the goals were, far less the operational basis for delivering social and emotional learning. The evaluation report found that there was a significant reduction in pupils' trust and respect for teachers and also their liking for school. The national evaluation of SEAL in secondary schools recommended that future school-based social and emotional learning initiatives should more accurately reflect the research literature about 'what works'. Humphrey *et al.* (2010: 3) concluded that a 'greater emphasis needs to be given to the rigorous collection and use of evidence to inform developments in policy and practice in this area; in particular, there should be proper trialling of initiatives like SEAL before they are rolled out on a national level.'

SEAL was perceived as a failure and had cost taxpayers over £100 million. Ecclestone and Hayes (2008: 136) argued at the time of SEAL's introduction that there had been a decline in self-determination among young people resulting in a situation which 'erodes the idea of humans as conscious agents who realise their potential for individual and social change through projects to transform themselves and their world'. Ecclestone and Hayes (2008) perceived that the emotional curriculum has been prioritised over the intellectual and they warned that such developments engender an unhealthy preoccupation with the self, leading to increased emotional vulnerability, anxiety and fearfulness. However, SEAL was not simply about preventing negative outcomes, but rather about emphasising positive development of human potential. SEAL was terminated in 2013 as schooling became more focused on academic subjects and testing. Character education has largely replaced SEAL as the preferred policy of government, but various networks, such as the SEAL Community, continue to promote social and emotional learning in schools and see the new emphasis on character as a way to re-introduce social and emotional learning.

The political driver of SEAL was part of the larger political agenda relating to well-being (see Humphrey, 2013: 47) and it could, therefore, be argued that the advocates of social and emotional learning were opportunists whose window of opportunity had opened with the election of the New Labour government in 1997 and were 'bandwagon' types who cling to the issue once it had been placed on the political agenda (see Weissert, 1991). The litany of alarm (see Arthur, 2003: 3) concerning youth included concerns about marginalisation, unemployment, mental illness, poverty and anti-social behavior, which fed into a sense of youth in crisis. Young people were seen as broken and in need of fixing, and SEAL could potentially equip students to become more resilient (Humphrey, 2013: 48). But this was also the period of standards and accountability, which appeared to be incompatible with SEAL, as it emphasised that the most important outcome of schooling was academic attainment. There was no shortage of policy advocates from the academy to press for the introduction of social and emotional learning, and the window of opportunity opened with the new emotion-friendly *zeitgeist* of New Labour policies in education, no matter how contradictory. Expert voices and 'research' from the academy were used to justify the SEAL policy and its many 'benefits' to schools. There were clearly multiple and different kinds of policy entrepreneurs at work here at each stage, from initiation of ideas to implementation of policy.

The case of citizenship education

One of the first education initiatives of the New Labour government (1997–2010) was for David Blunkett, the new Secretary of State for Education (1997–2001), to commission a report from Professor (later Sir) Bernard Crick, a political theorist, on the introduction of citizenship education into English schools in 1998. Members of the Citizenship Advisory Group represented a cross-party approach, since a degree of consensus was considered essential if the project was to succeed. Apart from Crick, there were only two other members of the sixteen who were drawn from higher education – Dr. Marianne Talbot, a philosophy lecturer from Oxford University, and Dr. Alex Porter, an education lecturer from the Institute of Education in London. Crick had to strongly argue for Porter's inclusion. Talbot had previously chaired the National Forum on Values in Education and the Community between 1996 and 1997, at a time of on-going societal concerns about values and the personal development of students. The final report of the Advisory Group, entitled *Education for Citizenship and the Teaching of Democracy in Schools* (DfES, 1998: 93), recommended the introduction of citizenship education as a subject into secondary schools and defined it as comprising: 'social and moral responsibility, community involvement and political literacy.' The government accepted the recommendation and it was introduced as a statutory subject to secondary schools in September 2002. Within the lens of policy entrepreneurship it is interesting to ask where the motivation to introduce a government policy on citizenship education came from.

While there had previously been no explicit tradition of teaching citizenship education in English schools, there had been a great deal of advocacy for its introduction from pressure groups and some academics (see Heater, 2004). The

Association for Education in Citizenship was founded in the mid-1930s to advocate citizenship education in English schools, but despite its membership comprising a coalition or network of distinguished academics and policy makers of the time it had little success – no window of opportunity opened for them. The Association produced a statement on *Education for Citizenship in Secondary Schools* in 1935, but the government rejected any direct teaching of citizenship education in schools because it was controversial and lacked a consensus of definition.

Little happened until Derek Heater, a history school teacher and subsequently a university education lecturer, founded a professional association of teachers in the form of the Politics Association in 1969 with Bernard Crick as President and himself as Chair. It campaigned for civics education in schools and sought to promote political literacy in education, but it was narrowly focused on 'A' level politics and political literacy, as can be seen from the content of its *Programme for Political Education 1974–1978*. Debates about what actually constituted citizenship education within different traditions of thought continued within academe and were essentially philosophical and historical in nature rather than empirical. These academic attempts to discuss and define citizenship education were largely born either out of a perceived problem in society – the erosion of both participation in civic life and moral standards in a rapidly changing society, particularly among the young – or the desire to promote some form of education broadly related to citizenship, such as peace education, global education, environmental education or human rights education. It is also significant that the vocabulary of 'citizenship' was conspicuous by its absence in academic writing from the 1960s to the early 1980s. As Beck (2012: 5–6) notes:

> The word does not appear at all in the index of Crick and Heater's 1977 book, nor in Crick and Porter's influential 'Political Education and Political Literacy' (1978), nor was it included among Crick's 'basic concepts for political education' (Crick, 1974) which was foundational to his key educational idea: the development of political literacy among young people.

Nevertheless, by 1990 the Conservative government had introduced citizenship education as a cross-curricular theme in the National Curriculum, but it was largely ignored by schools. Citizenship education had arrived on the political agenda and political lobbying by pressure groups for its inclusion as a subject in secondary schools intensified. Jack Straw, who was Shadow Secretary of State for Education at the time, announced that: 'I hold the view that citizenship should be taught in every school, to every child, in a systematic way' (see Heater, 1991: 140). Discussion on the merits of compulsory citizenship education took place within a wider political debate, and Ben Kisby (2007: 187) identifies two distinct policy communities which he claims played a key role in the campaign for citizenship education. The first group he calls the 'Intellectuals', made up of Geoff Mulgan, David Miliband, Tom Bentley and David Hargreaves, who together were inspired by the work of Robert Putnam on social capital. The think tank DEMOS, he claims, also played a role and worked with this group, who predominantly were policy advisers rather than 'intellectuals', so as to emphasise a communitarian focus on community cohesion and moral responsibility. This group set the backdrop for citizenship education to enter more seriously into the political agenda. The second group he calls the 'The Social Education Community' (197), comprising pre-existing pressure groups and a range of actors with concerns about the disengagement of young people from political involvement, particularly the decline in voting at elections. Kisby (2007: 196) observes that there is no evidence of any significant interaction between these two groups, but that both campaigned for citizenship education lessons.

The new citizenship education initiative of New Labour in 1998 represented a window of opportunity that advocates of citizenship education had been waiting for, and it was promoted as a solution to the problem of youth participation in society. The relationship and different understandings of citizenship between David Blunkett and Bernard Crick were significant. Blunkett had been Crick's student in politics at the University of Sheffield, so they knew and trusted each other – an essential ingredient for policy development and influence. Blunkett's personal beliefs were much influenced by the Third Way ideas of the period, which included a communitarian rhetoric with a particular emphasis on civic morality. Blunkett wanted morally motivated citizens who were responsible and active in their communities, something that fitted well with the Prime Minister's emphasis on 'shared values', social inclusion and the enabling role of the state.

His view was a combination of communitarian and republican ideas in the sense that he did not believe the state should be neutral about what constituted the 'good life' – he adopted a proactive agenda to promote a range of civic virtues and encouraged citizens to espouse 'shared values'. Kisby (2007: 277) refers to Blunkett as a 'policy entrepreneur', saying that 'Blunkett is best seen as a policy entrepreneur who was able to "sell" the policy both to the cabinet and to the Prime Minister by presenting the initiative as being concerned with the promotion of "good" citizens as much as "active" citizens'. This was a normative approach to policy development reflecting the government's understanding of the concept of citizenship to which Crick was less sympathetic; he was more associated with the tradition of liberalism and wanted to encourage greater political literacy in citizenship education in schools. There were differences between Crick and Blunkett, so it might be more accurate to refer to Blunkett as a 'political entrepreneur' with the pressure group actors around him as the 'policy entrepreneurs', together forming an entrepreneurial network that strategically advanced their policy ideas. They were certainly more than advocates of a policy on citizenship education, and Blunkett encouraged them to come together around an idea which he was prepared to promote in government. Blunkett was firmly in the driving seat, but was prepared to allow these different actors and groups a say in shaping definitions of citizenship education and in the design, formulation and development of a distinct policy.

The policy on citizenship education which the government adopted in the end was largely top-down, and was enthusiastically supported by an array of policy coalitions and networks in the field: the Citizenship Foundation, the Politics Association, the Association for Citizenship Teaching, Citized, Community Service Volunteers, the Institute for Citizenship, the Hansard Society and the Council for Education in World Citizenship, all of which overlapped with each other in terms of goals and membership. This collection of policy entrepreneurs was small in number and they all knew each other. They were based in London and were in regular contact, developing ties and connections and feeding into policy debates on citizenship. They forged alliances with each other and one pressure group, the Citizenship Foundation, even attempted to get them all to sign up to a joint statement through a Citizenship 2000 Group – in other words, it tried to exert control over the evidence and messages to government about citizenship education. Citizenship education is not a neutral concept, and debates about policy implementation ought to be subject to dispute and struggle. I felt that this was not happening at the time because it was simply assumed that Crick and his networking followers had already decided the policy. Key figures in the Community Service Volunteers, the Citizenship Foundation and DEMOS even secured membership of the Citizenship Advisory Group.

However, the example of one individual, David Kerr, illustrates the interconnectedness of these organisations and also the multi-faceted dimensions of policy making in citizenship education. First, while not a member of the Citizenship Advisory Group, he acted as the professional officer and worked with Crick to produce various position papers for the Group to discuss. He worked as a senior research officer and then Research Director at the National Foundation for Educational Research. He then became a citizenship consultant to the DfES (now the Department for Education). He taught and wrote on citizenship education for short periods at the Institute of Education in London and was then funded by the government as Research Director of the Citizenship Education Longitudinal Study. He then became a member of the board of trustees of the Citizenship Foundation and is currently the UK representative for the Council of Europe's Education for Democratic Citizenship and Human Rights Education Project. His roles in citizenship education have been multiple: from membership of independent enquiries, consultant and adviser to government, university teacher and writer, membership of advisory boards, advocate and researcher, as well as evaluator. He was not the only academic to hold various advisory positions in citizenship, but he represented a small group of people who were open about advocating for policy change and using their own persuasive arguments in citizenship education simultaneously. He was involved in every aspect of the process to get citizenship education into schools from research, policy formulation and design, implementation and finally evaluating what he himself had advised. This interchangeability of roles was a feature of the policy networks at the time. The key actors from the various interest groups in the on-going development of citizenship education policy shared common beliefs and knowledge and had a common interest in pursuing certain solutions to it. We can define them as policy entrepreneurs in that they were actors who dedicated their professional lives to achieving a narrowly targeted set of policy goals (in citizenship education) through the political system.

Other academics, such as Professor John Annette, found themselves advising the Home Office as a citizenship expert, as did Jan Newton, Chief Executive of the Citizenship Foundation, who became a government adviser. Consequently, we had a very small number of academics and members of pressure groups becoming expert policy advisers and consultants to government Ministers and particularly to the policy civil servants. Their advocacy ideas gained influence because they were able to secure positions of authority within decision-making processes in government and its agencies. As policy networkers, they had access to government Ministers and civil servants and enjoyed both formal and informal linkages with government policy making. An array of different initiatives came from various government departments to encourage active citizenship and participation, all designed by external advisers and civil servants. Blunkett's move to the Home Office encouraged some of these initiatives as he maintained his personal interest in citizenship, broadly defined. These included: the Civil Renewal Unit in the Home Office, Civic Pioneers, Year of the Volunteer, Citizenship Day, National Community Forum, Neighbourhood Renewal Fund, the New Deal for Communities, Millennium Volunteers, Young Volunteers Challenge, Go Givers, Community Champions, and many others. Efforts in this area have continued with the Coalition Government establishing the National Citizenship Service for 16 year olds as part of their 'Big Society' initiative. In all of this activity it is difficult to identify any empirical research outputs that fed directly into these initiatives.

Research was thin on the ground; indeed, Gearon (2003: 5) argues that actual research into citizenship education only became active after the introduction of citizenship education in schools in September 2002. Research prior to this might be termed implicit citizenship research in the sense that it concerned peace education, human rights and global studies, but there was nothing in terms of research knowledge directly related to justifying or supporting specific citizenship education lessons (see Halstead and Taylor, 2000). I myself had become Director of Citized in 2002, an organisation made up of all citizenship teacher educators within universities and funded by the Teacher Training Agency to develop curriculum materials and a national approach to teacher training for citizenship education. The citizenship curriculum was introduced to secondary schools in 2002 as a subject in the National Curriculum without any specialist teachers. The number of teachers being trained to teach citizenship education never rose above 260 annually. As a member of the Citizenship Working Party sub-group on initial teacher education and continuing professional development, we conducted a survey of head teachers to ascertain whether there was a demand for citizenship teachers – the results indicated that it was low. This was used by the Teacher Training Agency to limit the numbers training to become citizenship teachers.

As Director of Citized, I used some of the funding to establish the Citizenship Education Research Strategy Group, which began a systematic review of the impact of citizenship education on the provision of schooling in 2003 – essentially because I was aware of the lack of research in the area. The systematic review was conducted with the EPPI Centre and was led by Dr. Ruth Deakin Crick at Bristol University with whom I was working on another project at the time. The review demonstrated that there had been little sustained research on citizenship education prior to the Crick report, and therefore no significant body of research-based knowledge existed to justify or support a policy on citizenship education. In 2005, I accompanied Sir Bernard Crick to meet the Shadow Secretary of State for Education, David Willetts, and Nick Gibb, another shadow education Minister, to brief them on the progress of citizenship education in schools prior to the General Election of that year. We had been sent by the DfES and I was asked to gather together a number of students whom I had taught and who were now teaching citizenship education. At the time, it was the case that one in three of all students nationally were being taught citizenship education by Andrew Peterson and myself in Canterbury, including Teach First students. The meeting was a general success, with both shadow ministers agreeing that citizenship education had merit.

With Ian Davies, I also edited the four volumes of *Citizenship Education* for Sage in 2008, which contained 77 academic articles chosen from over 300, but few of these were empirical studies of citizenship education and almost none focused on 'what works' in citizenship education. The same could be said of my editing of *Education for Citizenship and Democracy*, also for Sage (2008), which contained 42 newly commissioned articles and, again, there was little that could feed directly into policy making in citizenship education. Another collection of essays entitled *Debates in Citizenship Education*, which I edited with Hilary Cremin in 2012, provided further evidence that research did not play a role in the case for citizenship education. This paucity of research for policy making was demonstrated by the National Foundation for Educational Research's submission to the Education and Skills Select Committee in March 2006, which listed seven research items that the NFER had been involved in. Four were international in orientation, one was a small UK evaluation project, another a small project on resources and the final one was the government's funding of the on-going longitudinal study of citizenship education. The report was written by David Kerr and evidence from the UK was weak. Despite his intention to 'present the research evidence', the report excludes all references to other research and yet it makes a huge number of claims for the benefits of citizenship education in schools. There was a very weak research base for citizenship education in the UK – the report said far more about promoting the NFER itself. The report of the House of Commons Education and Skills Committee's enquiry revealed an uneven pattern of provision in citizenship education and noted 'the evidence we have received on the … quality of CE … describes a field that is patchy at best', and the Ofsted report *Towards Consensus* (2006: i) emphasised that there was 'not yet a strong consensus about the aims of citizenship education'.

Don Rowe of the Citizenship Foundation claimed that the 'moral and community' aspects of the new citizenship curriculum framework were 'directly what we argued for' in the evidence submitted to the Advisory Group (see Kisby,

2007: 232). However, as a member of the Group, Marianne Talbot had argued strongly against moral relativism and for a strong moral component to citizenship education. Elizabeth Hoodless, Executive Director of Community Service Volunteers, also a member of the Group, had argued strongly for community involvement. There were many claims made by the various pressure groups in citizenship education about their impact or influence on the new policy on citizenship education, but without supporting evidence being provided. The Crick Report that recommended citizenship education as a subject in secondary schools was inevitably a compromise, despite Crick's very ambitious hope that it could represent a 'change in the political culture of the country' (DfE, 1998: 93). Crick had accepted a broader understanding of citizenship education and accommodated different perspectives within the Advisory Group. The result was that the kind of citizenship education that emerged from the Group represented a communitarian-republican model that reflected the prevailing government *zeitgeist*. The future of this policy is in doubt as many secondary schools have become academies and have effectively dropped compulsory citizenship lessons as they are freed from implementing the National Curriculum. The DfE also announced in November 2014 that the primary vehicle for promoting British civic values would be through spiritual, moral, social and cultural education, which leaves questions hanging on the purpose of citizenship education. The moral and community dimensions have also been given a new stimulus through the DfE's major aim to build character education in schools and through the work of Step Up To Serve to increase volunteering in the community among young people – neither of these requires the implementation of explicit citizenship education. Add to this the decline in the number of teachers being trained to teach citizenship education and the future for the subject is not secure. The influence and impact of the policy entrepreneur networkers in citizenship education have not been sustained.

In summary, we can identify a pre-existing and narrowly focused policy community in citizenship education from the election of the Labour government in 1997 that maintained close cooperative relationships with a mainly self-selected group. This tight group, comprised of policy entrepreneurs, represented an insider pressure group that established formal and informal links with the civil service and relevant Ministers and government committees in order to strengthen its policy-making influence. Indeed, key individuals from these interest groups were actively co-opted into the policy machinery of government. The groups made a conscious effort to build consensus and coordinate multiple channels of influence within their own network. As Kingdon (1984: 123) had observed, this idea of a policy community was 'composed of specialists in a given policy area [citizenship education] ... scattered both through and outside of government'. However, I would say that these like-minded individuals were more like lobbyists than experts on citizenship education; they presented persuasive arguments to government rather than research knowledge or 'what works'. Research evidence was usually not their first port of call, especially since little explicit citizenship education research existed, and they restricted access to critical voices and dissenting perspectives in an attempt to present a manufactured consensus and coherence among a small grouping of inter-related policy actors. After all, these interest groups had waited a very long time for their 'window of opportunity' to open and they had no intention of allowing any outsider participation, whether by individuals or groups, to have some control of the agenda. They had, as Maloney *et al.* (1994: 28) said, 'developed the necessary political skills required for insider status'. This gave them a privileged status and, therefore, considerable say over how policy on citizenship education was developed in government: only their ideas were used by government as a basis for making decisions about policy. As entrepreneurial actors, they adjusted their policy positions in order to effect policy change by opportunistically intervening in the policy process.

Conclusion

The three case studies described in this chapter illustrate different actors operating in different policy communities, and we have considered the effect of their interactions on policy. The actors in each case study developed different networks and used research-based knowledge, where available, for different purposes. Some actors involved themselves in every aspect of the decision-making process and established insider status in policy making, while others limited themselves to what might be termed entrepreneurial activities. They all had linkages to politicians, civil servants and interest groups, while one case study was largely dependent on a political entrepreneur to drive a policy forward. One was restricted to a few influential academics, while another had a diverse base of support, and the third represented a tight group of professional lobbyists. As we have seen, not all participants in policy-making influence are considered equal. The citizenship case study in policy development indicated that some of the entrepreneurial actors did disagree with each other over the relative importance of different objectives, but the focus was on consensus. It corresponds to what Christopoulos (2006: 773) observes: 'an actor's network provides a framework within which the actor can project power, control information flows and attempt to influence political outcomes or other actors.'

The best example of an educational academic engaging in policy entrepreneurship is Andrew Pollard. He can be associated with a large number of entrepreneurial characteristics and activities which included:

1. He was well connected and authoritative with a good reputation in the education world.
2. He had the resources and a long time frame in which to operate.
3. He had a breadth of involvement from the education community and encouraged and created stakeholders in his research project.
4. His senior team developed a sense of ownership of the ideas and could be trusted to communicate them to diverse audiences.
5. He co-opted international experts to help advance the merits of his project.

6. He was able to translate ideas from research into accessible presentations.
7. He could straddle academic and practitioner involvement.
8. He had good access to politicians and civil servants.
9. He addressed real education issues with practical suggestions on how to solve them.
10. He articulated a compelling vision for the project.
11. He established strong allies and partnerships with others.
12. He developed a range of public engagement and communication strategies.
13. He was flexible, persistent and aware of the political sensitivities in the work.

However, the other two case studies employed different methods to pursue policy change, which involved direct access to civil servants and Ministers and they were more ideologically motivated. In the case study of citizenship, it consisted of closely connected individuals who shared both ideas and access to the machinery of policy making.

5

CASE STUDY: THE JUBILEE CENTRE FOR CHARACTER AND VIRTUES

Bridging research and policy

Introduction

This chapter provides a case study of the Jubilee Centre for Character and Virtues, which seeks to provide a real-life example of the practical steps one can take to engage with practitioners and policy makers in the field of education. It chronicles the Centre's major accomplishments to date, challenges faced and the lessons learned with regard to policy ideas, generating impact and influence. Details of the ways in which the Centre set out to establish itself as a leading authority in the field of character education are outlined. It provides an account of the strategies and approaches that I have tried to develop and initiate so that the Centre is seen as a free and neutral space to ask fundamental questions both to challenge and support debates on the role of character and virtues in public life. The chapter provides a detailed account of the creation of the Jubilee Centre, since its inception in 2012, and it describes how we have engaged with policy makers, practitioners, charities and the wider community at all levels. It provides real-life examples of policy entrepreneurship in action within a multi-disciplinary centre, using multiple sources of impact evidence.

The Centre neither deploys nor supports a one-size-fits-all strategy for policy entrepreneurship. In creating and establishing the Jubilee Centre for Character and Virtues, I set out to undertake rigorous academic research, to discover new insights in the research outcomes, and begin to bring about change in terms of impact on policy, practitioners and the academy. We recognised early on that the worlds of the researcher, practitioner and policy maker need not be three different worlds, but could interact with one another for mutual benefit. This case study offers a critical examination of the strategies and processes adopted in creating, establishing and maintaining the Jubilee Centre as a leading voice in the field of character education. In the process, it provides interpretation and analysis of the Centre's efforts to influence and impact schools' policy in the UK, but mainly within England. It is intended to contribute to our understanding of policy entrepreneurship, and challenges some of the definitions that have been offered of its practice. This case study investigates policy entrepreneurs within a real-life context. It is designed to tell a story, and while my selection of materials and examples is intended to be comprehensive, it is also open to interpretation. It is the study of the particularity and the complexity of the Jubilee Centre, combined with ideas about policy entrepreneurship.

From the very beginning, the Centre focused on relationship-building with decision makers within the academy, government, business and civil society. These relationships were, and continue to be, built, maintained, and managed as effectively as possible, so as to influence these decision makers with our research findings and principles. Our starting aim was to alter the prevailing conception of character and virtues education in schools, in higher education, in the professions, and in communities more broadly, across Great Britain. Influence in sensitive policy areas rarely leaves an audit trail, but this case study records the evolution of the Centre and its connections and networks. We understand that educational research does not provide the kinds of prescriptions one might expect in medical research, so our efforts to influence educational policy had to be more assertive and strategic. The Centre's independence was essential for us to be taken seriously by all policy makers. Our adherence to established academic standards and research methods was also vital at the outset, as research findings that help legitimate policy come from recognised universities and experts. This continues today, but the status that the University of Birmingham holds as a significant research-led university, and the calibre of academic experts that we recruited were important factors in establishing the credibility of our ideas.

Determining whether research is impactful or influential on policy is often a subjective exercise, and is, of course, not immediately obvious. We recognised that in order to gain influence on policy, we should accept that messages and findings are often modified and adapted by the dynamics of the civil service and other political considerations. What we might consider relevant may not be influential in policy terms. Equally, research that is not of direct utility today may still be influential in the future. The Jubilee Centre has had great success with its research outcomes so far, and has engaged and led the debate on the role of character in schools, in particular, and in society more broadly. How we measure our success has been challenging, and it is not simply about counting citations, newspaper references, numbers of meetings with civil servants or politicians, evidence to committees, etc. These indicators of success only represent potential correlates of research recognition. Measuring and evaluating our impact as individual researchers, and as a centre, is notoriously difficult to accomplish, but we made a decision early on to focus on the larger goal of attempting to influence educational policy, and to transcend party political commitments by working pragmatically across different fields of knowledge.

This chapter, therefore, needs to be read in conjunction with the previous chapters. I acknowledge that there is some repetition of themes between materials presented in Chapter 3 and my discussion in this case study. The reason for this is that, while intended to form part of the narrative across this whole text, some readers will be interested in reading this section as a stand-alone chapter. The advantage of the case study approach is that it provides an opportunity to look at both the strategies and outputs from the Centre, as well as the precipitating events which have occurred both pre-2012 and since. The way that the Centre has responded to challenges is chronicled, as well as key milestones and events orchestrated by the Centre intended to raise our profile and engage in policy influence. I will begin with my early preparations in this field.

Developing the idea

A preparation in policy studies

In 1988, after completing seven years teaching in a large Birmingham comprehensive school I began a Master of Science degree in educational governance at the University of Oxford. Successfully completing the course, which focused on educational policy, I embarked on a doctorate at Oriel College that examined the philosophy, policy and practice of Catholic education in England. My supervisors for the next three years included Professor Basil Mitchell, the eminent chair in the philosophy of religion at Oriel College, and Professor Richard Pring, the first ever professor of education at Oxford. However, my principal tutor was Dr. Vivian Williams, a brilliant education policy analyst, who guided me in and through a deep understanding of educational policy development. It was not, therefore, surprising that my first book, *The Ebbing Tide: Policy and Principles of Catholic Education* (1995), addressed an important question of educational policy of the day – namely faith schools. The training in policy analysis and development that I received at Oxford became an essential preparation for my later work in the field of policy research on character.

After moving to Canterbury to take up my first substantive academic position in higher education in 1993, I became an active member of the National Forum for Values in Education and the Community in 1996. This Forum led to the publication of the important National Statement of Values in 1997, which played a significant role in schooling as it was incorporated into the revised National Curriculum for England. The Forum was established at a time when moral issues in public life had reached almost panic dimensions. The Conservative government was trying to recover from the failed 'Back to Basics' campaign, but still remained interested in the question of morality within education policy. It was also the time of Quentin Tarantino's *Pulp Fiction* (1995), which had raised issues about whether Western 'postmodern' society had descended into 'nihilism'. The New Labour government, elected in 1997, continued the political interest in moral education through a proposed citizenship education curriculum, but chiefly through the influence of communitarianism on its social policies made popular by Professor Amitai Etzioni, a sociologist and social critic whose advice was eagerly sought by New Labour.

Dr. Nick Tate, who had established the National Forum as Head of the School Curriculum and Assessment Authority (SCAA), was retained by the New Labour government in 1997, and he became Director of the successor organisation to SCAA – the Qualifications and Curriculum Authority (QCA). In early 1998, both Dr. Tate and I were invited by Professor Etzioni to attend and speak at the fifth annual White House/Congressional 'Conference on Character Building' in Washington, DC. Tate knew me from my membership in the Forum and invited me to his offices in London to discuss what we might say in Washington, DC. Both of us were interested in virtue education and, while we would obviously give different presentations, we agreed that there was some mileage in considering character virtues as a way forward in the moral and citizenship education debate. My talk to over 300 delegates suggested that character education was an emerging policy agenda item for New Labour. It could be said that I was alert to the latent public demand for character education that was not fully formed, nor even fully understood by others, which points to a characteristic of a policy entrepreneur: to sense an emerging demand from the public and to do something about a perceived problem.

On my return to the UK, I joined various consultation groups with the QCA on personal, spiritual and moral education, on the future of history teaching as a member of the History Task Group in 1999, and in teacher education with the Teacher Training Agency. In 2000, Jacqui Smith, Minister of Education, invited me to become a member of a sub-group of the Citizenship Working Party and to look at developing a policy for the training of citizenship teachers. I was able to bring my concerns about the ethical dimensions of citizenship as well as the question of character education to the table. I was also a member of the personal and social education group that met at the Department for Education with civil servants. Throughout 1999, my direct access to government discussions on all of these issues, but especially teacher and citizenship education, together with the increasing influence of communitarianism on New Labour allowed me to write *The Communitarian Agenda in Education* (2000), in which I clearly articulated a summary of how New Labour was interested in character education. I summarised the communitarian approach to education and school life as follows:

* We should restore an Aristotelian approach to education in which the virtues have a central place.
* The family should be the primary moral educator of children.
* 'Character education' includes the systematic teaching of virtues in schools.
* The ethos of the community has an educative function in school life.
* Schools should promote the rights and responsibilities inherent within citizenship.
* Community service is an important part of a child's education in school.
* A major purpose of the school curriculum is to teach social and political life-skills.
* Schools should provide an active understanding of the common good.

- Religious schools are able to operate a strong version of the communitarian perspective.
- Many existing community-based education practices reflect the features of the communitarian perspective.

It was, therefore, no surprise to me that in the year following the publication of my book on communitarian education the government published its Green and White Papers detailing how it would seek to promote 'education with character' and to 'build the character' of students in schools. My prediction of this in my speech at the White House conference a few years previous was becoming a reality. These government papers spurred me on to write my next book, *Education with Character: The Moral Economy of Schooling* (2003), with the title taken directly from the text of the government's Green and White Papers of 2001. This was the first book in the UK to be dedicated wholly to an understanding of character education for over 50 years.

The New Labour government brought thought leaders into government as advisers, and consequently, increased the potential of policy entrepreneurs to shape and influence both the way policy is made and the content of policies themselves. Civil servants were also encouraged to contribute ideas to the policy-making process under New Labour, and both adviser and civil servant involvement in policy making has continued under subsequent governments. Building and maintaining good relations with senior civil servants is a key element of policy entrepreneurship, as they write briefs and speeches for Ministers, and they can invite academics into the inner circles of decision making. Labour's 'Third Way', ideas based on American communitarianism, became the *zeitgeist* for the period in which ideas of character education were floating around.

Whitty (2008: 178) believes that this Third Way did not deliver any significant changes in the overall direction of educational policy, as there was considerable continuity between the substantive policies pursued by the New Labour government and those of the Conservative governments that immediately proceeded it. For Tony Blair (1998), the Third Way project was essentially about a modernised social democracy through a flexible commitment to social justice. The concern in New Labour was to make ideas operable as concrete social policies, and ministerial speeches began a subtle change of emphasis in politics which shifted the tide of opinion. A more scientific criterion, it appeared, for policy determination was increasingly adopted by the New Labour government; this replaced appeals to class loyalties or ideological stances. Policy makers wanted legitimacy for their policies and sought 'scientific evidence and knowledge' from some academics, but mainly from think tanks. In this context, although working under a coalition and now Conservative government, the Centre is able to conduct academic research, produce rigorous research reports and publications and, because of its independent source of funding, enjoy a large degree of autonomy and support with an excellent research infrastructure. This means that we are able to maintain a degree of separation from government and political parties. We also seek to resist both the temptation to recycle ideas and present short sound bites to politicians to win favour. We have consciously resisted pressure to over-simplify research findings, while trying to present findings honestly and in an intelligent way, together with building positive relationships at the political and bureaucratic levels. As Winch (2001) reminds us, 'to maintain research integrity while maximising impact requires a careful balance between maximising influence and remaining "excessively true to oneself"'.

Early academic connections and Templeton

Professor Karen Bohlin, who was Director of Boston University's Center for the Advancement of Ethics and Character, was my first serious academic contact in the US. After meeting many communitarian scholars at George Washington University in 1998, I wanted to seek out academics specifically working in the field of character and virtues education. Karen visited me in Canterbury in 1999 and then invited me to Boston. I visited her centre for the first time in November 2001. The Center contains a small specialist library on character and virtues literature, named after Professor Kevin Ryan, which is a veritable smorgasbord of information. I used it intensively, and in between reading my way through the collection, I had productive meetings with Karen Bohlin, Professor Charles Glenn and her other colleagues, discussing the state of character education in the US. Karen later introduced me to Professor Kevin Ryan, one of the modern fathers of character education in the US. I returned to the Boston Center in March 2002 and gave a seminar on the emergence of character education as a government policy initiative in the UK. In the audience was Dr. Arthur Schwartz from the John Templeton Foundation (JTF) and he invited me to join him and Karen for lunch. Over lunch we discussed character and moral education in the UK and Dr. Schwartz said he would contact me – I had no idea at the time that this fortuitous meeting would eventually lead to the establishment of the Jubilee Centre. So, while luck is an important factor in policy entrepreneurship, it is important to be proactive and position oneself, both to be able to respond to unexpected developments, and lobby and advocate for the changes one wishes to see.

Dr. Schwartz phoned a month or so later and encouraged a proposal of funding to the JTF and we discussed what this proposal might look like. I successfully submitted a proposal to look at the character qualities of 16–19 year olds in three large Bristol secondary schools, between 2004 and 2006. We collaborated with academic colleagues at the University of Bristol, particularly Dr. Ruth Deakin-Crick, and, interestingly, we held most of our meetings at the University of Birmingham. This was my first grant from JTF and involved a two-year study which led to a report published in 2006: *Character Education: The Formation of Virtues and Dispositions in 16–19 Year Olds*. The research sought both to explore how 16 to 19-year-old students understand virtues and values and what they perceive to be the main influences on the formation of their own character and to understand how schools can inhibit or facilitate the formation of virtues and values in this age group. Two important lessons were learnt from this first study that would increase the impact of the research itself.

First, the significance of collaboration and networks with other academics cannot be underestimated. Recruiting support from other academics in the pursuit of research and potential policy change is an important ingredient of policy entrepreneurship. Character education specialists in academe are rare in the UK, and this was especially the case in 2004. Dr. Ruth Deakin-Crick is such an academic, interested in values education, and was making her name in this field at the time. It was therefore important to connect with her, and we agreed to collaborate on the research. As such, Bristol schools were chosen to be part of the study rather than schools in Canterbury, where I was based. The research collaboration extended to teachers and schools, as it was important at the early stage to link researchers and teachers. Second, the proposal to JTF contained a pledge to establish an expert advisory body for the research, and this consisted of:

- Lord Alan Watson of Richmond
- Stephen Brenninkmeijer, Chair of the Enterprise Education Trust
- Patrick Coldstream, Director of the Council for Industry and Higher Education
- Jane Leek, The Derwent Consultancy
- Gary Powell, UK Managing Director of NM Rothschild Bank
- Monica Taylor, Editor, *Journal of Moral Education*

Dr. Kenneth Wilson, the former Principal of Westminster College in Oxford, was instrumental in assisting with the creation of the Advisory Board and became a member of the research team. Lord Watson acted as Chair, and the report was launched on 28 November 2006 in the House of Lords. Both the academic collaboration and the members of the Advisory Board ensured that the report would reach audiences beyond academe, and members of the Advisory Board did not simply offer advice but provided other resources – the Derwent Consultancy (now Porticus) in particular offered office space in London for meetings together with significant grants to further the work. This also led to new sources of research funding from other charitable foundations, such as the Esmée Fairbairn Foundation and Westfield Trust, which funded other research projects including a large survey of what student teachers expected from their training in the area of moral and values education.

Another partnership that was created at this time, and that has since become very significant to the work of the Jubilee Centre, was with David Lorimer, who ran a project called 'Learning for Life Values Poster Award Programme', principally in Scotland. David and I had first met in 2003 when he had reviewed my book on character education and we began an early collaboration. David edited a book of student writing from the project, *Learning for Life: From Inspiration to Aspiration*. We managed to launch the book in the Scottish Parliament with Alex Salmond, First Minister of Scotland, in March 2008. Our collaboration ensured that the idea of character education was being taken seriously by policy makers in both England

and Scotland. We created and established a charity together called Character Scotland, with David as Chief Executive and me as Chair. The work continues today, with new trustees, and character education is promoted in Scotland.

The *British Journal of Educational Studies* published my article on 'Character Education in British Education Policy' in 2005, and the *Journal of Moral Education* published my article on 'Character and Teacher Education' in 2007 – two early forays into the academic field which employed the research findings from the first JTF research project and the Esmée Fairbairn funded research on teacher education. As has been noted previously, policy entrepreneurship must stress 'the importance of creating a groundswell of interest and a body of evidence to make a compelling case for policy change' (Mintrom, 2014: 430) and these early publications helped promote interest within the academy, while the partnerships and collaborations that I was building outside of the academy helped promote and sustain the interest of key stakeholders.

Despite these early research findings not being particularly encouraging, in terms of how and what character virtues the young people involved were developing, we discovered that the major finding was that most students lacked a language of virtue and viewed their school as a place only to succeed in examinations and not to flourish as people. This was an important early discovery, which I conveyed to the JTF, who thankfully continued their interest in our work. I was invited to meet with Dr. Jack Templeton in London to discuss our research findings. This led eventually to securing another grant to run a more ambitious programme of research entitled 'Learning for Life: Strengthening Character in UK Civil Society', which was launched in October 2007. The research covered all phases of formal education. Lord Watson remained as chair of the Advisory Board, and two politicians from the main parties joined – Rt. Hon. Liam Byrne MP (Labour) and Mary McLeod MP (Conservative). Lord Watson, who is a member of the Liberal Democratic Party, described the underlying philosophy of the research when he said 'competence without character is unlikely to survive under stress. Know-how without values can be a dangerous thing and qualifications without the quality of self-knowledge ill prepares individuals for modern life' (JTF Capabilities Report, 2008: 166). This major project, which used the Learning for Life designation from the Scottish programme (and included a development of the Values Poster Programme), was the predecessor of the Jubilee Centre. The operational model later adopted by the Jubilee Centre began with the Learning for Life project. It also started with a commitment to frame issues in a way that appealed to stakeholders from diverse backgrounds, while actively seeking out and engaging with those who potentially might disagree with us: two other important features of successful policy entrepreneurship.

Learning for Life was not an official research centre, but still employed a number of research fellows to assist in carrying out the research in four specific phases of education: (a) the development of a character perspective in early years education, (b) the continuity of experience with regard to values in the transition between the primary and secondary phases of schooling, (c) the character formation of young people in schools 14–16, and (d) values in higher education and employment 18–24. The range of projects covered the ages 3–25 years, and, collectively, was a major study with over 70,000 participants. This research complemented the 16 to 19-year-olds project that had already been completed; we had to re-print this due to the demand for copies! The research in all cases sought to explore, descriptively, the current situation with regard to character development in different locations. It also sought to investigate character education through interventions that place a central emphasis on character formation.

Importantly, and from the outset, teaching and learning materials were developed by the research team and practising teachers with an interest and knowledge of the (re)emerging field of character education. The aim was to influence society not simply through research-informed policy (top-down), but also through research-informed practice (bottom-up). The first materials included a publication called 'Character First' (a guide for students about character and employment) and, 'Becoming Value-able' and 'Building Character', which were all precursors to the character education resources later developed by the Jubilee Centre. It was clear from the outset that these learning and teaching materials were popular with teachers and students. The research combined qualitative and quantitative methods to investigate and map out the issues in character education in each phase of schooling, as the field was light in this area. The research moved from descriptive to evaluative methods as it assessed the moral education policies in schools. We also employed some prescriptive research by testing our interventions, which introduced new ideas and proposals to address some of the issues that had arisen in character education.

A website was created to communicate the ideas of the project, and we contacted the local MPs in the areas where we conducted the research to inform them of our purpose and to outline our intentions. All were supportive, irrespective of political party, and even helped facilitate entry to schools and attended the launch of the final reports. For example, Liam Byrne MP invited us to survey all six secondary schools in his Birmingham constituency (Hodge Hill), so we conducted the research on 14 to 16 year olds exclusively within his constituency. The study explored the attitudes, dispositions and values of young people living in one of the most socially and economically deprived areas in the UK. Liam took a continuing interest in the research, and I was able to brief him in the Cabinet Office while he was the Cabinet Minister, and then in the Treasury when he became First Secretary to the Treasury. He was wholly supportive, launching the final report, 'Citizens of Character: The Values and Character Dispositions of 14–16 Year Olds in the Hodge Hill Constituency', at Westminster Abbey with many of the children from the six schools present. Speaking at the launch, Liam stated that:

> The research that the University of Birmingham undertook is, quite honestly, probably still the most influential piece of research I have ever seen in ten years as a public servant, as an MP, and as a Minister. It also showed that in our education system we have to equip our kids, not just with an

understanding of the world around them, but with an understanding of what is inside them.

(Rt Hon Liam Byrne MP, 2009)

Julian Brazier (2010), the Conservative MP for Canterbury, launched the transition from primary to secondary school report in a local school. In doing so, he commented that:

> Learning for Life is right to start from the premise that education is not just about the acquisition of academic credentials and social skills, but also, crucially, about active character development. My congratulations to Learning for Life for its insight into the minds of the next generation.

At the same time, the then leader of the opposition, the Rt. Hon. David Cameron (2009) also commented on Learning for Life, stating that:

> we all have a shared responsibility for our shared future, and for our neighbours, our country and our planet. That is what social responsibility is all about. It is great that Learning for Life encourages pupils to reflect not only on how to improve their own lives, but also on the values they need to make a contribution to wider society.

We learned that reaching out to an MP or other high-profile figure, and inviting them to launch a report, could assist with bringing additional media interest and coverage, and increase the dissemination, influence and impact of the study. We also learned that securing broad, cross-partisan support is a key component of a successful policy entrepreneur's ability to promote policy change. Striving for a bipartisan convergence remains crucial, and we were able to point to earlier government support/commitment for character education as evidence of the cross-party support our character education recommendations enjoyed. Many became increasingly convinced of the value of character education, and this emerging policy idea often proceeded without serious opposing voices. There was no counter-mobilisation (see Jones and Baumgartner , 2009: 5) at play, but the idea of character education did not go completely uncontested.

Landry *et al.* (2003: 22) provide an interesting list of six uses of research involving policy makers. By way of illustration we can consider these six uses of research with regard to the influence on Liam Byrne MP: 1) *reception* (the research outputs are received by Liam); 2) *cognition* (Liam reads and understand the research); 3) *discussion* (the research is the subject of meetings in Liam's office at the Cabinet Office and subsequently at the Treasury); 4) *reference* (the research is cited in internal documents as Liam writes to other ministers to spread the research); 5) *adoption* (efforts are made by Liam to use the research at Fabian Society meetings and in speeches); and 6) *influence* (the research influences decisions made, and change can be evidenced). It is this final stage that is difficult to audit; in any event, the number of policy ideas from reception to adoption stages is reduced. It was certainly the case that my pre-existing relations with Liam Byrne (2013) contributed to greater use of our research findings in political circles, as he would give speeches to the Fabian Society quoting from our research. This confirms Lomas *et al.*'s (2005) view that research is most likely to be used in policy if policy makers have been involved in its development. While the decisions to interact and engage with high-profile policy makers and MPs from the outset was a conscious decision, the ways in which we achieved the most success through the Learning for Life project were noted and adopted in the creation and establishment of the Jubilee Centre.

The Learning for Life project moved from Canterbury to the University of Birmingham in October 2009 and two other smaller research projects were approved by JTF at Birmingham in 2011. The first project was called 'My Character' and examined the idea of 'future-mindedness', the capacity of students to set goals and make plans to achieve them, which had become popular in the UK at this time. The aspiration was to not simply develop new teaching and learning programmes, but also evaluate their effectiveness, as we knew this would make the research more attractive to policy makers and practitioners. The 'My Character' programme consisted of an online and hard copy character journal in which 11–14 year olds were required to record their character development against eight moral virtues. The programme was subjected to a feasibility trial (randomised and controlled) from which much was learnt, not only about the programme itself but also the challenges of measuring character. The report on the 'My Character' programme was the first to be published by the Jubilee Centre in 2014.

The second project, 'Knightly Virtues', consisted of a taught programme for 9–11 year olds using selected stories to teach character. The programme has proven to be hugely popular, and has so far reached over 30,000 pupils worldwide. Expertise gained during the 'My Character' trial informed the methodology used to evaluate 'Knightly Virtues', and the results were reported in the second research report to be published by the Centre, again in 2014. The trial involved over 3,200 pupils from 55 schools, and provided substantial empirical evidence for the effectiveness of using stories to develop virtue literacy – the knowledge, understanding and application of virtue terms and concepts. The research also found that the 'Knightly Virtues' programme closed the gap between pupils in faith and non-faith schools in terms of their grasp of virtue language and concepts in personal contexts, or 'virtue literacy'. The report was launched by Dr. Jack Templeton himself at the Union League Club in Philadelphia at a dinner in autumn 2014, with many invited academics from Ivy League universities. The programme continues to be popular both in Britain as well as in schools across the world. Replica programmes have since been initiated in Britain and other countries, and a book published by the Centre, *Educating Character Through Stories* (Carr and Harrison, 2015), was inspired by this programme.

In September 2010, I had been invited to the Advisers' Meeting in Oxford of the JTF by Dr. Kent Hill, who was the Vice President for Character Education. The intention was to launch a summary research report of the Learning for Life initiative,

Of Good Character (2010), and our whole Advisory Board attended and spoke about different parts of the short book. They included Lord Watson, Liam Byrne MP, Mary MacLeod MP, Dr. John Hall, Dean of Westminster and Stephen Brenninkmeijer. At this meeting, Mary MacLeod read out a statement from the Secretary of State for Education, Michael Gove, endorsing the research insights provided by the Learning for Life project. The research on which *Of Good Character* is based represents probably the largest study of character education in the UK to date, involving – both formally and informally – responses from over 70,000 participants. The project was largely funded by the JTF and Porticus UK, but initial funding was provided by the Esmée Fairburn Foundation, and a further ten UK charities also provided support. The major part of the research involved an extensive empirical investigation – by means of semi-structured group discussions/interviews and semi-structured individual and questionnaire surveys – of the thoughts on values and character education of young people in different parts of the UK, across the entire spectrum of formal education and beyond. It therefore covered children of nursery age, the earlier and later stages of primary education, secondary education, further education, tertiary education and into employment. Immediately after the launch meeting on 30 September, I met Dr. Templeton the next morning for a private discussion about the research. Dr. Templeton was clearly eager to convey to me his desire for more research in the UK context on character virtues.

During 2011, Dr. Templeton initiated a series of discussions with me 'about the full scope of JFT's commitment to a 10-year horizon of multiple grants' in researching character virtues. We met on numerous occasions with his wife Pina and with Barnaby Marsh. Barnaby, who was a Vice President of JTF, led on the detail of the discussions. Essentially Dr. Templeton wanted to honour his father in 2012, as this was his centenary as well as the 25th anniversary of the award of his knighthood from the Queen. It was also the Diamond Jubilee of the Queen herself, and these two events were behind his thinking and motivation for establishing a Centre. The Centre idea gradually emerged in the discussions, and Dr. Templeton sought to continue the work of the Learning for Life project, which he appreciated. It was finally agreed that the establishment of a large research centre would be the best vehicle to advance the cause for character education in the UK by conducting multiple, simultaneous research projects under one roof. The name of the Centre was agreed with Dr. Templeton to honour the Diamond Jubilee, and the anniversary of his father's knighthood. In early 2012, plans were laid to launch this multi-million pound centre, to be based at the University of Birmingham, in the Houses of Parliament. It was launched on 16 May 2012 in the Attlee Room of the House of Lords with many distinguished guests, including Sir David Eastwood, the Vice Chancellor of the University of Birmingham, Drs. Jack and Pina Templeton, Heather – their daughter, Lord Watson, and many MPs. It was a major occasion, and the large party moved to the Athenaeum Club, to be hosted by Dr. Templeton for a celebration dinner. The next morning I realised I had only one member of staff, Aidan Thompson, with Tom Harrison, acting as a consultant. Both had worked with me at Birmingham on the Learning for Life project: Aidan is an extremely competent administrator and Tom had great experience from the voluntary sector having worked for Community Service Volunteers. The Centre officially came into existence on 1 June 2012 at the University of Birmingham and Dr. Templeton announced that he would be visiting the Centre on the 30 September – I had to get a move on!

Creating the Jubilee Centre

Founding philosophy

My early book on communitarian education (Arthur, 2000: 23, 87, 89) argued that many of the assumptions of communitarianism are rooted in an Aristotelian virtue ethics approach to education. The revival of virtue ethics within the policy domain was generally optimistic – that life can get better and that the individual can achieve coherence and flourishing in life through a search for the common good. Included within this movement were ideas from positive psychology and well-being advocates, and by 2012 there were a number from left and right in politics who cited Aristotle as a key influence on their politics of virtue. In his blog of 24 May 2012, Jules Evans cites them as Jon Cruddas, Liam Byrne, Geoff Mulgan, James O'Shaughnessy, Lord Richard Layard, Anthony Seldon and Oliver Letwin. This was a broad movement that believed that economic growth could be a means to virtue and flourishing, rather than an end in itself. Following an Aristotelian line of thinking, it endorsed the idea that we can change ourselves through the use of reason, that we can create new habits of thinking, feeling and doing, that we can build flourishing lives and that this search is social, communal and political. Richard Reeves (Cleary and Reeves, 2009), then Director of DEMOS, edited a report on building character in which he spoke of the 'Neo-Aristotelian consensus' in policy circles. There was an Aristotelian turn in many policy ideas and the think tanks – DEMOS, ResPublica and The Young Foundation – led the way. All seemed to desire the same end in public policy, which was to cultivate *eudaimonia* (flourishing) among citizens, even if they disagreed on the means. The Conservative MP Jesse Norman (2010: 11) wrote that his intention in writing his *Big Society* was to explain 'how an ancient theory of human flourishing can be used to develop a far richer conception of human character and well-being' and how it can be used to guide public policy. This all matched the ethos that the Jubilee Centre was built on; that character and virtues can be developed through:

> the contexts of the family, school, community, university, professions, voluntary organisations and the wider workplace. From the outset, the Centre believe that virtues such as courage, justice, honesty, compassion, self-discipline, gratitude, generosity and humility 1) are critical to individual excellence; 2) contribute to societal flourishing; 3) can be exercised within all human contexts; 4) are educable.
>
> *(Jubilee Centre for Character and Virtues, 2012)*

Selecting staff

Well-qualified staff are vital for any research project, and from the beginning the Jubilee Centre was concerned with being an interdisciplinary endeavour, and therefore required expertise across a range of academic disciplines. I was conscious that the staff selected to work in the Centre would be the face of the Centre's ideas and that their academic qualities would only give credibility to the work of the Centre if they developed ownership of these ideas. Hence my first concern, in any policy entrepreneurship sense, was the staff I recruited. The staff needed to become strong allies and partners in the vision that I had for the Centre, and be able to link this vision to our research programme as well as our potential influence on policy. Members of staff could not be allowed to mutate the ideas in the original vision; a degree of development, yes, but not a misrepresentation.

The creation of a coalition of interested and invested parties required a strong narrative of virtue and character education throughout any communication and dissemination, and that process began within the Centre itself. A carefully planned and considered induction process was created for all incoming staff, so as to educate and immerse them in the Centre's ethos, approach and direction. We also needed people who had the potential to translate research results into plain language for distribution to non-specialist audiences. We planned a role for someone with expertise in media relations to build our media connections. While we didn't, in the end, recruit such a person, we have utilised many different contacts and approaches with regard to media, and have been extremely successful to date. While it was time consuming to have planned and strategised in advance for the recruitment of different 'types' of personnel and roles, this became incredibly beneficial once the actual research was underway, and is an essential feature when thinking about policy entrepreneurship.

The first requirement was to secure the services of outstanding philosophers of education; Professor John Haldane at St. Andrews University reminded me that they were in short supply. Professor David Carr had recently retired from the University of Edinburgh and is another outstanding contributor in the field of moral education. He had worked with us on the 'Knightly Virtues' project, and he accepted the position of Chair in Ethics and Education. Professor Kristján Kristjánsson had been writing about Aristotelian ethics and character for a number of years, and in 2012 was on a sabbatical from his native Iceland at St. Edmund's College, Cambridge, writing another philosophical text. I contacted him and invited him to apply, which he did, and after some gentle persuasion he accepted an offer and became our first academic appointment as Chair in Character Education and Virtue Ethics. He became the Centre's Deputy Director, and has since been elected as a member of the Royal Institute of Philosophy's Council. The Royal Institute of Philosophy became one of the first strategic partners of the Jubilee Centre. It is an institute dedicated to the advancement of philosophy in all its branches through the organisation and promotion of teaching, discussion and research of all things philosophical. In discussion with Professor John Haldane, we secured a joint chair with the Royal Institute of Philosophy – something unprecedented that would lead to the appointment of Professor Randy Curren of Rochester University, who had written extensively on Aristotle and education.

We had secured three truly outstanding appointments in philosophy of education. We began the recruitment process of research fellows, a task which took the whole of the summer and early autumn of 2012. We had a huge number of exceptionally well-qualified applications, and, with the assistance of Aidan Thompson, who became the manager of the Centre, I was able to short-list a credible field of candidates for each of the posts. Each candidate had to provide a written statement on why they were interested in character virtues, and at interview make a five-minute presentation on this theme. By this method, we secured the appointment of eight research fellows by September 2012, together with a number of support staff. I was keenly aware that a highly motivated team could do much to advance policy ideas, in addition to undertaking and producing high-quality academic research. We were conscious that university practices, in terms of promotion, are sometimes counterproductive to generating research and increasing its impact, but the University of Birmingham often gives engaged academics the opportunity to develop position and prestige through highlighting their successes in civic engagement, dissemination and impact – in other words, research impact is valued in this university. The University of Birmingham's institutional capacity and infrastructure to support effective sharing of research findings is second-to-none, and our Centre has benefited from a well-organised and coordinated effort to turn research outcomes into policy ideas. We made a deliberate effort to broaden the experience of incoming staff, and to school them in the language and techniques of dissemination, from the very start, through involvement in outreach activities.

Following extensive induction programmes for all staff in the autumn of 2012, we officially launched the Centre to the international academic community in December 2012, deliberately and proactively engaging with some of the most senior figures in the field of character and moral education. These included James Davison Hunter, William Damon, Howard Gardner, Marvin Berkowitz, Lord Richard Layard and John Haldane – all of whom gave keynote addresses at our inaugural conference. Our ambition was, and still is, to become the leading voice on character, not just in the UK but internationally. We therefore engaged with the leading scholars already in the area to get them on board with our work and our vision. We were acutely aware that it was the Centre's cross-disciplinary focus that would set us apart from other centres and scholars; we were bringing together the leading thinkers from philosophy, psychology, education and sociology to speak about character, which was something that had not been done before. Our annual conference at Oriel College in the University of Oxford has become a much-desired and very well-attended event, with expert colleagues from around the world.

We did not want to confine our interactions to the academy. We wanted the staff of the Centre to understand both research and practice, to interact regularly with teachers and other professionals, and be able to communicate effectively with them. This combination of an academic and practical focus has been of great benefit to the Centre. It was vital to our plans for generating impact, and we continue to give it priority.

Our research: scope and reach

The initial motivation for creating the Centre was to promote, through rigorous research, the importance of character in British society. Our approach involved both basic and use-inspired research. We sought to engage in systematic study directed towards fuller knowledge and understanding of character and virtues in public life, with specific application always in mind. However, some elements of our research were motivated by ultimate application. From the outset, we recognised that education is an 'applied, multi-disciplinary field' and that use-inspired research within it pursues use and influence. We are concerned with policy ideas, not policy formulation in the form of ready-made policies. We prioritised, and continue to prioritise, traditional routes for academic publication and dissemination, via publications in peer-reviewed journals and presentations at national and international academic conferences. However, we had the resources and staff to disseminate to a wider, non-academic audience in policy-relevant terms – in other words, we were able to translate much of our research into policy ideas, as we produced research findings. Our key message is that good character matters to individuals and society and that the qualities that make up good character can be both learnt and taught. Our guiding, but not exclusive, philosophy is Aristotelian virtue ethics, which is being concerned with how people might best live virtuously – this is about how people acquire and act reflectively on well-chosen habits in order to flourish as human beings.

We began with the belief that we needed a new emphasis on these virtue qualities in schools and in professional education. We set out to present three defining arguments. First, that good character has multiple benefits for individuals and society. This first argument reasoned that the virtues which make up character enable us to enjoy rewarding and productive lives and that the more people with good character the healthier our society. However, we took care not to couch this argument in merely instrumental terms, also highlighting the intrinsic worth of a virtuous life. In our professions, we argued that integrity, as well as knowledge, is vital. We also reasoned, at the start, that the virtues could be found in all the great faiths, but equally that they are not restricted to religions. Second, that character can be taught, learnt and reinforced, and needs to be placed at the heart of education. We wanted to demonstrate that the academic research literature had already shown that teaching character is both possible and practicable. We believed that it was about empowering young people, not limiting them, but rather helped give them the judgement to make the right decisions. Third, that the Jubilee Centre would engage in cross-disciplinary and innovative research, work in partnership with schools and the professions, and promote the importance of good character against a background in society that had grown increasingly sceptical about the moral integrity of both the professional classes and politicians.

As a centre, we began every research project with systematic reviews, critically appraising and collating all available relevant studies in character and virtues education, both in Britain and internationally. We wanted to identify practice needs for evidence, and worked with practitioners from the outset to refine the research questions. The teachers we work with are not just seen as the 'users' of the research, but co-creators of it. We involved teachers and professionals as members of our initial expert panels, to help produce policy statements and guide our work on curriculum development. We later created the post of Teaching Fellow to recruit practising teachers interested in the area to work full-time in the Centre each term. By this means, we secured, and continue to secure, user involvement. We welcomed their comments on our research methods, involved them in data collection, and they in turn tested ideas in the classroom. We posed questions to users both prior to conducting research and prior to publication of findings. We sought opportunities for participatory research, which meant we had to think beyond our normal circles of collaboration. Anderson and Freebody (2014) call this 'partnership research', and the intention is to close the gap between researchers, practitioners and policy makers. It is ultimately about making research outcomes count. We adopted a push and pull strategy: to push research information out to target audiences and to pull people into the character education movement, sharing ideas through engagement and involvement.

Our public relations strategy was, and continues to be, one which encourages audiences to recognise the Jubilee Centre as a leading voice on the subject of character and virtues in British society, through the publication of rigorous research reports, academic papers in high-ranking journals, innovative statements and first-class teaching resources. It was, therefore, essential that the whole team was outward looking from the start, in terms of recognising dissemination strategies and opportunities beyond the 'traditional' academic outlets. We knew that excellent research could easily sit on the shelf without an engaged, interested and active audience. We wanted people, especially teachers and professionals, to use our resources and to visit our website for advice and guidance on character virtues and how they can be taught, promoted and developed in classrooms, universities and places of work. Above all, we wanted our audiences to view us as a centre of research excellence that was objective, multi-disciplinary, robust, rigorous and non-political, and we wanted the media to come to the Centre for comment, analysis and information. A hallmark of the Centre is our focus on academic excellence in conducting research, scholarship and development work. We began to build a clearly defined profile that set out a compelling vision of what the Centre was about, the research that we were beginning to conduct, and the audiences that we sought to engage with. We crafted a clear message, which we presented as a narrative for change. We worked as a team, and we understood the role of evidence in making compelling arguments. We had recruited both distinguished and developing academics, and we were confident that the academic merits of the Centre and its refereed outputs would speak for themselves.

However, our impact on public policy was never assured. While, on reflection, the Centre has done much to interact with, engage and impact education policy in the UK and internationally, and continues to do so, policy evolves and changes – it also transforms through a constant articulation and re-articulation of the ideas. These processes give rise to impact that is not entirely predictable even when our staff have a remit to support the use, impact and dissemination of our research. We sought, from the start, to craft a distinctive message of what the Centre was about and what it had to offer. Our focus was not simply on traditional social science research projects, but also on 'development' work, where we engaged directly with schools and young people, creating resources and materials; this has helped raise our profile in areas we might not otherwise have engaged in. We sought positive publicity, as anyone would, but responded positively to any negative publicity, either specifically about the Centre or our approach to character education. We understood that some people would believe that our approach was misguided, narrow, or just different, but we always put our focus on developing the agenda of the debate and engaging with people who were defining the issues. We did not ask 'can this be done?' but rather 'how can this be done?' to emphasise our sense of mission and of what was possible. That said, we continue to understand the importance of being aware of all sides of any debate, and how best to engage with each side. One way of doing this has been our regular research seminars, where we invite some of the leading academic names in the field to speak to our team and the rest of the University, so that we can learn more about the field of work, and give a chance for our researchers to challenge them and ask questions.

Our initial research aims were to amass evidence on different areas of character and virtues education for use in the development of policy ideas that we would later place into the public domain. We wanted to build a strong, evidence-based, intellectual argument for our initiatives. We understood that this approach requires input from many people, so that arguments and counter-arguments can be broadly canvassed before a decision is taken in terms of policy creation. From the very start of our work, we considered whether there could be any significant effects on character education policy. We believed that there would be, so we have kept the potential impact and influence of any research findings on policy makers at the front of our minds when planning for dissemination. However, our principal aim, at least initially, was to use credible academic arguments to influence how others thought about character education in schools. At the outset, we sought to forge strategic networks with key stakeholders, organisations and schools, bringing their knowledge and skills to bear on the policy debate. In establishing our reputation as a credible and reliable research and development centre, we are able to build and maintain good relations with influential policy makers and leading practitioners through regular dialogue and dissemination of research outputs. As Mintrom *et al.* (2014: 424) said, 'policy entrepreneurs tend to work hard at (1) defining and framing problems; (2) building powerful teams that tap relevant knowledge networks; (3) amassing evidence to show the workability of their proposals and (4) creating strong coalitions of diverse supporters'. By these means we attempted to educate both members of the policy community and the general public as a whole. We are conscious that research findings ought to be debated and tested, as part of the academic dialogue, and also before a consensus is reached on concrete policy recommendations.

In the Centre, we have always identified the major stakeholders that we wish to influence as schools, education stakeholders, social action organisations and wider communities, but also government officials and policy makers. We set out to increase the interest in character and virtues in public life by attempting to:

1. Stimulate public debate that is informed by our research.
2. Affect the awareness, attitudes and understanding of practitioners and policy makers through our research insights.
3. Improve best practice in schools and the professions through engagement.
4. Make changes to education and professional training through our research and development work.
5. Encourage policy decisions or changes to government regulations or guidance that has been informed by our research.
6. Promote decisions by practitioners that have been enlightened by our research insights.
7. Make changes to professional standards or training informed by our research.
8. Encourage professionals and professional bodies using our research and development work to improve their working practices.
9. Increase public interest, discussion, debate and engagement in character education.

These objectives, together with all our other goals, have been continually measured, reviewed and revised as we have progressed.

Research evidence and findings can often be interpreted subjectively, and used to further an existing line of argument, rather than create a new one. The field of character education has suffered from a lack of a consistent language, among both academics and policy makers. One of the first challenges for the Jubilee Centre was to standardise the language within the field and make sure our own use of terminology was consistent. The Centre set out to shape this language, both in defining the use of particular terms and in using umbrella terms to encompass the array of different notions of character education. I recall early on in the Centre's existence Prince Charles asking me what people meant by 'character education'. Roberts and King (1991: 170), using ideas from Rogers and Kim (1985: 88), have cautioned that ideas from policy entrepreneurs may be difficult to understand and have multiple meanings. It is important for a policy entrepreneur to be clear and consistent about the ideas and evidence that they are presenting. Roberts and King accepted that ideas generated by policy entrepreneurs would be more readily adopted than others to the extent that they are perceived to have:

1. *Reduced complexity* – the Centre views character education broadly, in that it was generally consistent with existing, but not explicit, values and experiences in schools.
2. *Greater triability* – the Centre has tested ideas in practice, to demonstrate 'what works', e.g. our 'Knightly Virtues' curriculum intervention and research project.
3. *Greater observability* – we wanted our research and its findings to be visible and widely disseminated.
4. *Greater relative advantage* – we wanted our recommendations to be perceived as better than the practices that preceded them.

We also wanted to ensure that our focus spanned across a range of related activities. Roberts and King (1991: 158ff) helpfully categorise these activities as follows:

a. *Ideas generation activities* – policy entrepreneurs generate and trade in ideas, and some ideas have the power to change the course of policy development.
b. *Problem-framing activities* – engagement in problem framing and definition to convince policy makers that our ideas represent sound policy options.
c. *Dissemination activities* – spreading our ideas to a wider audience than the academy, in the form of statements, reports and newsletters.
d. *Strategic activities* – increasing and maintaining the momentum by attracting support, and developing both a long-term strategy and a short-term strategy to deal with changing political realities.
e. *Activities to cultivate bureaucratic insiders and advocates* – building positive relationships with civil servants.
f. *Collaborative activities with high-profile, elite groups* – working with thought leaders and securing their commitment to our ideas.
g. *Activities to enlist support from elected officials* – seeking support from interested political figures.
h. *Lobbying activities* – a focus on spreading our message and generating interest among the general public.
i. *Activities to attract media attention* – convincing the media of our case.

Mintrom and Vergari (1996: 423) argue that the standard to which these activities are undertaken is critical in successfully influencing the policy debate. They recognise that those policy entrepreneurs who are based in universities often use their institutions as 'safe havens' to exercise their intellectual freedom, but this may reduce their ability to be influential in policy environments. However, direct lobbying of politicians may be at the other end of the spectrum for an academic. Clearly, lobbying entails letting those who make decisions know what you think, and it can assist with agenda setting. It obviously requires academics to communicate a clear message before establishing links and making themselves known in policy circles. One needs to garner support from others and support what they are doing, and the policy entrepreneur needs to navigate often volatile political waters in such a way that they do not appear as merely partisan. They also need to know that there are different ways of presenting the same piece of research. Finally, they need to know that it is not always possible to convince policy makers on every point, and that it is sometimes necessary to meet people half-way, to begin to lead them to where you want them to go, to build a bridge between the current perceived wisdom to new ways of thinking and understanding.

The Centre set out to undertake a number of tasks in relation to our research agenda. These included the same three roles identified by Ward *et al.* (2009): knowledge management (finding and disseminating information about character virtues in public life), linkage and exchange (facilitating discussion between researchers, practitioners and decision makers on character), and capacity building (developing capacity for future knowledge exchange). The Centre involved itself in a range of activities which brought people together to exchange information and ideas, as well as monitoring and evaluating character education interventions in schools and in the professions to identify success or where changes were needed.

The work of Oborn *et al.* (2011: 325) also helps shed light on the process of turning academic outputs into policy development. They identified two key shifts in the way health policy was being made, which seem applicable to the education context. First, they quote Harrison and Wood (1999) who referred to 'manipulated emergence', which is the recognition that there is no blueprint in policy reform, once designed and exclusively overseen by civil servants in central government. They believe that the process of policy development and change 'emerges' from the interaction between stakeholders. In our case, it was shaped by incentives, interventions and findings designed and reported by the Centre. So in character education, this consisted of the government adopting character as an aim of the DfE, awarding grants for research in character education, and creating national character awards, without a centralised guidance or curriculum for character education in schools. The second shift that they identify is the greater involvement of external 'experts' and others, bringing them together to advise and construct policy ideas – in character education this is exactly what happened. The Centre has been able to mobilise international support for character education through its academic contacts. As Secretary of State for Education, Nicky Morgan visited the same countries where we have developed strong links, like Japan, to discuss character education at the highest levels.

The research was, from the beginning, broken up into four phases. The first phase we called 'Gratitude Britain', and this initially consisted of five major research projects. A brief summary of all five is warranted here, but through the eyes of the five public figures who launched the final research reports in late 2014 and early 2015. First, Lord Neuberger, President of the Supreme Court of the UK, launched the *Virtuous Character for the Practice of Law* report (Arthur *et al.*, 2014b) at the Supreme Court in London and commented 'the research report which we are here to launch is an interesting, important and impressive document'. Second, Professor David Haslam, Chair of the National Institute of Health and Care Excellence, launched the *Virtuous Medical Practice* report (Arthur *et al.*, 2015c) at the Royal

College of General Practitioners, and commented, 'the time is absolutely spot-on for this report. It deserves to have a major impact.' The Rt. Hon. Baroness Morris of Yardley, a former Secretary of State for Education, launched *The Good Teacher: Understanding Virtues in Practice* report (Arthur *et al.*, 2015a) at the City of Birmingham Council House and commented 'this report gives us the stepping stones and permission to recover the language of moral values in teaching'.

Sir Anthony Seldon, then Master of Wellington College and himself a strong advocate of character education, launched the *Character Education in UK Schools* report (Arthur *et al.*, 2015d) in February 2015. This particular research project conducted the largest single study of character education in the UK, looking to triangulate data from over 10,000 participants between the self-reporting in surveys of pupils, completion of moral dilemmas, and interview and focus group discussions of both teachers and pupils. Sir Anthony commented that the research 'shows a huge desire from teachers to engage in character education'. The final major research report, *An Attitude for Gratitude* (Arthur *et al.*, 2015b), was launched at the British Academy by Dr. Michael Moseley, a well-known British television journalist, also in February 2015. The research again involved over 10,000 participants and examined how the British public understand, experience and value gratitude. Dr. Moseley commented that, 'I think that gratitude is a skill that can be taught … I look forward to further research and the recommendations of the report being put into practice.' All of these reports captured significant press attention. The study of education needs to speak to society, to teachers, and policy makers, and not encourage a separation between the two, as the most important channel of communication is between educational researchers and schools. It is vital that schools feel part of the research and absorb the findings and recommendations, transforming them into practice. There is often a wide gap between educational research and educational practice (see McLoughlin, 2000). This gap is not restricted to educational research; you will find it in nearly all the social sciences.

We always intended to develop a close working relationship with teachers and schools. We knew that without the active participation of practitioners, our research would not generate findings that are useful in improving schools. The research of the Centre has developed a strong research–practitioner interface, even when such interactions are not explicitly research orientated. We were ready to forge new alliances and to bring together networks with which we had no previous contact. In a sense, we wanted to establish a coalition of policy entrepreneurs from across the sector. Our focus began with influencing the initial stages of policy formulation, not in the political implementation of policies – at the latter stage, we believed that it is best for academics to remain distant from actual decision making. So, while we wished to remain firmly within our domain of academic expertise, we recognised the importance of contributing to the public debate on character education and, as a result, being prepared for 'blowback' – ready to receive criticism. We recognise that we have had quite unprecedented access to politicians – this is rare in academia, let alone the social sciences, and especially so in a niche area of education. However, this access and influence has been deliberately planned and carefully managed in order to achieve maximum impact and influence, while remaining true to the principles of the Centre and our research. The main areas of political influence are discussed in greater detail below.

Policy entrepreneurship and the Jubilee Centre

The University of Birmingham School

In 2010, the new Coalition Government issued its education White Paper 'The Importance of Teaching', in which I noticed one sentence at 2.25 saying that the DfE would 'invite some of the best higher education providers of initial teacher training to open University Training Schools'. I had in that year become Head of the School of Education at Birmingham, and shortly after received a visit from Ofsted to inspect our teacher training provision. This inspection resulted, for the first time, in the award of 'outstanding' for both our primary and secondary courses. I had introduced character education as part of the training of all teachers at Birmingham, the first university in the UK to do so. I began discussions with the DfE in London on new ways that universities could be involved in teacher training. These discussions were taking place at the same time that I began discussions with the JTF about establishing a possible research centre to advance character education in the UK. I therefore combined both interests and set out to propose the establishment of a University Training School dedicated to the development of character. In early 2011, I presented my proposal first to the Vice-Chancellor at the University of Birmingham, who was supportive. He asked me to present my arguments to the University Executive Board and subsequently to the Council of the University. All parties agreed with and supported the proposal, which contained an explicit intention that the school would be a site for character education and research.

A proposal was submitted to the DfE, and after a number of visits to London to argue the case, the then Secretary of State, Michael Gove, agreed to fund a new secondary school in Birmingham. Michael Gove had developed a strong reputation as a defender of academic attainment, but we had lobbied him for years and had provided international research evidence that emphasised the usefulness and link between character education and attainment. Over the course of the next two years, the Jubilee Centre worked with teachers to produce a bespoke curriculum on character education specifically for the new school. Working with the architects, I was able to help design a school for the development of character, as I believe that character education requires not only a rich culture, but a consciously designed space for it to benefit students. The teaching staff recruited have a dedication and belief in the positive development of character virtues, both in their pupils and in themselves.

The school was opened in September 2015 by Secretary of State Nicky Morgan, who strongly praised the school's commitment to character education. The school is now one of the most over-subscribed in the country and its dedication to character education has been extremely popular with parents and students. The theory of change that the school adopts is not a simplistic model of instilling character into students in the hope that all will be well, rather it provides new experiential contexts for character building which expose pupils to new roles, responsibilities and relationships, as well as dedicated time for reflection. The Jubilee Centre is at the heart of the pre-service and in-service training of the teachers. Further, many of the teachers are involved with Jubilee Centre research projects, either as advisers or active participants. The school has become an excellent exempla of the Centre's research in practice for the many policy makers and educational leaders who have requested a visit.

Royal awareness and support

Some members of the Royal Family became aware of the existence of the Jubilee Centre in 2013 through two separate initiatives. The first was through discussions with William Nye, the Private Secretary to Prince Charles, about the possibility of Prince Charles awarding the annual Templeton Prize. His father, the Duke of Edinburgh, awarded the prize between 1973 and 2011. Dr. Jack Templeton had asked me to accompany him to Clarence House and participate in the discussions. The second was through the establishment of the Step Up To Serve campaign, co-founded by Dame Julia Cleverdon, whom I had met for the first time in June 2013 to discuss how the Jubilee Centre and this new national youth initiative could collaborate with each other. It was at this meeting in St. James's Palace with Julia that we spoke about the 'double benefit' of youth social action in terms of assisting society while also building the character of those who volunteered. Julia afforded me the opportunity to help influence the goals and direction of this national initiative at an early stage. I was then asked to take a hand-delivered letter from Prince Charles to Dr. Templeton in Rio de Janeiro, where the JTF advisers were meeting in 2013. I had been appointed an adviser to the JTF in 2011, so I was due to attend this meeting in any case. In this letter, the Prince hoped that his new campaign for youth social action would include 'challenging opportunities to build character and virtues of a far more positive and constructive sort' and reminded Dr. Templeton that the Prince had personally made a speech in the House of Lords in 1975 promoting building the character of young people.

Prince Charles' letter was written to invite Dr. Templeton to Buckingham Palace on 21 November to attend the launch of the Youth Social Action campaign. Dr. Templeton was unable to attend, but I was also invited by the Prince and was introduced to him in Buckingham Palace, where we had our first conversation about the Jubilee Centre. He later asked William Nye to write and convey his thanks to Dr. Templeton for supporting the Jubilee Centre. I was subsequently asked to sit on the Advisory Board of the Step Up To Serve campaign, and was invited to Clarence House to brief the Prince, chair of the Step Up To Serve's Advisory Board, on the progress of character education around his dining table with the other advisers. I met the Prince again in 2015 to discuss, briefly, the work at Birmingham, and since then, we have met at other advisers' meetings in Clarence

House and Buckingham Palace. Two Fellows of the Centre have also been introduced to Prince Charles – Dr. Tom Harrison and Emma Taylor – and both were able to talk about the Centre's work and the positive impact of the research and development programmes.

Prince William has also been made aware of the work of the Centre through our collaboration with SkillForce, of which the Prince is Patron. The Centre has collaborated with SkillForce as its key research partner in evaluating the Prince's Award for character in young people aged between 5 and 14, and we continue to work alongside SkillForce to improve the award, to the satisfaction of Prince William. Indeed, it was the Jubilee Centre that first recommended the need for such an award to SkillForce, to celebrate the character of young people. Prince William officially established the award on 1 March 2017 when I was able to discuss the importance of character education with him. In addition, the Duchess of Cornwall visited Montenegro in 2016 with Prince Charles, and she was introduced to the work that the Jubilee Centre had carried out in partnership with UNICEF and the Montenegro Ministry of Education. Support from influential actors is one of the characteristics that distinguish policy entrepreneur activity, and Prince Charles and Prince William have certainly supported character building activities of the Jubilee Centre.

International influences

The Centre has enhanced its impact in global research networks through its strategic partnerships with international organisations in America, Australia, Japan, South Korea, Singapore, Malaysia, Taiwan and China, with increasing connections to Latin America and Europe. Establishing these partnerships and building collaborations around ideas has resulted in the generation of evidence and produced a momentum for change globally. The Jubilee Centre has welcomed a large number of distinguished academics in the field of virtue ethics, moral development, character education and professional ethics to spend a week or two at the Centre. During that time, they have delivered a seminar paper in the Centre's bi-weekly seminar series and, on occasion, given an open lecture. Most importantly, they have collaborated with the teams working on different research projects within the Centre and provided their expertise as consultants on various aspects of our on-going research. They have also taken away the ideas and findings that the Centre is generating, which has had a formative influence on their own scholarship.

We have received numerous invitations from foreign governments to visit and engage; I was invited to Singapore when the Singapore Minister of Education launched the Character and Citizenship programme for schools. I delivered a keynote lecture when the policy was announced by the Minister, and we have been able to maintain these strong links. At the government's invitation, I also visited Tokyo to meet civil servants designing the new character programme for schools to be introduced in Japan in 2018. Nicky Morgan subsequently visited the

Japanese Ministry of Education to discuss the same idea. There is a good deal of consensus on the broad aims for character education between our international partners, but considerable variation in the political operation and processes of character education, resulting in divergence of content, practices, teaching approaches and assessment within these different East Asian countries.

Another area of significant partnership and development in East Asia has been in Malaysia. At the invitation of the one of the largest foundations in Malaysia, YTL, I was invited to speak at a conference in Kuala Lumpur in November 2016. During this conference, I addressed over 500 teachers from across the country about the Centre's Framework for Character Education and how it might be adapted to suit their schools. During the conference the Malaysian Minister for Education presented a new national character education award to a teacher who had made a significant contribution to the field: this award was modelled on the work of the Jubilee Centre. I was also privileged to be able to hold a private meeting with the Minister, who explained how character was central to the government's blueprint for education in the future. The YTL Foundation owns and runs the Frog online platform which has been instilled in every school in the country. The Foundation has asked the Jubilee Centre to co-create character education resources and materials that will be hosted on this platform and available to all teachers.

Our work with American academics has been extensive. We assisted in the creation of the Institute for the Study of Human Flourishing at the University of Oklahoma in 2014, and have maintained strong networks and partnerships with the scholars there. We worked with the newly established Virtue, Happiness and Meaning project at the University of Chicago under the direction of Professor Candace Vogler and we collaborated with Professor Christian Miller at Wake Forest University on his project on character. In June 2015, the Jubilee Centre held a conference on character, non-cognitive skills and K-12 education, in partnership with a leading education think tank in New York. The conference took place at Roosevelt House, New York, and brought together leading authorities from a variety of backgrounds, including research, school leadership, teaching, the voluntary sector and policy. The conference examined the theoretical basis for character education, explored its application to policy and practice, and generated a great deal of debate about the terminological and conceptual variance between fields in both the UK and US. The launch of the report by DEMOS with the Jubilee Centre, *Character Nation*, also took place as part of the conference, highlighting some key recommendations for policy makers in the UK.

In 2016, the Centre collaborated with an international research network on character education established by Bill Damon from Stanford University and Richard Lerner from Tufts University. The Jubilee Centre was the first centre approached to join, and the network aims to include five research centres with strong international presence in the field of character and virtues education. The Centre is also working with the Simon Center for Professional Military Ethics at West Point Military Academy, and we have welcomed lecturers from the Academy

to our Centre for periods of time to study, as well as our staff visiting West Point.
. Influence abroad has impacted charities such as the The Kern Family Foundation,
a multi-million US charity, which adopted part of the Jubilee Centre's *Framework
for Character Education in Schools* as its criterion for future grant awards in the area of
character education. We also partnered, at their invitation, with the National
Liberty Museum in Philadelphia in researching the character virtues of inner city
school children, and this report was launched in February 2016 with the Mayor
issuing a proclamation in recognition of the importance of the research.

Our work and collaborations in Europe have been extensive and included
lecturing visits to government departments in Poland, Lithuania, Spain, France,
Slovenia, Bulgaria, Romania, Italy, and close connections with the new Centre for
Virtue at the University of Genoa, Italy. We have received numerous delegations,
including a major charitable approach from Porticus Amsterdam, the Vogelgezang
Foundation and the Goldschmeding Foundation, to consider establishing a similar
centre in the Netherlands. The work in Europe, particularly with UNICEF in
Montenegro, is worthy of special mention. In July 2014, I gave a keynote address
at the UNICEF Quality Education for Better Schools, Results and Future
conference in Podgorica, Montenegro. The Prime Minister of Montenegro, Milo
Jukanovic, gave an introductory speech at the event and UNICEF Montenegro
Representative Benjamin Perks also spoke. The British Foreign Office and
UNICEF invited the Centre to become involved in an education project in
Montenegro. The Foreign Office paid for us to attend and even hosted an evening
drinks party at the Embassy, where we met members of the Montenegrin Parliament
including the Minister of Education.

British Ambassador to Montenegro, Mr. Ian Whitting OBE, spoke at the
Conference, saying:

> the Jubilee Centre at the University of Birmingham has brought the essence
> of 'character' to the heart of educational innovation in the UK. Putting
> pupils at the centre of the process, acknowledging that our behaviours and
> our values shape our potential and our reality; recognising that education
> should always be rooted in character and virtue – and that developing this is
> not something that happens by chance, but is something that, with the right
> efforts, inputs, and understanding, we can cultivate in our schools and in our
> communities. I feel these themes of 'innovation' and 'character' in education
> have a special relevance for Montenegro at this time.

UNICEF and the Montenegrin Ministry of Education invited the Centre to work
with teachers and psychologists in the country to develop a virtues-based education
curriculum, grounded in the work that we were undertaking in Birmingham. This
has led to a collaboration with UNICEF, the Bureau of Education and Ministry of
Education in Montenegro. Ben Perks, the Representative in Montenegro for
UNICEF, put us in contact with educationalists in the Bureau and Ministry, who
arranged for us to work with teachers and educational psychologists in primary

schools across the country. The Montenegrin team have travelled on numerous occasions to the Centre in Birmingham to receive training in character education.

Aidan Thompson visited Podgorica in June 2015 to deliver presentations at the Quality Education 'My Virtues and Values' workshop at the Bureau of Education. The two-day seminar, run in partnership between the Bureau, UNICEF Montenegro and the Jubilee Centre, brought together primary teachers in Montenegro and the project team working to develop a primary curriculum for character education in the country. Centre staff gave presentations to introduce the Centre's work, with a particular focus on how the *Framework for Character Education in Schools* was developed, as well as introducing the Programmes of Study that the Centre has created, and how a 'whole school' approach to character education can be developed. The workshops mixed the theoretical and practical approaches to developing character in the classroom, and the teachers involved in the project shared their insights into experiences, successes and challenges faced in adopting a moral focus to education. In October 2015, Aidan Thompson again presented at the UNICEF Montenegro Quality Education conference on 'Quality, Inclusion and Innovation – Foundations for the Future' in Podgorica. Over 250 delegates attended, including the Minister of Education, Predrag Bošković, who opened the conference. The British Ambassador to Montenegro, members of the Cabinet Office, UNICEF, the Ministry of Education, the Bureau of Education and teachers and directors from schools across the country were in attendance, and the occasion brought together Montenegrin education stakeholders involved in pre-school, primary and secondary education for the first time to discuss character education reforms in the country. Aidan gave a presentation on 'The Call for Character' on the role of schools in developing the character of young people.

The Montenegrin research project has led to our influence being extended to Eastern Europe. In November 2015, I presented at the UNICEF Central and Eastern Europe Regional Meeting in Geneva. The conference was for all the UNICEF representatives in 20 countries from Uzbekistan to Croatia. The focus was knowledge exchange in the area of understanding key concepts in adolescent development. The case study of character education in Montenegro was presented to delegates and many of the representatives began to think about what they could do in this area – Bulgaria was the first to begin to experiment in character education soon to be followed by Macedonia.

In March 2016, HRH The Duchess of Cornwall visited schools in Montenegro to see how they are implementing this joint UNICEF and Jubilee Centre project on character education. The project launched its *My Character and Values* research report in February 2016, and looks at the 'role of schools in developing students' character, values and skills'.

The Centre has sought to command a strong and distinctive international reputation for the quality of its work, particularly the impact of its research work and its service of character education. Kristján Kristjánsson and David Carr made major contributions to this work. The Centre places particular emphasis upon producing research of international impact and significance, welcoming researchers from across the world, enabling its staff to engage international cultures, and promoting partnership with international universities, funding bodies and other private and public organisations. International exchange of staff and expertise is a feature of our work and enhances our entrepreneurial approach.

Media and social media

From the beginning, media interest in the Centre has been intense and continues to date. On radio, from the *Sunday Programme* to the *Moral Maze*, members of the Centre have participated in interviews and documentaries. The Centre has participated in a documentary and taken part in discussions of character development in young people for BBC Radio 4's *Bringing up Britain* programme. In November 2015, the Jubilee Centre featured in the University of Birmingham Heroes campaign, which was re-run in May 2016. It included poster campaigns on the London Underground to promote the work of character education, with the strap line 'We are teaching a generation Character Matters – so our children excel in life and not just in exams.' This was the University of Birmingham's most successful campaign in terms of hits on the University website. The Centre was delighted to have been selected to feature in this prominent campaign, which was promoted on local public transport and the London Underground throughout November 2015 and May 2016. The Centre has developed a subsequent campaign which takes four quotes from Greek philosophers and challenges the public to think about them as they go about their daily business. Quotes such as 'Gratitude is not only the greatest of all virtues, but the parent of all others' (Cicero) and 'It is better to suffer injustice than to commit it' (Socrates) challenge members of the public to think about the role of character and virtue in their own lives. The campaign has been very successful, generating increased traffic to our website, accessing our resources, creating interactions and generating debates and conversations. The campaign was brought together under a 'Character Matters' title, and appeared online, at Birmingham New Street railway station, and across the London Underground for six weeks in October and November 2016. The campaign drew many positive and favourable responses, and included one from the Chartered Institute of Personnel and Development (CIPD), who asked for access to the posters to use both in their 'in-house' workshops and on their community discussion boards. It was a combination of the thought-provoking questions and the 'Character Matters' tagline that chimed with CIPD principles of 'work matters', 'people matter' and 'professionalism matters'. We have been featured in many articles in newspapers and trade magazines and interviews by journalists from the *Times Educational Supplement* to the *Guardian*. All members of the Centre have been specifically trained in media relations to support their skills in dealing with these enquiries.

Central to the flow and spread of the Centre's work has been the importance we place on social media. Social media gives a sense of immediacy and even 'freshness' to the issue. We wanted to go beyond basic Twitter and Facebook interactions so as to understand social media engagement broadly in terms of any interactions where we create, share and exchange information and ideas in virtual communities and networks. We sought to enhance participation in the Centre's work, as we saw a need to reach out to the public to inform policy ideas and enhance public awareness of the role of character and virtues in public life. By providing sound bites, catchy headlines and crafting short 'opinion pieces' for blogs, the message of the Centre was, and continues to be, promoted broadly. Interacting on social media allows us to appeal directly to the public in an effort to change the climate of opinion on ideas about promoting good character, and we have been able to channel more traffic through to our main website, create greater exposure for our research reports, and increase the number of practitioners engaging with our teaching resources. Our website is regularly updated, with new content added on an almost daily basis. Significantly, we have been able to use the website to target particular audiences – students, practitioners, policy makers, journalists and researchers – we have produced the largest portal of publications in the area. Our monthly policy and research digest newsletter is read by over 3,000 policy makers, academics and practitioners, and we regularly receive praise and feedback, with comments from subscribers that it not only provides a comprehensive digest of the field of character and virtues education, but that the richness of the content is the best in the field, both nationally and internationally.

Consultations, statements and publications

In the early stages, an embryonic form of the Centre, using the evidence from the Learning for Life project, participated in providing evidence to the Riots, Communities and Victims Panel, established by the Prime Minister in 2011. The Panel was established following widespread rioting, predominantly by young people, across the country in August 2011, resulting in over 3,000 arrests. In the aftermath, there was a feeling of moral decay in society, perhaps best summed up by the cartoonist Ingram Pinn who depicted a Union Flag being broken through by a looter in a hoodie carrying a stolen box of Adidas trainers, preceded by two men in suits carrying piles of cash, one saying 'MP's Expenses' and another 'Banker's Bonus'. Inevitably, questions were raised about what is taught in schools to young people and what kind of character building is needed. As a new research centre, we did not try to exploit the situation by declaring a moral crisis in our schools in order to advance character education as an immediate policy solution. Our aim was to frame issues in ways that appeal to broader audiences and to diverse interests, because we knew that there were no clear definitions of the issues that we could promote with confidence at that stage. The final report of the Riots, Communities and Victims Panel in 2012 recommended what it called a 'new approach' – building character. The report stated that:

> The Panel has seen strong potential in programmes delivered through schools in the UK, US and Australia which are designed to help children build resilience and self-confidence as part of normal school life. We propose that

there should be a new requirement for schools to develop and publish their policies on building character. This would raise the profile of this issue and ensure that schools engage in a review of their approaches to nurturing character attributes among their pupils. We also recommend that Ofsted undertake a thematic review of character building in schools. To inform interventions tailored to individual pupils' needs the Panel recommends primary and secondary schools should undertake regular assessments of pupils' strength of character.

The Panel accepted our arguments that character education should be at the core of education in schools, but we did not recommend that it should be assessed on a regular basis. We recognised that our expert evidence at these enquiries gives intellectual credibility to the ideas that we knew were already circulating within and outside of Parliament. The All Party Parliamentary Group on Social Mobility received evidence from the Jubilee Centre on a regular basis, and we attended all their public meetings. We have proposed the establishment of an All Party-Parliamentary Group on Character Education and both Tristram Hunt and Nicky Morgan agreed to co-chair before Hunt resigned as an MP. This APPG also ensures a level of cross-party support for character education and allows high-level discussion of our research, and the research of others in the field, among policy makers.

Our first public statement as a centre was issued in 2013 entitled *A Framework for Character Education in Schools,* after a period of consultation with teachers and members of the public. In the statement we declared that:

> flourishing is the aim of character education, which is critical to its achievement. Human flourishing requires moral, intellectual and civic virtues, excellence specific to diverse domains of practice or human endeavour, and generic virtues of self-management (known as enabling and performance virtues). All are necessary to achieve the highest potential in life. Character education is about the acquisition and strengthening of virtues: the traits that sustain a well-rounded life and a thriving society.

The statement was sent to over 5,000 schools and to politicians, policy makers and scholars, and generated a huge response, particularly from head teachers who wanted to know how they could turn the framework into a practical reality in their schools. We have since published statements on *Character Education and Teacher Education, Character Building and Youth Social Action,* and *Character, Virtue and the Professions.* It has become apparent that these statements, grounded in the research and informed by practitioners, are an excellent way to influence both policy and practice.

Another successful strategy has been the use of polling companies to undertake surveys on behalf of the Centre on topics of national interest. A ComRes poll of MPs in Westminster undertaken both before and after the 2015 General Election showed cross-party support for character development in schools and in training. This poll has helped with the creation of the APPG in character education. Researchers from the team have worked with Populus to shape the questions. For example, we asked Populus to survey parents on whether they thought schools should 'teach' character education. Key findings in the poll include:

- 87 per cent of parents felt that schools should focus on character development and academic study, not simply academic study alone.
- 84 per cent of parents felt that teachers should encourage good morals and values in students.
- 95 per cent of parents felt that it is possible to teach a child values and shape their character in a positive sense, through lessons and dedicated projects or exercises at school.
- 81 per cent of parents wanted schools to have a core statement of the values that schools instilled in their pupils.

The poll demonstrated that there was overwhelming support for character education from parents. The results of the survey were included as a story on the BBC website and staff were interviewed about the results on eight local radio programmes in a single day. A later poll on social media attracted similar attention and was featured in several online newspapers. The success of these polls was based on finding issues relating to character that the public, more broadly defined, would be interested in. Indeed, the combination of polls and statements did much to draw attention to policy issues in character education. Short statements with key messages arising from our research were tightly targeted and included a call to action. By this means, the character movement that we had helped initiate has gained greater traction by reaching wider audiences.

Collectively, academics in the Centre have published over 200 books, articles and scholarly papers since 2012. These have included publications intended for policy makers, practitioners, and students in the form of popular textbooks. In addition to more 'traditional' academic outputs in journals, they have included specialist academic texts and edited collections, together with conference proceedings and policy statements. Professor Kristjansson was appointed editor of the prestigious *Journal of Moral Education* in 2017. We have produced short research policy briefs that have allowed us to communicate the results of our research in the form of easy-to-understand, concise and persuasive recommendations. This has been an effective way to engage the interest of policy makers. We have succeeded in capturing a policy maker's interest in this way, which also increases the chances that our findings will enter policy agendas and debates – the first policy brief was sent to the Secretary of State, Michael Gove, in 2012, summarising the international research findings on the link between character and attainment.

The Centre has always attempted to address education audiences consistently and regularly – namely speaking directly to teachers. We wanted to present the same idea about character to multiple audiences across the country, and, to this end, we developed a bank of slides for presentation purposes. Each member of staff in the Centre has access to pre-prepared materials that present a consistent message on what the Centre teaches about character. This has ensured consistent communication and each member of staff has received bespoke training in both media interactions and more broadly on public speaking. We understand that giving presentations is a way of communicating ideas and information to different groups and that they allow immediate interaction between all the participants. We have sought to ensure that our presentations to the public contained information that people needed, that can be understood, and is easy to take away and apply. A good live presentation will be remembered much more vividly than a good report.

Conferences and political networks

We have engaged in a great range of conferences to promote character building in British society. A number of illustrative examples are worth mentioning. Sir Anthony Seldon gave the Priestley Lecture in the School of Education at Birmingham in 2013 on 'Why the Development of Good Character Matters More Than the Passing of Exams'. He echoed what the Centre has been advocating when he said that 'exam success is a necessary but not a sufficient condition for being an educated human being. This is because human beings are not machines but flesh and blood, with capacious minds, with bodies, with emotions, and with a soul.' In December 2014, the Jubilee Centre hosted a joint conference on character with DEMOS, Britain's leading cross-party think tank. The conference, titled 'The Character Conference', was held at the Institute of Directors in London. The conference explored different aspects of character and society and opened with a keynote speech from Tristram Hunt MP on the 'character gap' and the need for more emphasis on character throughout the education system. The Centre's Director of Education, Dr. Tom Harrison, presented at the 'Future Prepared: Building Character by Doing in Schools' event organised by the Scouts in February 2016. This event, held at the Institute of Education in London, formed a debate about how the Scouts and other voluntary sector organisations can enhance schools' character education provision. The debate was shaped and informed by the Jubilee Centre's *Framework for Character Education in Schools* and individuals were invited to speak about either moral, civic, performance or intellectual virtues. While these examples specifically illustrate the policy interactions of the Centre, we have held a large number of other seminars, workshops and conferences around the country for different audiences.

Contact with politicians has been a feature of our dissemination and influence strategies from the start, with the objective of garnering support in the pursuit of policy change in character education. Writing to local MPs and councillors to make them aware of our research projects was the beginning of political networking, always on a non-partisan basis. As Head of the School of Education, I was able to invite a series of politicians, from all the main parties, to deliver the annual Priestley Lecture, which is the University's most prestigious invited lecture in education. The series began with the Rt. Hon. Liam Byrne MP, who had worked closely with us in Learning for Life, and continued his support of the Jubilee Centre. He was followed by Lord Watson of Richmond, who chaired our Advisory Board, and then the former Secretary of State for Education, Baroness Morris of Yardley. None was invited to speak specifically about character education, but all did so in positive terms, praising the efforts of the Jubilee Centre and the contribution it was making to public life in promoting character and virtue. Lord Blunkett, another former Secretary of State for Education, also gave the Priestley Lecture and spoke warmly about character education. We had invited Michael Gove, then Secretary of State for Education, to deliver the Priestley Lecture and had also kept him informed of our work. He was focused on raising numeracy and literacy levels in schools and did not make character education a priority during his tenure, even though he had endorsed our *Of Good Character* text in September 2010 and approved our new school at the University of Birmingham dedicated to character education.

The Labour opposition, in contrast, did speak explicitly about character education and the Shadow Secretary of State for Education, Tristram Hunt, made numerous references to it, keeping the idea alive in the political realm. However, Michael Gove did not completely ignore character education, and towards the end of his period as Secretary of State for Education began to make frequent references to why schools ought to promote 'character virtues' – significantly, he used the language of the research briefs we had sent to him. He subsequently accepted an invitation to give the Priestley Lecture in 2014, but was moved to the Ministry of Justice in a Cabinet reshuffle shortly before the date of the lecture. In 2016, Michael Gove spoke, along with Nicky Morgan, Tristram Hunt and Estelle Morris, at the Character Matters II event at the University of Birmingham. During this event, Michael Gove admitted he had not taken character education seriously enough when he was Secretary of State and applauded Nicky Morgan's promotion of it while in office. Gove, along with the other speakers at the event, spoke warmly about how character education could and should be both taught and caught.

His successor was Nicky Morgan, whom we immediately invited to give the lecture in Michael Gove's place. She accepted and gave the lecture in November 2014, in which she said that much of her work on building the character of young people:

> was inspired by the Jubilee Centre at Birmingham University and its innovative research on character education and its work with schools to build best practice in this area. Organisations like the Jubilee Centre have been pioneering in recognising that character can be taught ... like the Jubilee Centre we passionately believe that we owe it to today's young people to help them marry the highest standards of academic rigour with the character foundation needed to help them flourish.

This was a major change of emphasis in education policy by the government and Nicky Morgan subsequently invited me to her office for a roundtable discussion on character, at which she employed the definition of character education from the Jubilee Centre:

> Character is a set of personal traits that produce specific moral emotions, inform motivation and guide conduct. Character education is an umbrella term for all explicit and implicit educational activities that help young people develop positive personal strengths called virtues. Policy entrepreneurs know that changes in the political climate and in personnel can result in new groups forming, new arguments being made and even dramatic turns in policy design.

The Minister for Civic Society visited the Jubilee Centre to see our work for himself. In addition, the Secretary of State for Education made character building in schools one of the five major aims of the Department for Education. A reference group on character education was established by the DfE, which I was invited to join, together with Ed Timpson, a Minister of Education, being given specific responsibilities for character education. A national character award was announced so that schools could submit an outline of what they were doing to build the character of their pupils, and I was asked to become a judge both in 2015 and 2016. I was invited by the Minister of Education to read out the winners when they were presented as part of the 2016 Association of Character Education inaugural conference. A unit for character education was created in the DfE, and civil servants began to explore how the government could promote it in schools. Character education also featured strongly in the government White Paper entitled *Education Excellence Everywhere,* published in March 2016. The executive summary stated that 'education should prepare children for adult life, giving them the skills and character traits needed to succeed academically, have a fulfilling career, and make a positive contribution to British society' (DfE, 2016: 20). Character education had become mainstream, with change coming from different directions and other policy entrepreneurs. We recognised from the outset that there were other important actors and players in the field who would assist with our attempt to demonstrate the merit of developing and delivering character education in schools.

My advice to Nicky Morgan was to make sure that character education did not appear as a top-down policy, nor to detail what should be included within a character education programme. Rather, I suggested that it should be bottom-up, with schools and teachers being encouraged to develop their own approach to character education, with best practice being shared and highlighted by the DfE among schools. I believe that while top-down pressures contribute to change, there is also an important role for bottom-up pressures, initiatives and issues. This is exactly the policy that has been followed by the government. At the same time, we in the Jubilee Centre were anxious to cooperate with the Opposition, and we invited the then Shadow Secretary of State for Education, Tristram Hunt, to visit the Jubilee Centre. Mr. Hunt spent a full day with our team in Birmingham, learning that we had introduced character education as part of the teacher education courses run at the University, and he decided to make this a specific pledge in the Labour manifesto of 2015. In fact, both the Conservative and Labour manifestos of 2015 made reference to building the character of young people in schools. Character education had made it onto the political agenda of both the Conservative and Labour parties. Since the election of 2015, we have continued to brief local MPs and national spokespersons on education for most political parties. For example, we briefed the MP for Edgbaston, Gisela Stuart, on our work and she asked Nicky Morgan a question in the House of Commons during Education Questions. She asked the Secretary of State about how we could bring character education into every level of schooling. The Secretary of State answered that she had met me and thought the Jubilee Centre was doing 'fantastic work' and that our Centre would be part of her plans to build character approaches in every school.

In December 2015, the Secretary of State for Education, Nicky Morgan MP, gave evidence to the Social Mobility Select Committee in the House of Lords and cited the work of the Jubilee Centre. Speaking in response to Baroness Claire Tyler asking about the need for character development in schools, Ms. Morgan cited the Centre working with the University of Birmingham School to 'embed character education into the curriculum'. Ms. Morgan also cited the 'moral virtues' that the Centre focuses on. We have met with the Shadow Secretary of State for Education, Lucy Powell, who fully supports a character education approach in schools, as does John Pugh MP, the Liberal Democrat education spokesperson. By this means we have attempted to encourage what Mintrom *et al.* (2014: 428) calls 'the norm-shaping nature of discourse within coalitions over a sustained period generates ideas for policy change and aligns political forces needed to achieve that change'. We have defined and refined our messages about the importance of character education with each politician that we have met. We have also had to learn to understand the information needs of policy makers. This was especially important in submitting evidence to the Education Select Committee in 2016 when it was considering personal and social education in schools.

We commissioned a study of 150 Members of Parliament undertaken by ComRes on behalf of the Jubilee Centre to assess the views of MPs about character and virtue education in schools, and within the world of work, to establish a baseline for future research. The survey results show a broad and firm support across all three major political parties for character education, with two-thirds of the MPs surveyed agreeing that character education should be taught in schools and 80 per cent of the MPs surveyed agreeing that developing a sense of moral values is as important for school children as good GCSE and A-level results, with 30 per cent indicating that they strongly agree, and 65 per cent agreeing that character education should be taught in schools, with 24 per cent strongly agreeing. The MPs were more divided on whether young people are leaving school without a strong enough sense of moral values, with half of the MPs (51 per cent) agreeing and more than a third of the MPs (37 per cent) disagreeing. In response to other questions, six out of ten of the MPs agree that it is important that school teachers (61 per cent) and those working in the medical (59 per cent) and legal (56 per cent) professions have had training in character education. Around a quarter disagreed with the statement.

Professor Kristján Kristjánsson and I attended the Positive Education Summit at 10 Downing Street on 2 October 2013. The Jubilee Centre was a sponsor of the event, with 30 of the world's leaders in education, academia and psychology lending their expertise and opinions to the discussion. The roundtable was organised and chaired by James O'Shaughnessy (now Lord O'Shaughnessy) and the Summit programme was organised by Professor Martin Seligman, Director of the Positive Psychology Center at the University of Pennsylvania. This was an opportunity to speak with different government departments – this cross-cutting approach to policy entrepreneurship allowed us to speak with senior civil servants from the Cabinet Office and the Health Department. Kristjan and I later joined the Steering Group of the International Positive Education Network, which organised its first major international conference in Atlanta in 2016.

The Jubilee Centre co-hosted an event at the Labour Party Conference with leading UK policy think tank DEMOS in September 2015. The event, which promoted the DEMOS and Jubilee Centre *Character Nation* report, provided an opportunity for delegates to engage with the debate on character education. I joined the Secretary of State for Education, Nicky Morgan MP, on a discussion panel in October 2015 during a fringe event at the Conservative Party Conference. The event was also co-hosted by the Jubilee Centre and DEMOS and aimed to address the question 'How can Britain become a leader in character education?', with a particular focus on the *Character Nation* report. We were joined by Lucy Frazer MP, Lord Chris Holmes, and Ralph Scott (Head of Citizenship and Political Participation at DEMOS). The panel discussed the importance of character education, how it is both caught and taught, the barriers faced by both teachers and schools in delivering character education and how these might be overcome. Nicky Morgan MP emphasised the role of a clear school ethos, one that runs throughout the curriculum, in providing the foundation for character education. Following contributions by each panel member, members of the audience engaged in the debate with questions posed to the panel about the role of parents in character education, the contribution youth social action can make to character education and the issue of measurement for determining the success of any character education initiatives. We again attended the Labour and Conservative Party Conferences in 2016.

I attended a second roundtable at the DfE in December 2015, this time with Ed Timpson, the Minister of State for Children and Families. The meeting brought together key individuals and officials in the field of character education to discuss initiatives planned by the Department in this area. The roundtable was held ahead of a Character Symposium that the DfE hosted in London in January 2016, at which the Secretary of State for Education outlined new government initiatives on character education and resilience.

With the change of Prime Minister and Secretary of State for Education in July 2016, we had to reassess our political contacts. I had positive contacts with No. 10 Downing Street through the new Chief of Staff, Nick Timothy and new education advisor to the Prime Minister Mike Crowhurst. We attended the Conservative Party Conference in October 2016 in Birmingham, and spoke with government Ministers at a DEMOS panel meeting at which we once again promoted the work of the Centre. Following the change of PM, other relevant Ministers of Education, Ed Timpson and Lord Nash, remained in post and have continued to support character education. On 20 March 2017 I was able to meet with the new Prime Minister at a reception in 10 Downing Street and briefly discuss the importance of character education.

Our centre has not conducted research for the government, so our research questions have not come from policy makers. We have been free to set our own research questions and objectives. Our independence from government, and from all other political groups, has been important in establishing the credibility of our research. Our membership of the University of Birmingham, within the School of Education, College of Social Sciences, has allowed us important flexibility and the ability to increase capacity when needed. The continuity and consistency of our research staff has also contributed to the quality and quantity of research; it allowed us to mix 'have to do' projects with 'want to do' work to sustain the interest of research staff.

Civil servants have the potential to facilitate or hinder policy ideas coming from the academy. Since the Centre has sought to foster research utilisation within a policy context, we have needed to build trust with civil servants, while recognising that we often use a different language. The ability of civil servants to use research evidence often depends on their level of scientific literacy and expertise, but they first have to recognise the value of the research itself. This is something we were keen to address. There have been times when we have had to guide civil servants through our research, while on other occasions they simply did not see the relevance of the research, nor its findings. Civil servants appear to be concerned about managing risk for Ministers, which can mean that while the Minister is seeking innovative and perhaps even risky options in policy, the civil servants act as a kind of counter balance and are more concerned about what they see as the realities of delivering the policy – in developing policies that will work in practice. They can also make their own political judgements on the relative acceptability of the approach. Their influence on how a policy is shaped cannot be underestimated. Their influence will depend on how often a Minister is changed, the Minister's knowledge of a particular subject, the Minister's instructions to civil servants, and how much this allows for collaboration with the civil servant. The term policy maker includes both politicians and civil servants who have decision-making roles at various levels of government. Our experience has been to engage with both civil servants and politicians, refining our messages for each camp when engaging in dissemination activities. The stronger the relationship with the politician or civil servant, the greater the likelihood of creating impact on policy.

Convincing arguments and relevant research findings are not sufficient to change policy, so active policy entrepreneurship is crucial, which involves cultivating relationships with civil servants. The civil servants that we met and worked with have been policy officials, not those who perform operational roles. At ministerial meetings that we attended, these policy civil servants were always present and had already briefed Ministers before our arrival. Hence, it was essential to ensure there was an open communication between the civil servants and members of the Centre. We have tried to be entrepreneurial in our approach to keeping this particular line of communication open. Civil servants from the Character Unit visited the Centre and another from the Character Unit actually spent time within the Centre on sabbatical and another civil servant from the Ministry of Education in Singapore has also spent time in the Centre. We are conscious that problem definition is not restricted to the start of the policy process; it is possible that some parts are left to civil servants during policy formulation. We have worked hard to cultivate all of our links with politicians and civil servants, both in and out of government, and of all political persuasions. We were delighted when the new Chief of Staff at No. 10 Downing Street wrote in July 2016 to say that No. 10 was supportive of the work of the Jubilee Centre. We have put many hours and a great deal of effort into developing links within policy circles, and it is pleasing and humbling to receive such commendation.

Association of Character Education

In 2015, the Jubilee Centre established a national Association of Character Education (ACE), which held its first meeting in the Jubilee Centre in 2015. The founding executive members included head teachers nationally recognised for their work on character education – including Sir Iain Hall, Gary Lewis and Michael Roden. The purpose of ACE is to build and strengthen the grassroots support for character education. Within six months, ACE had over 100 subscribing members (mainly schools and voluntary sector organisations), and had organised a 'sold out' conference. This helped convince policy makers that there was genuine grassroots interest in character education, as well as providing the DfE with an audience for some of their initiatives – including the awards, grant scheme and an online networking platform.

The constitution of ACE followed the *Framework for Character Education in Schools* outlined by the Jubilee Centre, and included the following statement:

> Character is a set of personal traits that produce specific emotions, inform motivation and guide conduct. Character education is an umbrella term for all explicit and implicit educational activities that help young people develop positive personal strengths called virtues. Character education is more than just a subject. It has a place in the culture and functions of families, classrooms, schools and other institutions. Character education is about helping students grasp what is ethically important in situations and how to act for the right

reasons, so that they become more autonomous and reflective. Students need to decide the kind of person they wish to become and to learn to choose between alternatives. In this process, the ultimate aim of character education is the development of good sense or practical wisdom: the capacity to choose intelligently between alternatives.

ACE held its inaugural conference at the University of Birmingham School in July 2016, with the Minister of Education responsible for character education present to deliver a speech and announce the winners of the National Character Awards. ACE continues to grow, and is planning a kite mark for schools of character (it is also considering an international award), and it is significant that the judges of the national character awards have always included representation from the Jubilee Centre.

Teaching and learning resources

The growing interest by policy makers in character education has been matched by a growing demand from schools and teachers for high-quality character education resources and materials. The success of the Knightly Virtues programme had provided confidence that the Centre was capable of developing high-quality resources that would be attractive to teachers. The Jubilee Centre has always been keen to respond to the demand, but was always at pains to stress that there is no blueprint for character education, so that teaching and learning materials should be adapted to suit the individual contexts and needs of the schools that use them. Curriculum materials of note include Programmes of Study for primary and secondary schools that are built around a distinctly neo-Aristotelian philosophical foundation. They also encompass many of the whole-school concerns including PSHE, citizenship, employability and behaviour. We have distributed well over 100 hard copies of the Programmes of Study to teachers in schools, with many more accessing the resources electronically on our website. We have also produced a *Handbook for Character Development Evaluation*, including a framework for schools to self-evaluate their character education provision, both taught and caught. An early effort was our *Schools of Character* publication, which showcases seven schools, both private and state, that make character education a conscious part of their everyday practice through a variety of approaches. The case studies presented were designed to highlight the most pertinent features of character education in each of the schools, aiming to provide both inspiration and examples for other schools.

The DfE funded a project run by the Jubilee Centre on teaching character through subjects at the secondary level. This project created new, innovative teaching resources to develop key character virtues in students through and within 14 specialist school subjects. The project was launched at the ACE inaugural conference in June 2016. The Centre also developed a primary version of the materials, with a particular focus on primary to secondary transition. Both the primary and secondary resources have been produced by teachers, for teachers, ensuring greater interest and interaction with the project from teachers. We have since secured a second grant from the DfE, as the Jubilee Centre, but intended for ACE to develop more curriculum materials for character education.

The Centre has also sought to reach out and engage with new audiences through several high-profile awards programmes. These included the Thank You Letter and Film Awards, in which, to date, nearly 100,000 children and young people have participated. These awards invite young people to think about how they experience the virtue of gratitude in their everyday lives. We have held award ceremonies for the winners in cinemas and other venues across Britain. In addition, we have initiated public sector awards to recognise those that undertake meaningful and beneficial service to others and a very popular youth service award held annually at the House of Lords. In partnership with Step Up To Serve, we have also selected and recognised 150 Social Action Ambassadors – 10 to 20 year olds from across Britain who have undertaken meaningful action in the service of others. The ambassadors have featured in publications which include forewords by HRH The Prince of Wales and Sir Nick Parker. We have also brought our message to the community, hosting and participating in many community-based activities, including the celebration of World Gratitude Day in September 2014, with an event in Birmingham city centre where members of the public were encouraged to write notes to the people that they were grateful to on large blackboards and posters, which drew the attention of local media.

Education and training in the professions

The Centre has a broader remit than research and development work in schools – it also works extensively in the training of professions (Arthur *et al.*, 2014 a-c, 2015 a-e, 2016). Research projects looking at the training and practice of teachers, business people, doctors, nurses, lawyers and army officers have been published, with a cross-sectional approach looking at junior trainees, those graduating university, and those with five to ten years of professional practice. The role of virtue in each profession has been explored, with comparisons in each cohort between the virtues each participant believes that the ideal professional requires with the virtues each participant believes that they demonstrate themselves. Similar projects with social workers, the police and journalists are planned for future phases. In doing this, we have worked with many professional associations including The Law Society, The Bar Council, The General Medical Council, teaching unions, and the Ministry of Defence, who gave us approval to examine the ethical character and virtues of army officers at various stages of their training.

The Centre understood that professionalism entails understanding that one has responsibilities to society at large, not simply to one's own profession, employer or family. The honourable undertaking of these wide responsibilities places fundamental demands on a person's character. The service required by society of a professional does not merely mean the successful completion of a training programme equipping them with the minimum skills for membership of a particular profession. While such a qualification is a necessary condition for entry into a profession, it is not sufficient for the proper exercise of professional responsibilities. For example, scientific knowledge in the case of a medical practitioner, legal competence for a lawyer, and scrupulous attention to financial practice in compliance with the law for the banker, are not enough. A professional is involved in service to the wider community extending beyond the profession, beyond the client and beyond his own personal interests; professional practice demands attention to the virtues – truth, justice, courage, generosity, etc. Every good practitioner becomes aware of this as his own experience develops and of the potential conflict between public service and the limited demands of professional standards of compliance. Such constructive engagement will bring forth not just a closer and re-affirmed tie to the moral calling of one's profession, but also a stronger inner moral character – in both adversity and opportunity. It raises questions such as: What sort of a person am I? What sort of parent, sibling, son, daughter, or colleague am I? What are my core values? What are the virtues I wish to embody in my practice as a professional and beyond?

We wanted to ask some fundamental questions during the research, including: What are the traditions in which a profession believes itself to stand? Do professionals recognise their role in building trust and affirming the essential contribution of personal relationships to society's well-being? What do members of a profession themselves feel grateful for? For what do members of various different professions believe that their clients should be grateful to them? Are some professions more likely to develop a sense of gratitude among their members than others? If so, which professions and why? Are some professions more likely to receive expressions of gratitude than others? What difference would it make to society or to the professions if they were, in fact, non-existent or were only functionaries? What form of evaluation could be devised within each profession to enable members of that profession to be judged for their character and their recognition of the importance of their personal responsibility to society? These questions need to be asked of key professions that both shape and serve British society with integrity.

There is considerable evidence that compliance with the 'letter' of professional rules predominates over service in much if not all contemporary professional practice. Our starting hypothesis was that training programmes and early guided experiences of professional practice will be greatly enhanced by giving more attention to the character dimensions and demands of professional practice. This cannot simply be subsumed within, for example, traditional 'medical ethics', 'business ethics', or in the relationship between the law and morality – important as these may be. They do not in themselves address the personal life of practitioners, nor their need to grow in character if they are to accept full responsibility for their actions and judgements as servants of their professional society and society as a whole. Moreover, as the professional's experience expands, so the demands on their character will grow, not the least in their family and personal life. The research projects investigated the extent to which the recruitment, training and continuing education and practice in professional life also need to take account of the crucial aspect of personal and public character in the professions. In the light of these investigations, we have proposed ways in which attention can be focused on a higher standard of virtue – not simply in one's personal life, but in professional practice and a commitment to the overall reputation of the professions. To the extent that this can be achieved, professional service will be enhanced, as will the developing quality of public life.

We assembled and critiqued ethical statements regarding professional practice together with the mission statements of the respective societies, associations and institutes. We investigated the processes by which professional practice standards were put together and the thinking behind their publication. We conducted an examination of recruitment patterns into the professions – application form, interview practice, etc., in order to discover the ways in which personal qualities, virtues and attitudes are (or are not) taken into account. We reviewed the training/ education (including continuing education) programmes leading to qualification and professional membership. It was particularly important to review the role of universities, alongside the criteria of professional membership. We set out to discover whether, when, to what extent and for what purpose attention is directed towards the fundamental values/virtues/attitudes that can be drawn from practice as opposed to exclusive focus on practical short-term outcomes. The investigations included questionnaires involving persons: a) in training, b) after three years, and c) after five to ten years of practice. In most cases, there were follow-up in-depth interviews. The outcomes included published reports, conferences and seminars, and the development of materials to enhance professional practice.

We have also been invited by a number of organisations, schools and professions to conduct research into their ethical standards. In 2013, the Jubilee Centre was invited by the Psychology Unit in the British Army to conduct a study to investigate the extent to which regular junior officers display and aspire to attitudes and personal characteristics in line with those set out in the Army Values and Standards Guide, both as the officers see it and in terms of their moral reasoning in response to moral dilemmas. This was part of the Jubilee Centre's study of the professions to research the ideal of serving the common or public good in contemporary British society and in professional life. A secondary aim was to investigate a much broader range of character strengths among the officers, and to canvas their views and experiences of Army Values and Standards among their leaders and their soldiers. The preparation of soldiers to face ethically challenging situations in a variety of settings (operational and non-operational) is vital. The study by the Jubilee Centre is intended to provide the Army with empirical data that it may incorporate into its planning of and training for future operations, which may enable soldiers to handle ethically challenging situations appropriately. Although we were invited to conduct this research, we were still required to submit a proposal through the normal Ministry of Defence procedures for research, and the project was eventually approved in early 2016.

Our aim was not to simply study the professions but, where possible, to undertake activities that would help educate and transform them. This has led the staff at the centre to develop a number of training programmes. These include a Massive Open Online Course (MOOC) called 'What is Character?: Virtue Ethics in Education'. To date, over 20,000 individuals from around the world have registered for the MOOC, and it has become a platform for practitioners to learn about and debate issues related to character education. The Centre has also developed and trialled, with universities across Britain, a series of online courses for teachers, doctors and lawyers focusing on the virtuous professional. We hope that these courses will become integrated within the teaching of each of these three professions, both at university and beyond into professional training. Finally, in September 2016 the Centre launched the world's first MA in Character Education, a distance learning, Masters-level course with students from around the world signing up. All of these teaching and training programmes have included the production of professional films showcasing the work of the Jubilee Centre and attracting new audiences to our research. The Centre has made films one of our key outputs, not only as teaching resources but also as documentaries for scholars and the general public so they can come to understand more about our work and our approach to researching character and virtue.

Our intention was always to approach the teaching unions to share our ideas, as we were initially uncertain of their support for character education in schools. So we were surprised when they approached us first. Both the National Association of Schoolmasters Union of Women Teachers (NASUWT) and the National Association of Head Teachers (NAHT) made early contact with us. We considered these some of the most important people we could engage with because they had the potential to oppose our ideas. Hence, it was natural for us to want to find out what they were thinking and what their arguments against character education might be. The unions were very interested in our arguments and we held numerous early meetings with them and kept them informed at every stage. We found no explicit opposition to our research and they were in fact supportive, if cautious. This general support was demonstrated when we were invited to write articles for their members in their house journals as well as attend seminars to talk about character education.

Conclusion

As a university-based, free-standing research and development centre with a focus primarily on conducting research, we have sought to translate and disseminate our research findings to policy makers and practitioners. Having solid research behind your advocacy both establishes your credibility and gives you substantive reasons for advocating your key messages. It helps to counter opposition arguments, and to address concerns and emotion-driven objections. Furthermore, it reassures that you know what you're talking about. The Centre has received enquiries for advice and guidance from around the world. Within a short space of time the Centre had established itself as a leading research resource, and has increasingly become a source of both solutions and answers for teachers and professionals. We have emphasised the importance of evidence that speaks to practitioners' own circumstances and we have attempted to resolve issues for head teachers, teachers and professionals by clarifying what character is and how it could be introduced to schools. We have effectively become the 'go-to' centre, with thousands of enquires each year and, as a result, many international visits to the Centre. Nevertheless, rather than expecting key audiences to come to us, we have continually pushed information out to them, through the traditional and more modern channels. As a result, we have been able to reach more audiences, and they in turn can share our content through their own networks.

We might claim that the Jubilee Centre has developed a range of communications to various audiences to meet their user needs. Our goal was to engage practitioners and policy makers – a goal which remains – and we can claim a good measure of success. We are aware that it takes time for contacts to develop, for take-up of ideas to occur and for diffusion to take place. We have enjoyed a great deal of support and good fortune and have benefited from our strong alliances and strategic partnerships. That said, we have put in a great deal of hard work and strategic thought into developing both our key messages and our strategic dissemination plans and partnerships. We had to ask ourselves whether we were engaging in policy entrepreneurship for our own personal benefit or for the benefit of others. Did we have a notion of the good that we were trying to realise? As a centre, we sought to become a leader in the field, one who is seen to put good ends ahead of ambitions for power or influence. In order to create a sense of momentum for the Centre, we began by setting out what we hoped to achieve, by identifying specific aims and goals, creating key milestones against which to judge our development, and building personal and professional credibility through our work. The Centre was, and remains, focused, disciplined and innovative and has had a sense of mission from the start. We developed a compelling vision, which we have argued for, and a solid, focused strategy.

We had the benefit of resources and a long time frame in which to operate, but we have been flexible, as well as persistent, in our advocacy. We established powerful alliances and partnerships at local, national and international levels, and used these connections to give us credibility and authority. We have straddled working with practitioners, politicians, civil servants, charity workers and many others – we effectively work both inside and outside the policy process. We have not worked in isolation, but engaged the public, particularly parents, with communication and engagement strategies. We continue to enjoy broad political support, but that has come about through our hard work and targeted dissemination. We have established a breadth of involvement from other academics by focusing on academic publications and conferences. By these means we have developed wider ownership of the ideas we promote, while keeping close to the reality on the ground.

In terms of capacity building in those we have sought to influence, we run workshops, training events and professional development sessions all over the country, attracting thousands of teachers and other stakeholders to develop their knowledge and skills. This growing network of teachers and organisations has helped further the progress of our work. We realised quite early on that there was an appetite and demand for our efforts to promote character education across a range of subjects and areas. Our intention for this research project has been to turn the focus away from producing narrow studies, read only by other specialists. We adopted an alternative approach, use-inspired research, which has sought both to discover new knowledge and to enable society to put that knowledge to use. Our enquiry has been grounded in a genuine desire to improve people's lives. The term 'use-inspired research' aims to close the gap between pure basic research and applied research. It is not always possible to draw a clear line between research projects where a central aim is to increase knowledge and those aimed at application in society.

The policy impact of research is sometimes constrained by political factors, such as censorship, political disinterest, an intolerant political culture or a lack of public support for education and research. Not all of our academic researchers were working in policy-relevant areas, but we have created an ethos and mentality among them that considers the potential impact of each project within the broader context of the mission of the Centre. Our political networks have sometimes been cultivated and maintained in an *ad hoc* and on-going way, but we always learn from our experiences – what works and what doesn't – and participate as much as possible in a range of activities, such as roundtable discussions, one-to-one discussions, and memberships of panels, groups and committees. Influence outside the policy arena, and within general British culture, can also be documented through unexpected examples from writers on education. These include Tony Little, the former head master of Eton College, who highlighted the work of our Centre in his *An Intelligent Person's Guide to Education* (2015), and Janice Kaplan, a major US magazine editor, praising the Centre's work in her *The Gratitude Diaries* (2015). Liam Byrne MP has also used the research from the Centre in his book *Black Flag Down* (2016). The Legatum Institute in London has created a Centre for Character and Values with similar aims to the Jubilee Centre. We work very closely with this new centre, and it offers a further, and more current, example of the continuing impact of the Jubilee Centre. Our influence and impact as a centre will be sustained in the years to come. We hope that this continues to promote our key messages around the importance and benefit of character and virtues, not just in schooling, but across British society, and indeed internationally, for the benefit of human flourishing.

CONCLUSION

The political opinion and the behaviour of intellectuals are seldom to be taken
seriously.

W. H. Auden

In an age when more and more policy-relevant research is becoming available, the
Jubilee Centre set out to place the best evidence available at the heart of policy
development in character and virtues education, both in schooling and in the
professions. As Ozga (2004: 1) says, research is being steered towards problem-
solving and knowledge about 'what works', but she, like us, rejects the instrumental
or technical route of how research evidence informs policy. You cannot simply
side-step the normative goals and value conflicts associated with policy change, as
politics and ideology remain strong drivers of public policy decisions. The social
scientist generally prefers to focus on description and explanation and ignore
important values. Values are seen as subjective with little in the way of a rational
basis, which leads them to ignore normative questions such as what should be
done for the best, what is good or bad and how should we act in different
situations. These questions are at the heart of policy making and ought not to be
ignored in research.

We were conscious that policy in the area of character education is the result of
the cumulative impact of different initiatives around the country and that this
impact would take time to appear on the ground. This is why it is always difficult
to generate projects for impact and influence that are both measurable and
attributable. Assessing the impact that our research evidence has had on policy is a
complex and messy process because policy itself is often experimental, with
overlapping and competing agendas where fact and values are intertwined. Policy
is a political and not a purely technical process, so research evidence helps

understand the issues at hand. Policy making involves many facets and numerous actors, where some actions and decisions are observable and others hidden. Moreover, as an academic policy entrepreneur I was essentially a champion of an idea, had a degree of expertise, strong resources and a leadership role within an important university. I was well placed to advocate for character education over time and had certain skills to frame this idea. I recognised that the process of changing policy involved thousands of people – all actors who make choices in a democracy.

We were clear about why character education needs to be developed in the UK and consistently articulated our view. Our policy entrepreneurship helped leverage the intellectual, political and organisational resources of the Centre to generate our favoured policy outcome (see King and Roberts, 1992). We have discussed why successful policy entrepreneurs need to be good storytellers and how researchers who are good networkers are likely to have more policy influence than those who are not. We also worked to ensure that we became practically involved in testing our ideas before we could expect policy makers to heed our recommendations. So, while I acknowledge that it is difficult to demonstrate a causal link between our research and the real-world outcomes of policy, we can modestly claim a degree of success for the work of the Centre, as the following paragraphs explain.

Character education was increasingly seen to be responding to a perceived issue in education which involved the lack of a holistic approach to personal development in schools. The Centre's work included my first major text on character education published prior to the Centre's establishment, but became a pillar of the Centre's philosophy and approach (Arthur, 2003). Some of our written evidence for promoting character was accepted by the Riots Panel. Over 200 academic publications by Centre members on character promoted and helped to transform the view of character education in academe and in the public mind. Our research knowledge was used to 'back-up' a policy position, not necessarily instigate a policy idea. We provided detailed information, data, ideas and a degree of advocacy, and these new perspectives on character virtues were created and framed within a receptive policy environment for character education. We partnered with a strong constituency of support, both inside and outside government, advocating for character education on a united front. The work of Rt. Hon. Liam Byrne MP, Sir Anthony Seldon, Lord James O'Shaughnessy, Dame Julia Cleverdon, Step Up To Serve and many other youth charities helped to frame the issue of character in a manner that led to it gaining wider support in UK society.

We demonstrated our own credibility and status as advocates of character education with policy makers and practitioners through our commitment, knowledge and trustworthiness. The Centre established a reputation for being trusted as academics, and we used data, research and arguments to advance the idea of character development. We provided solutions, not problems, and helped create wins for schools in teaching character through our teaching and education statements, curriculum offers and pilot programmes. We built on existing policies and used political entry points through our understanding and experience of SEAL and

Citizenship programmes. We helped place character virtue issues on political agendas before elections and at party conferences as the concrete examples of the Labour manifesto on training teachers on character education testifies. We participated in numerous roundtable talks with the Secretary of State and Ministers as well as shadow Ministers. The Centre is a beacon for enthusiasm and commitment in the area of character education. We used every media form and we demonstrated that character education policy for schools was reliable – safe and efficient; valuable – it would change lives; acceptable – to the public; affordable – would cost little; feasible – it could be implemented; and accountable – responsible (Catford, 2006: 3).

Trying to change the terms of political debate on values and character education supposes that there are people and organisations that are open to new ways of thinking and are in a position to make a difference. I had a good relationship and knew personally three significant education Ministers in government: Lord Nash, Edward Timpson and Nicky Morgan and the various shadow secretaries of state. But there is no memory in government as Ministers and shadow Ministers generally have short tenures in office. Persistence on the part of those who advocate is all. One of the most significant meetings I ever had was at St. James' Palace to meet Dame Julia Cleverdon, a policy entrepreneur par excellence. She was setting up the Step Up To Serve charity at the time and we discussed for the first time the double benefit of service which included character building. This led to me becoming a member of the Step Up To Serve Advisory Council chaired by the Prince of Wales together with membership of the education sub-group. So from the outset, we engaged intelligently with the substance of the policy innovation of character education renewed under New Labour in the late 1990s and becoming more explicit in policy terms from 2014 onwards under the Coalition and subsequent Conservative governments.

The Jubilee Centre had an explicit intention to report our research results so as to inform policy decisions and improve practice on the ground. We formed relationships with policy makers that endured over a number of years and we tested our ideas with practitioners. We employed people in the Centre who had credibility in both the research and policy-making communities and were, thus, able to bridge the two. Taylor (2005: 748–750), former director of the Institute for Public Policy Research (IPPR), uses various examples, successes and failures from the UK to introduce five really helpful rules for successful policy entrepreneurship by researchers. In summary, they are: first, win the argument about what the problem is before trying to win the argument about what the solution is. Second, understand the vital importance of political context and look for political opportunities or, as Taylor puts it, always emphasise 'the need to frame research in relation to what might be called the political *zeitgeist* – in other words ... those issues that are at the front of people's minds'. Third, balance persistence and opportunism. Fourth, focus on application and implementation. Fifth, always be strategic, thinking about who might support and oppose a particular change.

To predict with any degree of assurance that research will influence policy decisions is a difficult and complex undertaking. Our work certainly helped to provide direction and stimulated a change in ways of thinking about character education in the UK. This work offered specific prescriptions, but more commonly brought a general enlightenment on character education as a public issue by offering ideas that helped inform and convince decision makers and practitioners to initiate new policies and practices in character education. We had the support of collaborators and strong advocates with policy networks, generous funding and a long period of time to disseminate our research outcomes. We were motivated and believed what we did benefited society, but we were realistic in the sense that we knew that our advice and information was sometimes expropriated to implement or argue for outcomes that did not reflect our preferences. We did not nor could we control the whole process of research-informed policy. Indeed, the main case study in this text has been as much about policy influencing research as it has been about research influencing policy. Recognising the interests and ideologies of the participants in the policy-making process, their normative background, is a key factor in understanding how policy is formulated. Understanding context is important as is interacting with all the policy players. Our research served to introduce new ideas, it helped policy makers and practitioners to identify problems and appropriate solutions in new ways, and it provided new frameworks to guide thinking and action on character building in schools and in the professions. We believe, from both a normative and empirical perspective, that character education is a worthy educational ideal and that the cultivation of the virtues which develop character is an appropriate aim of public policy.

REFERENCES

Adair, J. E. (1973) *Action-Centred Leadership*, London: McGraw-Hill.

Anderson, M. and Freebody, K. (2014) *Partnerships in Education Research: Creating Knowledge that Matters*, London: Bloomsbury.

Arthur, J. (1995) *The Ebbing Tide*, Leominster: Gracewing.

Arthur, J. with Bailey, R. (2000) *Schools and Community: The Communitarian Agenda in Education*, London: Routledge.

Arthur, J. (2003) *Education with Character: The Moral Economy of Schooling*, London: Routledge.

Arthur, J. (2005) 'The Re-emergence of Character Education in British Education Policy', *British Journal of Educational Studies*, 53(3), pp. 239–254.

Arthur, J. (2010) *Of Good Character*, Exeter: Imprint Academic.

Arthur, J. and Cremin, H. (Eds.) (2012) *Debates in Citizenship Education*, London: Routledge.

Arthur, J. and Davies, I. (2008) *Citizenship Education*, 4 volumes, London: Sage.

Arthur, J., Davies, I. and Hahn, C. (2008) *Education for Citizenship and Democracy*, London: Sage.

Arthur, J., Deakin-Crick, R., Samuel, E., Wilson, K., McGettrick, B. (2006), *Character Education: The Formation of Virtues and Dispositions in 16–19 Year Olds*, JTF.

Arthur, J., Harrison, T., Kristjánsson, K., Davison, I., Hayes, D., Higgins, J. and Ryan, K. (2014a) *My Character: Enhancing Future-mindedness in Young People*, University of Birmingham: Jubilee Centre for Character and Virtues.

Arthur, J., Kristjanssson, K., Thomas, H., Holdsworth, M. and Badini Confalonieri, L. (2014b) *Virtuous Character for the Practice of Law*, University of Birmingham: Jubilee Centre for Character and Virtues.

Arthur, J., Harrison, T., Carr, D., Kristjánsson, K., Davidson, I., Hayes, D., Higgins, J. and Davidson, J. (2014c) *Knightly Virtues: Enhancing Virtue Literacy Through Stories*, University of Birmingham: Jubilee Centre for Character and Virtues.

Arthur, J., Kristjánsson, K., Cooke, S., Brown, E. and Carr, D. (2015a) *The Good Teacher: Understanding Virtues in Practice*, University of Birmingham: Jubilee Centre for Character and Virtues.

Arthur, J., Kristjánsson, K., Gulliford, L., Morgan, B. and Roberts, R. C. (2015b) *An Attitude for Gratitude: How Gratitude is Understood, Experienced and Valued by the British Public,* University of Birmingham: Jubilee Centre for Character and Virtues.

Arthur, J., Kristjánsson, K., Thomas, H., Kotzee, B., Ignatowicz, A., Qiu, T. and Pringle, M. (2015c) *Virtuous Medical Practice,* University of Birmingham: Jubilee Centre for Character and Virtues.

Arthur, J., Kristjánsson, K., Walker, D., Sanderse, W., Jones, C., Thoma, S., Curren, R., Roberts, M. and Lickona, T. (2015d) *Character Education in UK Schools,* University of Birmingham: Jubilee Centre for Character and Virtues.

Arthur, J., Harrison, T. and Taylor, E. (2015e) *Building Character Through Youth Social Action,* University of Birmingham: Jubilee Centre for Character and Virtues.

Arthur, J., Kristjánsson, K., Harrison, T., Sanderse, W. and Wright, D. (2016) *Teaching Character and Virtue in Schools,* London: Routledge.

Audit Office (2001) *Modern Policy-Making: Ensuring Policies Deliver Value for Money,* London: National Audit Office.

Ball, S. J. (1994) *Education Reform,* Buckingham: Open University Press.

Ball, S. J. (1998) 'Educational Studies, Policy Entrepreneurship and Social Theory', in Slee, R., Tomlinson, S. and Weiner, G. (Eds.), *School Effectiveness for Whom? Challenges to the School Effectiveness and School Improvement Movements,* 70–84, London: Falmer.

Ball, S. J. (2008) 'New Philanthropy, New Networks and New Governance in Education', *Political Studies,* 56:4, 747–765.

Ball, S. J. (2009) 'Beyond Networks?: A Brief Response to Which Networks Matter in Education Governance?', *Political Studies,* 57:3, 688–691.

Ball, S. J. (2010) 'Making Policy with "Good Ideas": Policy Networks and the "Intellectuals" of New Labour', *Journal of Education Policy,* 25:2, 151–169.

Banfield, E .C. (1980) 'Policy Science as Metaphysical Madness', in Goldwin, R. A., *Bureaucrats, Policy Analysts, Statesmen: Who Leads?* Washington DC: American Enterprise Institute for Public Policy Research.

Bardach, E. (1972) *The Skill Factor in Politics: Repealing the Mental Law Commitment in California,* Berkeley and Los Angeles, CA: University of California Press.

Bartunek, J. M., Rynes, S. and Daft, R. (2001) 'Across the Great Divide: Knowledge Creation and Transfer Between Practitioners and Academics', *Academy of Management Journal,* 44:2, 340–355.

Bason, C. (2010) *Leading Public Innovation: Co-creating for a Better Society,* Bristol: The Policy Press.

Bastow, S., Dunleavy, P. and Tinkler, J. (2014) *The Impact of the Social Sciences: How Academics and Their Research Make a Difference,* London: Sage.

Bates, R. (2002) 'The Impact of Educational Research: Alternative Methodologies and Conclusions', *Research Papers in Education,* 17:4, 403–408.

Baumgarter, F. R. and Jones, B. D. (1993) *Agendas and Institutions in American Politics,* Chicago: University of Chicago Press.

Baumgartner, F. R., Green-Pedersen, C. and Jones, B. D. (2006) 'Comparative Studies of Policy Agendas', *Journal of European Public Policy,* 13:7, 959–974.

Beck, J. (2012) 'A Brief History of Citizenship Education in England and Wales', in Arthur, J. and Cremin, H. (Eds.), *Debates in Citizenship Education,* London: Routledge.

Beeson, M. and Stone, D. (2013) 'The Changing Fortunes of a Policy Entrepreneur: The Case of Ross Garaut', *Australian Journal of Political Science,* 48:1, 1–14.

Bell, L. and Stevenson, H. (2006) *Education Policy: Process, Themes and Impact,* London: Routledge.

Bennett, T. (2013) *Teacher Proof: Why Research in Education Doesn't Always Mean What it Claims, and What You Can do About It*, London: Routledge.

Benz, M. (2009) 'Entrepreneurship as a Non-profit Seeking Activity', *International Entrepreneurship and Management Journal*, 5, 23–44.

Bernier, L. (2014) 'Public Enterprises as Policy Instruments: The Importance of Public Entrepreneurship', *Journal of Economic Policy Reform*, 17:3, 253–266.

Beyer, J. M. (1997) 'Research Utilisation: Bridging the Gap Between Communities', *Journal of Management Enquiry*, 6, 17–22.

Beyer, J. M. and Trice, H. M. (1982) 'The Utilisation Process: A Conceptual Framework and Synthesis of Empirical Findings', *Administrative Science Quarterly*, 27:4, 591–622.

Birzer, B. J. (2015) *Russell Kirk: Conservative American*, Kentucky: University Press of Kentucky.

Blair, T. (1998) *New Politics for the New Century*, London: Fabian Society.

Blunkett, D. (1999) 'Excellence for the Many, Not Just the Few: Raising Standards and Extending Opportunities in Our Schools', *The CBI President's Reception Address by the Rt. Hon. David Blunkett MP 19 July 1999*, London: DfEE.

Blunkett, D. (2000) *Influence or Irrelevance: Can Social Science Improve Government?* Speech to the Economic and Social Research Council, 2 February.

Blunkett, D. (2002) *The Blunkett Tapes: My Life in the Bear Pit*, London: Bloomsbury.

Bogenschneider, K. and Corbett, T. J. (2011) *Evidenced-based Policymaking: Insights from Policy-minded Researchers and Research-minded Policymakers*, New York: Routledge.

Bond, R. and Paterson, L. (2005) 'Coming Down from the Ivory Tower?: Academics' Civic and Economic Engagement with the Community', *Oxford Review of Education*, 31:3, 331–351.

Boswell, C. (2009) *The Political Uses of Expert Knowledge: Immigration Policy and Social Research*, Cambridge: Cambridge University Press.

Bowe, R. and Ball, S. with Gold, A. (1992) *Reforming Education and Changing Schools: Case Studies in Policy Sociology*, London: Routledge.

Bowen, S. and Zwi, A. B. (2005) 'Pathways to "Evidence-informed" Policy and Practice: A Framework for Action', *Plos Medicine*, 2:7, 600–605.

Boyett, I. and Finley, D. (1993) 'The Emergence of the Educational Entrepreneur', *Long Range Planning*, 26:3, 114–122.

Brazier, J. (2010) Speech given at the launch of *Character in Transition*, Barton Court School, Canterbury: Learning for Life (26 February 2010).

Bridges, D. and Watts, M. (2009) 'Educational Research and Policy: Epistemological Considerations', in Bridges, D., Smeyer, P. and Smith, R. (Eds.), *Evidence-based Education Policy: What Evidence? What Basis? Whose Policy?* 36–57, Chichester: Wiley-Blackwell.

Briggle, A., Frodeman, R. and Holbrook, B. (2015) 'The Impact of Philosophy and the Philosophy of Impact: A Guide to Charting More Diffuse Influences Across Time', LSE Impact Blog; accessed online (02/11/16) at http://blogs.lse.ac.uk/impactofsocialsciences/2015/05/26/the-impact-of-philosophy-and-the-philosophy-of-impact/.

Brown, C. (2011) 'What Factors Affect the Adoption of Research within Educational Policy Making? How Might a Better Understanding of these Factors Improve Research Adoption and Aid the Development of Policy?' PhD Dissertation, University of Sussex.

Brown, C. (2013) *Making Evidence Matter: A New Perspective for Evidence-informed Policy Making in Education*, London, IOE Press.

Brown, C. (2015) *Evidence-informed Policy and Practice in Education: A Sociological Grounding*, London, Bloomsbury.

Bruce, B. and Eryaman, M. Y. (2016) *International Handbook of Progressive Education,* New York: Peter Lang.

Bryson, J. M. and Crosby, B. C. (2005) *Leadership for the Common Good: Tackling Public Problems in a Shared-power World*, San Francisco: Jossey Bass.

Bullock, H., Mountford, J. and Stanley, R. (2001) *Better Policy-making*, London: Cabinet Office.

Bulmer, M. (1982) *The Uses of Social Research*, London: George Allen and Unwin.

Byrne, L. (2013) *The Road to Full Employment*, London: The Fabian Society.

Byrne, L. (2016) *Black Flag Down,* London: Biteback Publishing.

Cabinet Office (1999) *Modernising Government*, White Paper, London: Cabinet Office.

Cahn, A. and Clemance, M. (2011) *The Whitehall Entrepreneur: Oxymoron or Hidden Army?* London: Institute for Government.

Cameron, D. (2009) quoted in Arthur, J., Harding, R. and Godfrey, R., *Citizens of Character: The Values and Character of 14-16 Year Olds in the Hodge Hill Constituency*, Birmingham: Learning for Life.

Carr, D. and Harrison, T. (2015) *Educating Character Through Stories*, Exeter: Imprint Academic.

Catford, J. (2006) 'Creating Political Will: Moving from Science to the Art of Health Promotion', *Health Promotion International*, 21:1, 1–4.

Catney, P. and Hennberry, J. (2015) 'Public Entrepreneurship and the Politics of Regeneration in Multi-level Governance', *Environment and Planning C: Government and Policy* 0:0, 1–20.

Christopoulos, D. C. (2006) 'Relational Attributes of Political Entrepreneurs: A Network Perspective', *Journal of European Public Policy*, 13:5, 757–778.

Cleary, H. and Reeves, R. (2009) *The 'Culture of Churn' for UK Ministers and the Price We Pay*, Research Briefing, London: Demos.

Cobb, R. W. and Elder, C. D. (1981) 'Communication and Public Policy', in Nimmo, D. D. and Sanders, K. R. (Eds.), *Handbook of Political Communication*, London: Sage.

Coburn, A. (1998) 'The Role of Health Services Research in Developing State Health Policy', *Health Affairs*, 139–151.

Cohen, B. C. (1963) *The Press and Foreign Policy*. Princeton: PUP.

Cohen, M. D., March, J. G. and Olsen, J. P. (1972) 'Garbage Can Model of Organisational Choice', *Administrative Science Quarterly*, 17:1, 1–25.

Cohn, D. (2006) 'Jumping into the Political Fray: Academics and Policy-making', *IRPP Policy Matters*, 7:3, 1–31.

Commission on the Social Sciences (2003) *Great Expectations: The Social Sciences in Britain,* London: Commission on the Social Sciences.

Craig, C. (2007) 'The Potential Dangers of a Systematic Explicit Approach to Teaching Social and Emotional Skills (SEAL)', The Centre for Confidence and Well-being, accessed online (30/10/16) at http://www.centreforconfidence.co.uk/docs/SEAL summary.pdf.

Crowley, J. E. (2003) *The Politics of Child Support in America*, New York: Cambridge University Press.

David, C-P. (2015) 'Policy Entrepreneurs and the Reorientation of National Security Policy under the G.W. Bush Administration', *Politics and Policy,* 43:1, 163–195.

Davies, P. (2012) 'The State of Evidence-based Policy Evaluation and its Role in Policy Formation', *National Institute Economic Review*, 219:1, 41–52.

Davies, P. (2015) 'Getting Evidence into Practice', *Journal of Development Effectiveness*, 7:4, 393–401.

Davies, H., Nutley, S. and Smith, P. (Eds.) (2000) *What Works? Evidence-based Public Policy and Practice*, Bristol: Policy Press.

Davis, G., Wanna, J., Warhurst, J. and Weller, P. (1993) *Public Policy in Australia* (2nd ed.), Sydney: Allen and Unwin.

DeMarco, R. and Adams Tufts, K. (2010) 'The Mechanics of Writing a Policy Brief', *Nursing Outlook,* 62:3, 219–224.

DfE (2016) *Educational Excellence Everywhere,* London: DfE.

DfES (1998) *Education for Citizenship and the Teaching of Democracy in Schools,* London: Qualifications & Curriculum Authority.

DfES (2003) *Primary National Strategy. Excellence and Enjoyment. Social, Emotional and Behavioural Skills,* Nottingham: DfES.

Diamond, P. (2015) 'New Labour, Politicisation and Depoliticisation: The Delivery Agenda in Public Services 1997–2007', *British Politics*, 10:4, 429–453.

Dror, Y. (2003) *Public Policy Making Re-examined,* New Brunswick, NJ: Transaction Publishers.

Ecclestone, K. and Hayes, D. (2008) *The Dangerous Rise of Therapeutic Education,* London: Routledge.

Economic and Social Research Council, (2009) *Research Ethics Framework,* Swindon: ESRC.

Elliott, J. (2009) 'Building Educational Theory through Action Research', in Somekh, B. and Noffke, S. (Eds.), *The SAGE Handbook of Educational Action Research,* Thousand Oaks, CA: Sage Publications, 28–38.

Etzkowitz, H. (1997) 'The Entrepreneurial University and the Emergence of Democratic Corporatism', in Etzkowitz, H. and Leydesdorff, L. (Eds.), *Universities and the Global Knowledge Economy: A Triple Helix of University – Industry – Government Relations,* London: Pinter Press.

Exworthy, M. and Powell, M. (2004) 'Big Windows and Little Windows: Implementation in the "Congested State"', *Public Administration*, 82:2, 263–281.

Figgis, J., Zubrick, A., Butorac, A. and Alderson, A. (2000) 'Backtracking Practice and Policies in Research', in *The Impact of Educational Research,* Canberra: Department of Education, Training and Youth Affairs.

Fischer, F. (1998) 'Beyond Empiricism: Policy Enquiry in Post-positivist Perspective', *Policy Studies Journal*, 26:1, 129–146.

Fischer, F. (2003) *Reframing Public Policy: Discourse Politics and Deliberative Practices,* Oxford: Oxford University Press.

Fischer, F. and Forester, J. (1993) *The Argumentative Turn in Policy Analysis and Planning,* London: Taylor & Francis.

Fish, S. (2003) 'Aim Low', *The Chronicle of Higher Education*, 16 May.

Gardner, H. (1983) *Frames of Mind: Theories of Multiple Intelligence,* New York: Basic Books.

Gearon, L. (2003) *Learning to Teach Citizenship in the Secondary School,* London: Routledge.

Ginsburg, M. B. and Gorostiaga, J. M. (2001) 'Relationships between Theorists/Researchers and Policy Makers/Practitioners: Rethinking the Two Cultures Thesis and the Possibility of Dialogue', *Comparative Education Review*, 45:2, 173–196.

Glendon, M. A. (2011) *The Forum and the Tower: How Scholars and Politicians Have Imagined the World, from Plato to Eleanor Roosevelt,* Oxford: Oxford University Press.

Goleman, D. (1995) *Emotional Intelligence: Why it Can Matter More than IQ,* London: Bloomsbury.

Gordon, I., Lewis, J. and Young, K. (1997) 'Perspectives on Policy Analysis', in Hill, M. (Ed.), *The Policy Process: A Reader,* 5–9, Hemel Hempstead: Harvester Wheatsheaf.

Griffiths, D. (2010) 'Academic Influence amongst the UK Public Elite', *Sociology*, 44:4, 734–750.

Griffiths, M. (1998) *Educational Research for Social Justice: Getting off the Fence,* Buckingham: Open University Press.

Haldane, L. (1918) *Report of the Machinery of Government Committee cd 9230,* London: HMSO.

Hallsworth, M. and Rutter, J. (2011) *Making Policy Better: Improving Whitehall's Core Business,* London: Institute for Government.

Hallsworth, M., Parker, S. and Rutter, J. (2011) *Policy Making in the Real World: Evidence and Analysis,* London: Institute for Government.

Halstead, M. and Taylor, M. (2000) *The Development of Values, Attitudes and Personal Qualities: A Review of Recent Research,* Slough: NFER.

Hammersley, M. (2001) 'Some Questions about Evidence-based Practice in Education', paper presented to the Annual Conference of the British Educational Research Association, University of Leeds, 15/09/2001.

Hammersley, M. (2005) 'The Myth of Research-based Practice: The Critical Case of Educational Inquiry', *International Journal of Social Science Methodology*, 8:2, 317–330.

Hargreaves, D. (1996) 'Teaching as a Research-Based Profession: Possibilities and Prospects', Teacher Training Agency Annual Lecture, London.

Harrison, S. and Wood, B. (1999) 'Designing Health Service Organization in the UK, 1968 to 1998: from Blueprint to Bright Idea and "Manipulated Emergence"', *Public Administration*, 77:4, 751–768.

Heater, D. (1991) 'Citizenship: A Remarkable Case of Sudden Interest', *Parliamentary Affairs*, 44:2, 140–156.

Heater, D. (1999) *What is Citizenship Education?* Cambridge: Polity Press.

Heater, D. (2004) *A History of Education for Citizenship,* London: Routledge.

Hess, M. F. (2007) 'The Case for Educational Entrepreneurship', *Phi Delta Kappa*, 89:1, 21–30.

Hess, M. F. (2015) *Educational Entrepreneurship,* Boston, MA: Harvard University Press.

Hess, M. F. and McShane, M. (2016) *Educational Entrepreneurship Today,* Boston, MA: Harvard University Press.

Hillage, J., Pearson, P., Anderson, A. and Tamkin, P. (1998) *Excellence in Research in Schools,* London: The Institute for Employment Studies/DfE Research Report 74.

Hilton, S. (2015) *More Human: Designing a World Where People Come First,* London: Penguin Random House.

Hogan, J. and Feeney, S. (2013) 'The Contribution of Political Entrepreneurs to Policy Change at Times of Crisis', working paper presented at the Annual Political Studies Association Conference, Cardiff University, Cardiff City Hall, 27/03/2013.

Holmes, J. and Clark, R. (2008) 'Enhancing the Use of Science in Environmental Policy-making and Regulation', *Environmental Science and Policy*, 11, 702–711.

Holzner, B., Knorr, K. D. and Strasser, H. (Eds.) (1983) *Realising Social Science Knowledge; the Political Realisation of Social Science Knowledge and Research: Toward New Scenarios,* Vienna: Physica Verlag.

Humphrey, N. (2013) *Social and Emotional Learning: A Critical Appraisal,* London: Sage.

Humphrey, N., Lendrum, A. and Wigelsworth, M. (2010) *Social and Emotional Aspects of Learning (SEAL) Programme for Secondary Schools: National Evaluation,* London: DfES.

Husen, T. and Kogan, M. (1984) *Educational Research and Policy: How Do They Relate?,* Oxford: Pergamon Press.

James, M. and Pollard, A. (2008) 'Learning and Teaching in Primary Schools, Insights from TLRP', accessed online (30/10/16) at http://cprtrust.org.uk/wp-content/uploads/2014/06/RS_2-4_briefing_160508_Learning_teaching_from_TLRP1.pdf.

Jobert, B. (1989) 'The Normative Frameworks of Public Policy', *Political Studies*, 37, 376–386.

John, P. (2003) 'Is There Life after Policy Streams, Advocacy Coalitions, and Punctuations? Using Evolutionary Theory to Explain Policy Change', *Policy Studies Journal*, 31:4, 481–498.

John Templeton Foundation (2008) 'Capabilities Report', accessed at: http://capabilities.templeton.org/2008/overview.html.

Jones, B. D. and Baumgartner, F. R. (1993) *Agendas and Instability in American Politics* (2nd ed.), Chicago: University of Chicago Press.

Jubilee Centre for Character and Virtues (2012) *Jubilee Centre for Character and Values*, Birmingham: University of Birmingham, accessed at http://www.jubileecentre.ac.uk/userfiles/jubileecentre/pdf/about-the-centre/Jubilee-Brochure.pdf.

Kaplan, J. (2015) *The Gratitude Diaries*, London: Yellow Kite.

King, P. J. and Roberts, N.C. (1992) 'An Investigation into the Personality Profile of Policy Entrepreneurs', *Public Productivity and Management Review*, 16:2, 173–190.

Kingdon, J. W. (1984) *Agendas, Alternatives and Public Policy* (1st ed.), Boston, MA: Little, Brown.

Kingdon, J. W. (1993) 'Politicians, Self-Interest, and Ideas', in Marcus, G. E. and Hanson, R. L. (Eds.), *In Reconsidering the Democratic Public*, University Park: Pennsylvania State University.

Kingdon, J. W. (2003) *Agendas, Alternatives and Public Policy* (2nd ed.), London: Longman Classics.

Kirp, D. (1982) 'Professionalization as a Policy Choice: British Special Education in a Comparative Perspective', *World Politics*, 31:2, 137–174.

Kirst, M. W. (2000) 'Bridging education research and education policymaking', *Oxford Review of Education*, 26:4, 379–391.

Kisby, B. (2007) 'New Labour and Citizenship Education: Social Capital, Policy Networks and the Introduction of Citizenship Lessons in Schools', PhD Thesis, University of Bristol.

Kissinger, A. H. (2007) *Current Trends and World Peace, Pontifical Academy of Social Sciences*, XIIIth Plenary Session, Vatican: Liberia Editrice Vaticana.

Klein, P. G., Mahoney, J., McGahan, T., Anita, M. and Pitelis, C. N. (2010) 'Towards a Theory of Public Entrepreneurship', *European Management Review*, 7, 1–15.

Knott, J. and Wildavsky, A. (1980) 'If Dissemination is the Solution, What is the Problem? Knowledge: Creation, Diffusion', *Utilisation*, 1:4, 537–578.

Kothari, A., MacLean, L. and Edwards, N. (2009) 'Increasing Capacity for Knowledge Translation: Understanding How Some Researchers Engage Policy Makers', *Evidence and Policy*, 5:1, 33–51.

Landry, R., Lamari, M. and Amara, N. (2003) 'The Extent and Determinants of the Utilisation of University Research in Government Agencies', *Public Administration Review* 63:2, 192–205.

Lasswell, H. (1951) 'The Policy Orientation' in Lerner, D. and Lasswell, H. S. (Eds.), *The Policy Sciences: Recent Trends in Scope and Method*, 3–15, Palo Alto: Stanford University Press.

Leadbeater, C. and Goss, S. (1998) *Civic Entrepreneurship*, London: Demos.

Lemay, M. and Sá, C. (2012) 'Complexity Science: Towards an Alternative Approach to Understanding the Use of Academic Research', *Evidence and Policy*, 8:4, 473–494.

Lewis, E. (1980) *Public Entrepreneurship: Toward a Theory of Bureaucratic Power*, Bloomington: Indiana University Press.

Lieberman, R. C. (2002) 'Ideas, Institutions, and Political Order: Explaining Political Change', *The American Political Science Review*, 96:4, 697–712.

Lindblom, C. (1959) 'The Science of "Muddling Through"', *Public Administrative Review*, 19:2, 79–88.

Lindblom, C. (1977) *Politics and Markets*, New York: Basic Books.

Lindblom, C. and Cohen, D. (1979) *Useable Knowledge: Social Science and Social Problem Solving*, Yale: Yale University Press.

Little, T. (2015) *An Intelligent Person's Guide to Education*, London: Bloomsbury.

Llewellyn, N., Lewis, P. and Woods, A. (2007) 'Public Management and the Expansion of an Entrepreneurial Ethos?', *Public Management Review*, 9:2, 253–267.

Lomas J. (2000) 'Connecting Research and Policy', *Canadian Journal of Policy Research*, 1, 140–144.

Lomas, J., Culyer, T., McCutcheon, C., McAuley, L. and Law, S. (2005) 'Conceptualising and Combining Evidence for Health System Guidance', accessed online (02/11/16) at http://www.cfhi-fcass.ca/migrated/pdf/insightAction/evidence_e.pdf.

Lorimer, D. (ed.) (2008) *Learning for Life: From Inspiration to Aspiration*, Learning for Life.

McComb, M. E. (2004) *Setting the Agenda: The Mass Media and Public Opinion*, Malden, MA: Blackwell.

Mackenzie, C. (2004) 'Policy Entrepreneurship in Australia: A Conceptual Review and Application', *Australian Journal of Political Science*, 39:2, 367–386.

McLoughlin, T. (2000) 'Philosophy and Educational Policy: Possibilities, Tensions and Tasks', *Journal of Education Policy*, 15:4, 441–457.

Majone, G. (1992) *Evidence, Argument, and Persuasion in the Policy Process*, New Haven, CT: Yale University Press.

Maloney, W. A., Jordan, G. and McLaughlin, A. M. (1994) 'Interest Groups and Public Policy: The Insider/Outsider Model Revisited', *Journal of Public Policy*, 14:1, 17–38.

Mazarr, M. J. (2007) 'The Iraq War and Agenda-Setting', *Foreign Policy Analysis*, 3, 1–23.

Meagher, L. R., Lyall, C. and Nutley, S. (2008) 'Flows of Knowledge, Expertise and Influence: A Method for Assessing Policy and Practice: Impacts From Social Science Research', *Research Evaluation*, 17, 163–173.

Miles, M. B. and Huberman, A. M. (1994) *Qualitative Data Analysis: An Expanded Sourcebook* (2nd ed.), Thousand Oaks, CA: Sage Publications.

Mintrom, M. (2000) *Policy Entrepreneurs and School Choice*, Washington, DC: Georgetown University Press.

Mintrom, M. (2009) 'Foundation Engagement in Education Policy-making: Assessing Philanthropic Support of School Choice Initiatives', in J. M. Ferris (Ed.), *Foundations and Public Policy*, New York: The Foundation Center, 243–278.

Mintrom, M. C. S. and Luetjens, J. (2014) 'Policy Entrepreneurs and Promotion of Australian State Knowledge Economies', *Australian Journal of Political Science*, 49:3, 423–438.

Mintrom, M. and Norman, P. (2009) 'Policy Entrepreneurship and Policy Change', *The Policy Studies Journal*, 37:4, 649–667.

Mintrom, M. and Vergari, S. (1996) 'Advocacy Coalitions, Policy Entrepreneurs, and Policy Change', *Policy Studies Journal*, 24:3, 420–434.

Mintrom, M. and Vergari S. (1998) 'Policy Networks and Innovation Diffusion: The Case of State Education Reforms', *The Journal of Politics, 60,* 126–148.

Molas, J., Tang, P. and Morrow, S. (2000) 'Assessing the Non-Academic Impact of Government-Funded Socio-economic Research: Results From a Pilot Study', *Research Evaluation,* 9:3, 172.

Molnar, T. (1994) *The Decline of the Intellectual,* New Brunswick, NJ: Transaction Publishers.

Monzo, L. A. and McLaren, P. (2016) 'The Future is Marx', in Bruce, B. and Eryaman, M. Y. (Eds.), *International Handbook of Progressive Education,* New York: Peter Lang.

Moore, M. H. (1988) 'What Sort of Ideas become Public Ideas?', in Reich, R. B. (ed.), *The Power of Public Ideas,* Cambridge, MA: Harvard University Press, 55–83.

Morgan, N. (2016) Speech at Character Symposium, 21 January 2016, accessed online (20/10/16) at https://www.gov.uk/government/speeches/nicky-morgan-opens-character-symposium-at-floreat-school.

Morris, M. and Jones, F. (1999) 'Entrepreneurship in Established Organisations: The Case of the Public Sector', *Entrepreneurship Theory and Practice,* Fall, 71–91.

Mulgan, G. (2003) 'Global Comparisons in Policy-making: The View from the Centre', accessed online (20/10/16) at https://www.opendemocracy.net/ecology-think_tank/article_1280.jsp.

Mulgan, G. (2006) 'Thinking in Tanks: The Changing Ecology of Political Ideas', *Political Quarterly,* 77:2, 147–155.

Mulgan, G. (2007) *Ready or Not? Taking Innovation in the Public Sector Seriously,* London: NESTA.

Munn, P. (2005) 'Researching Policy and Policy Research', *Scottish Educational Review,* 37:1, 17–28.

Norman, J. (2010) *The Big Society: The Anatomy of a New Politics,* Buckingham: University of Buckingham Press.

Nutley, S., Davies, H. and Walter, I. (2002) 'Evidence Based Policy and Practice: Cross Sector Lessons from the UK', ESRC UK Centre for Evidence Based Policy and Practice, St. Andrews: University of St. Andrews.

Nutley, S., Walter, I. and Davies, H. (2002) 'From Knowing to Doing, Discussion Paper 1, Research Unit for Research Utilisation', St. Andrews: University of St. Andrews.

Nutley, S., Walter, I. and Davies, H. (2007) *Using Evidence: How Research Can Inform Public Services,* Bristol: Policy Press.

Oborn, E., Barrett, M. and Exworthy, M. (2011) 'Policy Entrepreneurship in the Development of Public Sector Strategy: The Case of London Health Reform', *Public Administration,* 89:2, 325–344.

Ofsted (2006) *Towards Consensus: Citizenship in Secondary Schools,* London: Ofsted.

Oldham, G. and McLean, R. (1997) *Approaches to Knowledge-brokering,* London: International Institute for Sustainable Development.

Osborn, D. and Gaebler, T. (2000) *Re-inventing Government: How the Entrepreneurial Spirit is Transforming the Public Sector,* London: Longman.

Ozga, J. (2004) 'From Research to Policy and Practice: Some Issues in Knowledge Transfer', University of Edinburgh Initiative on Knowledge Transfer, Briefing No. 31, April 2004.

Parsons, J. D. and Burkey, S. (2011) 'Evaluation of the Teaching and Learning Research Programme (Second Phase)', Final Report of the Second Phase Review for the Economic and Social Research Council, Horsham: HOST Policy Research.

Parsons, W. (2002) 'From Muddling Through to Muddling Up – Evidenced Based Policy Making and the Modernisation of British Government', *Public Policy Administration,* 17:1, 43–60.

Pawson, R. (2006) *Evidence-based Policy: A Realist Perspective*, London: SAGE.

Pelikan, J. (1992) *The Idea of the University: A Re-examination*, New Haven, CT: Yale University Press.

Perry, A., Amadeo, C., Fletcher, M. and Walker, E. (2010) *Instinct or Reason: How Education Policy is Made and How We Might Make it Better*, London: CfBT Education Trust.

Pettigrew, A. (2011), 'Scholarship with Impact', *British Journal of Management*, 22, 347–354.

Policy Making Team on Professional Policy Making for the Twenty-First Century (1999) London: Cabinet Office.

Pollard, A. (2005) 'Taking the Initiative? TLRP and Educational Research', Educational Review Guest Lecture, University of Birmingham, 12/10/2015.

Pollard, A. (2008) 'Knowledge Transformation and Impact: Aspirations and Experiences from TLRP', *Cambridge Review of Education*, 38:1, 5–22.

Pollard, A. (2012) 'Exploring Strategies for Impact: Riding the Wave with TLRP', in Fenwick, T. and Farrell, L. (Eds.), *Knowledge Mobilisation and Educational Research: Politics, Languages and Responsibilities*, 30–43, Abingdon: Routledge.

Pollard, A. and Oancea, A. (2010) *Unlocking Learning? Towards Evidence-informed Policy and Practice in Education*, London: UK SFRE.

Revell, L. and Arthur, J. (2007) 'Character education in schools and the education of teachers', *Journal of Moral Education*, 36:1, 79–92.

Roberts, N. C. and King, P. J. (1991) 'Policy Entrepreneurs: Their Activity Structure and Function in the Policy Process', *Journal of Public Administration Research and Theory*, 1:2, 147–175.

Roberts, N. C. and King, P. J. (1996) *Transforming Public Policy: Dynamics of Policy Entrepreneurship and Innovation*, California: Jossey-Bass.

Rogers, E. and Kim, J. (1985) 'Diffusion of Innovations in Public Organisations', in R. L. Merritt and A. J. Merritt (Eds.), *Innovation in the Public Sector*, Beverley Hills: Sage Publications, 85–108.

Rogerson, L. (2015) *Give Thanks – Give Back: Exploring Gratitude and Service Among Communities*, Birmingham: Jubilee Centre for Character and Virtues, University of Birmingham, accessed online at http://www.jubileecentre.ac.uk/userfiles/jubileecentre/pdf/projects/Give_Thanks_Give_Back.pdf.

Sabatier, P. A. (1988) 'An Advocacy Coalition Framework of Policy Change and the Role of Policy-oriented Learning Therein', *Policy Sciences*, 21, 29–168.

Sabatier, P. A. (Ed.) (2007) *Theories of the Policy Process* (2nd ed.), Boulder, CO: Westview Press.

Sabatier, P. A., and Weible, C. M. (2007) 'The Advocacy Coalition Framework', in P. A. Sabatier (Ed.), *Theories of the Policy Process*, Boulder, CO: Westview Press.

Schneider, M. and Teske, P. (1992) 'Toward a Theory of the Political Entrepreneur, Evidence from Local Government', *American Political Science Review*, 86:3, 737–747.

Schneider M., Teske, P. and Mintrom M. (1995) *Public Entrepreneurs: Agents for Change in American Government*, Princeton, NJ: Princeton University Press.

Schon, D. (1971) *Beyond the Stable State*, New York: Norton.

Scott, P. (1990) *Knowledge and Nation*, Edinburgh: Edinburgh University Press.

Sebba, J. (2013) 'An Exploratory Review of the Role of Research Mediators in Social Science', *Evidence and Policy* 9:3, 391–408.

Slaughter, S. and Leslie, L. L. (1997) *Academic Capitalism: Politics, Policies and the Entrepreneurial University*, Baltimore, MD: Johns Hopkins University Press.

Solesbury, W. (2001) 'Evidence Based Policy: Whence it Came and Where it's Going', ESRC UK Centre for Evidence Based Policy and Practice, Working Paper 1, Queen Mary College, University of London.

Somers, A. (2013) 'The Emergence of Social Enterprise Policy in New Labour's Second Term', PhD Dissertation, accessed online (20/06/16) at http://research.gold.ac.uk/8051/1/POL_thesis_Somers_2013.pdf.

Stone, D. (2000) 'Private Authority, Scholarly Legitimacy and Political Credibility: Think Tanks and Informal Diplomacy', in Higgott, R., Underhill, G. and Bieler, A. (Eds.), *Non-state Actors and Authority in the Global System*, 211–225, London: Routledge.

Stone, D. (2007) 'Recycling Bins, Garbage Cans or Think Tanks? Three Myths Regarding Policy Analysis Institutes', *Public Administration*, 85:2, 259–278.

Taylor, M. (2005) 'Bridging Research and Policy: A UK Perspective', *Journal of International Development,* 17:6, 747–757.

Tooley, J. and Darby, D. (1998) *Educational Research: A Critique. A Survey of Published Educational Research,* London: Ofsted.

Torgerson, D. (2007) 'Promoting Policy Orientation: Laswell in Context', in Fischer, F., Miller, S. J. and Sidney, M. A. (Eds.), *Handbook of Public Policy Analysis: Theory, Politics and Methods,* 15–28, New York: CRC.

Twelve Acts to Professionalise Policy Making: A Report of the Policy Professions Board of the Civil Service (2013) London: Civil Service.

Van de Ven, A. H. (2007) *Engaged Scholarship: A Guide to Organizational and Social Research,* Oxford, UK: Oxford University Press.

Walker, J. L. (1981) 'The Diffusion of Knowledge, Policy Communities and Agenda Setting: The Relationship of Knowledge and Power', in Tropman, J. E., Dluhy, M. J. and Lind, R. M. (Eds.), *New Strategic Perspectives on Social Policy*, 75–96, London: Pergamon Press.

Ward, V., House, A. and Hamer, S. (2009) 'Knowledge Brokering: The Missing Link in the Evidence to Action?' *Evidence and Policy*, 5:3, 267–279.

Watermeyer, R. (2011) 'Challenges for University Engagement in the UK: Towards a Public Academe?' *Higher Education Quarterly*, 65:4, 386–410.

Weare, K. (2004) *Developing the Emotionally Literate School*, London: Paul Chapman Publishing.

Weare, K. and Grey, G. (2003) *What Works in Developing Children's Emotional and Social Competence*, London: DfES Research Report 456.

Weiss, C.H. (1977) *Using Social Research in Public Policy Making*, Lexington, MA: Lexington Books.

Weiss, C. H. (1979) 'The Many Meanings of Research Utilisation', *Public Administration Review*, 39, 426–431.

Weiss, C. H. (1982) 'Policy Research in the Context of Diffuse Decision Making', *Journal of Higher Education*, 53:6, 619–639.

Weiss, C. H. (1993) 'Where Politics and Evaluation Research Meet', *Evaluation Practice*, 14:1, 93–106.

Weiss, C. H. (1999) 'The Interface between Evaluation and Public Policy', *Evaluation*, 5:4, 468–486.

Weiss, C. H., Murphy-Graham, E. and Birkeland, S. (2005) 'An Alternate Route to Policy Influence: How Evaluations Affect D.A.R.E.', *American Journal of Evaluation*, 26:1, 12–30.

Weiss, C. H., Murphy-Graham, E., Petrosino, A., and Gandhi, A. G. (2008) 'The Fairy Godmother and Her Warts: Making the Dream of Evidence-based Policy Come True', *American Journal of Evaluation*, 29:1, 29–40.

Weissert, C. S. (1991) 'Policy Entrepreneurs, Policy Opportunists, and Legislative Effectiveness', *American Politics Quarterly*, 19:2, 262–274.

Whitty, G. (2007) 'Education(al) Research and Education Policy-making', in Saunders, L. (Ed.), *Educational Research and Policy Making: Exploring the Border Country Between Research and Policy*, Abingdon: Routledge.

Whitty, G. (2008) 'Twenty Years of Progress: English Education Policy 1988 to the Present', *Educational Management Administration and Leadership*, 36:2, 165–184.

Whitty, G. (2016) *Research and Policy in Education*, London: UCL IOE Press.

Willinsky, J. (2000) *If Only We Knew: Increasing the Public Value of Social-science Research*, London: Routledge.

Wilson, J. Q. (1981) '"Policy Intellectuals" and Public Policy', *The Public Interest*, 64, accessed online at: http://www.nationalaffairs.com/doclib/20080708_1981643policyin tellectualsandpublicpolicyjamesqwilson.pdf.

Winch, C. (2001) 'Accountability and Relevance in Educational Research', *Journal of Philosophy of Education*, 35, 443–459.

Woods, P. H. (2011) *Transforming Education Policy: Shaping a Democratic Future*, London: Policy Media.

Young, K. and Connelly, N. (1981) *Policy and Practice in the Multi-racial City*, London: Policy Studies Institute.

INDEX